THE GOVERNMENT EXPLAINS
A Study of the Information Services

In 1952 the Royal Institute of Public Administration
embarked on a series of major research projects to be carried
out by study groups. This book is the outcome of the sixth
project in the series. The other five are:

THE ORGANIZATION OF BRITISH
CENTRAL GOVERNMENT 1914-56

NEW SOURCES OF LOCAL REVENUE

BUDGETING IN PUBLIC AUTHORITIES

BUILDING BY LOCAL AUTHORITIES

OPERATIONAL RESEARCH IN LOCAL GOVERNMENT

George Allen & Unwin Ltd

The Government Explains

A STUDY OF THE INFORMATION SERVICES

A REPORT OF THE
ROYAL INSTITUTE OF PUBLIC ADMINISTRATION

WRITTEN BY
MARJORIE OGILVY-WEBB

FOREWORD BY SIR KENNETH GRUBB, CMG

London

GEORGE ALLEN AND UNWIN LTD
RUSKIN HOUSE · MUSEUM STREET

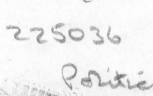
PRINTED IN GREAT BRITAIN
in 10 point Times Roman type
BY SIMSON SHAND LTD
LONDON, HERTFORD AND HARLOW

MEMBERS OF THE STUDY GROUP

Chairman
SIR KENNETH GRUBB, CMG
Controller, Ministry of Information, 1941–6
Publicity Consultant, Rank Organization, 1955–9

DR MARK ABRAMS, Director of Research, London Press Exchange Ltd.

F. A. BUTTERS, Member, Berkshire County Council.

IAN COX, CBE, Public Relations Adviser, Royal Dutch/Shell Group for UK and Eire.

T. FIFE CLARKE, CBE, Director-General, Central Office of Information.

J. E. FISHWICK, Town Clerk, Lambeth.

MARK HENIG, Alderman, Leicester City Council.

S. C. LESLIE, CBE, Consultant, Information Policy; Member, Northern Ireland Development Council; lately Head of Information Division, H.M. Treasury.

ERNEST LONG, lately Member, Central Electricity Generating Board.

JAMES E. MacCOLL, JP, Member of Parliament for Widnes Division of Lancashire.

DAME ALIX MEYNELL, DBE, formerly Under Secretary, Board of Trade.

SIR DAVID MILNE, KCB, lately Permanent Under Secretary of State for Scotland.

H. PERCIVALL POTT, Member of Parliament for Devizes Division of Wiltshire.

Research Officer
MARJORIE OGILVY-WEBB

FOREWORD

by *Sir Kenneth Grubb* CMG

My first duty and pleasure must be to make acknowledgements in three separate quarters. First a discussion group, whose names are given elsewhere, has worked hard and long on this subject. It was not always an easy group. It included persons whose own considerable experience and outlook had led them to firm views on information policy, but their views did not always accord with those of men of similar experience elsewhere. At one stage it seemed as if the whole enterprise of producing a work such as this was going to present almost unsurmountable difficulties. Few things seem to provoke such sincere divergences of opinion as information policy and practice. Those who have worked in this field have long been aware of this and the discussions in the group were largely the reflection of experience. But the continuing loyalty of all members to the enterprise has been beyond praise.

Second, Mrs Marjorie Ogilvy-Webb has not spared herself or her considerable skill and practical knowledge of this kind of work. It is quite certain that the book could not have been brought to the stage of completion without her unflagging energy and power both of criticism and summation. She has taken what was at one stage a considerable mass of material from a wide variety of sources and has developed it into a compassable form, suitable for a serious treatise.

Third, Mr Raymond Nottage (who makes his own acknowledgements in his Preface), the Director of the Royal Institute of Public Administration, has, with his colleagues, been unfailingly helpful. The enterprise started with the Royal Institute of Public Administration, but there is all the difference in the world between a Director or Secretary who helps to get a group together and then leaves them to sort it all out, and one who consistently assists the process of discussion and the meeting of minds. Mr Nottage is the latter type.

Why is it that this particular subject causes so much debate and difference of views? My own mind goes back to the period immediately prior to the Second World War when discussions were going on behind the scenes about what should be done if the war broke out. No one doubted that something was needed, but to secure agreement on just what, was tough. Radio had come into being, and the BBC was actively building up and expanding its great complex of overseas broadcasts which figured with such value during the war years. The

9

documentary film was another innovation. At home there was the problem of an adequate but not a laborious regional organization. The British Council had already established a substantial organization with its own connections in many countries. How much of all this ought to be centralized in wartime in a government department was a subject of earnest debate, and many of the questions posed were not resolved until the war had run its grim course for a year or two. Times had changed since Lord Northcliffe's enterprise in the First World War. There was little experience available and few had travelled that way before. In the event the form which the Ministry of Information acquired as the result of experience and early mistakes was substantially different from what had been originally conceived.

But there is more to it than the mere question of organization, which can always be solved with time. In peace-time, in ordinary years, information work raises the whole 'problem of communication' as modern jargon has it. This has become even more acute as the years go by, and it is the kind of subject which not unreasonably is apt to rouse the wrath of the average Englishman who thinks he is being 'got at'. To communicate information requires some knowledge of the audience. To acquire this knowledge, by the standard of modern techniques, may demand an investigation into the lives of citizens which is abhorrent to the average man. Shades of 'hidden persuaders' are conjured up, and although the picture is usually exaggerated (as the material in this volume dealing with Social Survey shows), there is something healthy about the suspicion itself. It is sufficient to say here, that this aspect of the total task of government explanation has been kept under timely control.

It is to the credit of the information services of the post-war period that they have operated, so to speak, under a self-denying ordinance. This is very clearly brought out in the body of the Report. They have not conceived their mission as that of 'pressure groups' or 'hidden persuaders'. They have imposed well-understood restrictions upon themselves. This has not made their task easier, but harder. Most people can get a sound out of a trumpet if they pick it up and blow it; few can conduct an orchestra.

Some may hold that such moderation is no longer possible in a world where unless one shouts one is not heard at all. This indeed, is one of the modern hazards of this peculiar scene. Modern man is bombarded by information, by views of all kinds and often of a very superficial kind, and by impressions conveyed to him by press, radio and TV. It is no answer to say that he can, if he wishes, cut himself off from all this. Much of it comes to him associated with his ration of news or his interval of entertainment and to cut himself off is to live the life of a hermit or anchorite. Many modern studies have been made of the effect of this constant writing, talking and acting. The general result seems to be little more than to produce a miscellany of fleeting impressions, and to create difficulties in every serious attempt by the citizen to evolve a sense of priorities for himself in his responsibilities and obligations.

How then can government information services which operate in this country with moderation and judgement, expect to be heard? And if they do not expect to be heard what are they there for? A large part of this book is taken up with giving the detailed answers to the first of these questions. To start with, as all sensible men recognize, government information is in a different position from a private enterprise which seeks to explain its action or make itself known. An aura of authority constantly rests upon government. The tendency of the average citizen may be to criticize the government whenever he can; this is an ancient human instinct which will happily continue, information service or no information service. But fair-minded citizens also want to hear both sides of the case, and the media of information are usually concerned to give it. This is the legitimate opportunity for the information services to take. It does not mean indulging in high-pressure propaganda. Occasionally a campaign of propaganda may be justified, and this study draws attention to questions which are generally above public dispute, such as inoculation against diphtheria or polio, which fall into this category. The Ministry of Health cannot reasonably be criticized for forcing such a matter as this on the public's attention.

But, more usually, what is needed is simply explanation. It is a familiar principle that ignorance of the law is no excuse for its contravention. The complications of modern legislation are such, reaching down to many things which affect the life of ordinary citizens, that it is almost unfair to expect the average man, who is no brighter than he should be, to understand all the things that may affect him in a massive Act of Parliament, or even the Order of a Minister. It has come to be generally recognized that here is a legitimate and very necessary duty for the information services and the evidence of this study is that generally they discharge it with skill, discretion and perspicacity.

Indeed, perhaps nothing in the findings of the study is more interesting than the demonstration that for many years now the information services have ceased to be an arena of political and public controversy. This is not to say that the situation does not call for that eternal vigilance which is said to be the price of our liberties. It is happily certain that if the information services lent themselves blatantly and deliberately to the purposes of party propaganda, a chorus of voices would be raised in protest. It is not likely that this will occur. The information services have found their place, an indispensable and invaluable one, in the machinery of modern government. Their relation to Parliament, to the Ministers of the departments, and the departments as a whole, have been carefully worked out in the English way, as a result of trial and error, and the information branches of the Ministries (to say nothing of the Central Office of Information) are led by men of proven experience and senior standing. The country as a whole and government in particular are well served by them.

It is not without considerable thought and experiment that this position has been reached. It has not been an easy row to hoe, because in the nature of the case, information work is directed to the public and is easily exposed to criticism. Nor have critics been lacking. But of recent years criticism, with some exceptions, has not been directed against the system as a whole, but against the particular incidents or questions, which, it is held, have been mishandled. On the whole, the political parties and the public, in so far as it is aware of how these things are done, have shown themselves prepared to accept the machinery of public information as a necessary part of the operations of government in a complicated modern state. It is to be hoped that in the general interest they will continue to do so. The information services have abundantly demonstrated that there are many ways of making one's voice heard apart from shouting.

It may be said, with some justification, that this is only possible in a relatively advanced democracy such as Great Britain, where, along with the duty of the Opposition to oppose, there is at the end of the day, a wide measure of agreement on what is necessary and good for the welfare of the country. It would be interesting, in this respect, to have a comparative study of how such services are performed in such countries as the United States or France. So far as I am aware, there is no recent study in existence.

Nevertheless, it is hoped that the present work will have some value for those who in other countries, where the techniques of modern government are less developed, are wrestling with similar problems. In travelling in the Commonwealth, I have been sometimes impressed with the lack of thought that is given to the handling of these delicate problems. The solutions so far found in the British scene may not everywhere be applicable for obvious reasons. But there is much in the British picture which, without giving ourselves airs, is suggestive, and one hopes, helpful.

For it is of the essence of the information services that they should neither usurp the functions of the free media, nor exaggerate the achievements and policies which they are concerned to explain. They are, therefore, in themselves a recognition of a certain maturity in a democracy. They testify to the existence of a society where facts are essential to the formation of views, where prejudice is to be combated by reason, and where policies should, nevertheless, be explained if they are to be understood. It will be an ill day for the Western World, not to speak of many other parts of the world, if it becomes impossible, through the sheer pressure of heated propaganda, exaggeration, distortion or suppression, to maintain this ideal. To the maintenance of it, the citizen himself, the free media, and the information services can all contribute, and *The Government Explains* is, in spite of its sub-title, concerned to a considerable extent with all these different parties.

CONTENTS

PREFACE

Some years ago the Royal Institute of Public Administration decided to undertake a series of major research projects on subjects of current importance to the public services. Public Relations was chosen as the sixth in that series.

The Institute selected this subject because of the important part which publicity and public relations play in the modern world, and the general recognition that public authorities must use these techniques to some extent if they are to carry out their duties effectively and to keep the public adequately informed of their activities. Special considerations must apply, however, to the ways in which some public authorities employ public relations techniques, especially those whose work comes within the area of political controversy. It would be contrary to prevailing constitutional theory for those at present in political power to be able to influence the electorate through the medium of publicity and information services supported by the general body of taxpayers. The objects of the study were, therefore, to examine the way in which information services had developed in public authorities, and to elucidate the principles on which they work in the party system operating in Britain. Finally, the Institute was conscious of the fact that the literature on public relations in public authorities was very limited, and it thought that a book resulting from a detailed study would be of wide interest.

The original plan was for the study to cover both central government and local government, since account would have to be taken in both of them of the activities of elected representatives and of political parties. As the study progressed, however, two facts became clear. First, the basic problems in central and local government were too dissimilar to make them easily comparable. The differences in the scale of operations was one important factor; another was the ability of local councillors to keep closely in touch with their constituents so much more easily than their national counterparts. Second, the great variety of practice in local authorities made it difficult to ascertain the facts and draw general conclusions. It was accordingly decided to confine the study, at least for its first stage, to central government and, as will be seen from the following pages, this limitation did not preclude a study of some magnitude on its own.

The study was also confined to the services provided for the direct

B

benefit of the citizens of the United Kingdom. It excluded the overseas information services, and those parts of the home information services which are primarily intended for overseas. This limitation was thought to be necessary since it would not have been practicable to undertake any part of the research abroad and to evaluate the effect of those services on those for whom they are intended.

Once again the Institute adopted the Study Group method of research, which it had successfully employed in other research projects it had undertaken. The Chairman of the Study Group for this inquiry was Sir Kenneth Grubb, a Controller in the Ministry of Information from 1941 to 1946, and Publicity Consultant to the Rank Organization from 1955 to 1959. The Institute greatly appreciates the wide knowledge and deep insight which he brought to this enterprise, and the vigorous leadership he imparted to it. The members of the Study Group are listed on a preceding page, and the Institute would like to emphasize the value of their contributions to the outcome of this work, particularly those of Dame Alix Meynell, Mr T. Fife Clark and Mr S. C. Leslie. The study took longer to complete than was originally expected, and the Institute would like to express its appreciation to Sir Kenneth Grubb and to the members of the Study Group for their sustained interest.

Each member of the Study Group served in a personal capacity, and nothing in this Report should be regarded as expressing the views of any organization with which he, or she, is connected. Nor, in a work of this kind, can it be assumed that every member would agree wholeheartedly with everything which is written in it.

The major part of the work on this inquiry was undertaken by Mrs Marjorie Ogilvy-Webb, a history graduate of Cambridge University who worked in the Cabinet Office on several volumes of the official economic history of the war. More recently she was engaged in research work for television and the press, and this brought her into close contact with government information services. The following pages will testify to the thoroughness of her research and quality of mind which she brought to the writing of the book.

Acknowledgement must also be made to the early work of investigation undertaken by Miss Ruth Butterworth, and to Mrs Margaret Garrard who carried out the research for Chapters VII and VIII and drafted them.

A book of this kind could not be produced without the help of many senior public officials and others who kindly allow themselves to be subjected to inquiries. Thanks are particularly due to the Chief Information Officers of the various departments investigated. They spent much time describing and demonstrating their work, the problems to which it gives rise and the personal satisfaction they derive from it. The Institute would also like to acknowledge the help it received from Sir Norman Brook (now Lord Normanbrook) who, as Head of the Civil Service, agreed that this would be a useful study to undertake and encouraged the departments to assist with it. Dr Hill (now Lord Hill of Luton) took an interest in the research and made available to the Study Group his experience as co-ordinator of information services. To all who have contributed in any way, the Institute expresses its warmest gratitude.

July 1963

CHAPTER I

The Channels of Communication

This book is about the government's public relations—the 'deliberate, planned and sustained effort to establish and maintain mutual understanding'[1] between itself and the people of this country. The major instrument of this deliberate effort is the information service; that is, the Information or Public Relations Divisions which exist within each of the major Departments of State, together with the Central Office of Information.

The main concern of the book is therefore with the government information services; their development from tentative beginnings to the present day in Chapters II and III; the way in which they are organized, the kind of work they have to do and the way in which they tackle it in Chapters IV, V and VI; the problems of staffing the information services are discussed in Chapter VII, and Chapter IX makes some attempt to assess the performance of the information services and the job they do on the home front.

But not all government public relations are the concern of the information services. A government department is making an impact on the public when the Minister addresses his fellow-members in Parliament, or the telephone operator at the Ministry switchboard answers an outside call; when one department issues a press statement on economic policy or another pays out a family allowance across the Post Office counter. They are all relations with the public, and in Chapter VIII we shall see how some of the ordinary civil servants are trained to do these kinds of public relations jobs.

In this first chapter, however, it has seemed to us worthwhile to describe briefly the whole range of government public relations—all the channels along which communications between the government and the governed can flow. We will look at the Minister's contacts with the citizens through Parliament and outside it; the officials' relations with the public, whether they are the advisory committees, the local authorities, the trade unions or the ordinary taxpayer; and the factual material issued by government departments, usually

[1] This is the definition of public relations used by the Institute of Public Relations.

21

through Her Majesty's Stationery Office. We can then see how the Information Divisions and the Central Office of Information fit in to this general pattern of government public relations. But when we go on to describe in detail in the rest of the book the functioning of the information services, it must not be forgotten that these more traditional methods of communication exist and go on side by side with the work of the information services.

THE MINISTER

His Relations with the Public through Parliament

The traditional contact between the government and the governed is through Parliament. Parliament is the forum for debate, for announcements of government policy, for elucidation of government action, for the consideration of grievances, for questioning the actions of the executive, and for the detailed examination of proposals for legislation and taxation which are likely to affect the mass of citizens—Bagehot's 'great engine of popular instruction and political controversy'. The Minister (including his Parliamentary Secretaries) is involved politically in all this as a member of the government in power. As the head of a department he is a member of the executive arm, and through him his department is also involved in the debates, Parliamentary Questions and Parliamentary Committees, and the Reports, Estimates and White Papers presented to Parliament.

Debates. In debate the Minister usually takes part on the subjects with which his department is concerned—setting out the government's policy, answering criticism of his department's activities, producing facts and arguments to persuade the House to reject the Opposition's proposals and accept his, or explain why his department will or will not take a certain line of action. On an ordinary day— December 21, 1961, for example—the President of the Board of Trade spoke in a debate on the future of the Lancashire cotton industry; the Financial Secretary to the Treasury on pensions for ex-overseas civil servants; the Attorney-General on the conduct of an inquiry into an aircraft accident at Southall; and the Minister of Labour and the President of the Board of Trade on the rise in industrial accidents. For such occasions the Minister involved will have been provided with a brief by the officials in his department concerned with industrial accidents or the cotton industry or whatever the subject may be, a brief he may have modified or changed according to his own policy or opinions or style, or which he may use virtually un-changed.

For a big debate involving some important changes in policy or legislation, a number of senior civil servants will probably be present in the official Box to follow the debate and be ready to supply notes to the Minister on any points arising from it and not covered by his brief.[1]

Questions. Answering Questions is different from taking part in a debate. Question time is the one occasion where the government has to stand up to day-to-day criticism and make day-to-day justifications for what it has done or failed to do. Question time in this country is the equivalent of a press conference in the United States.

Parliamentary Questions probably get a disproportionate share of press attention, partly because Question time is the only portion of the day's proceedings that can catch the evening papers and partly because answers are succinct and easy to understand. The information does not have to be dug out of some lengthy debate.

During a Parliamentary session about 12,000 to 15,000 Questions require either an oral or a written reply. Most Ministers appear on the roster to answer Questions once a week, although their junior Ministers often reply for them. A few, like the Chancellor, the Foreign Secretary and the President of the Board of Trade appear twice a week. The individual Member of Parliament is limited to asking two 'starred' questions a day—that is, Questions requiring an oral reply; any Questions over this maximum normally get only a written an-swer.[2] An oral reply is likely to take up more of a department's time than a written one, because the Minister must be given enough back-ground material to enable him to deal with any supplementary Questions. Although the department's turn only comes once a week, in most departments answering Questions has to take precedence over other work, so a civil servant may have to put aside something of greater long-term importance to deal with a Question.[3]

Questions can air grievances or press for action or ask for informa-tion. They are most frequently inspired by press reports, or are

[1] The official Box is a sort of pew on the floor of the House, reserved for civil servants; the House takes no cognizance of their presence. The Minister can talk to officials in the Box, or, if he is addressing the House, notes are passed back-wards and forwards by the Minister's Parliamentary Private Secretary.

[2] This maximum was reduced from three to two on February 15, 1960.

[3] It has been estimated that about 1,400 civil servants are involved in answering Questions; but not full-time. See Nevil Johnson, 'Parliamentary Questions and the Conduct of Public Business', Vol. 39, *Public Administration*, Summer 1961.

matters brought to MPs' notice by their constituents; they may also be initiated by pressure groups running special campaigns, or by local authorities; they may be asked by individual MPs with their own special enthusiasms or dislikes, or by a group, perhaps of forty Scottish members all putting down Questions to a Minister in the same day on a matter with which they are all concerned. In subject, Questions can range from items of purely local interest in an MP's own constituency—the siting of a new prison or even a new pillar box—to important topics like defence which are of major political importance. There are also 'inspired' Questions—that is, Questions which have been arranged by the department which has to answer them. The device of the planted or 'inspired' Question allows a department to publicize or explain its actions; or it can be used to announce the membership of a committee, or correct a mis-statement in the press. The inspired Question is employed partly to uphold the doctrine that all important announcements should first be made in the House of Commons. Members of Parliament are quick to resent anything that looks like an attempt to by-pass them, and many departments prefer to use the inspired Question rather than issue ministerial statements or hold a press conference. The inspired Question may often be followed, of course, by a lobby conference or an intimate talk with the lobby correspondents concerned.

Is the Question a useful instrument of public relations? The Question asked may not always be the most effective one possible; at its worst answering Parliamentary Questions is a game in which skilled civil servants block rather erratic bowling. A distinguished civil service lawyer is quoted as saying that a good many Questions are asked by people 'who, although they may have got hold of something that is worth looking into, are insufficiently briefed to make a case and lack the necessary skill or expert knowledge to press their points home'.[1] The sheer volume of public business makes Question time no longer the 'searchlight turned into every corner of the public service' that it was said to be fifty years ago.[2] Although the functions of government are much wider now than they were then, no more Parliamentary time is allotted to Questions. In fact fewer oral Questions can be asked nowadays because there are more supplementaries. Also the Parliamentary Question is probably more useful to remedy specific grievances or to get specific information than to change a department's general views or policy on an important point. For example, on the same day (November 4, 1958) the Prime Minister

[1] Francis Williams, *Parliament, Press and People*, Heinemann, 1946, p. 112.
[2] A. Lowell, *The Government of England*, Vol. 1, Macmillan, 1908, p. 332.

was asked to stop British nuclear tests and the Minister of Works was asked to thin a row of trees along Birdcage Walk. The latter was more likely to get results than the former. Nevertheless, the weekly flow of Questions probably keeps departments aware of the general tide of public opinion—or at least warns them when they are running against it. And Questions, by sheer reiteration of the same points—like Mr Nabarro's stream of Questions on purchase tax anomalies—may do more to pin-point public and departmental attention than the most lengthy debate.

Papers Laid before Parliament.[1] There are also the large number of papers initiated by the departments and laid before Parliament. As many as 280 may be issued in a single Parliamentary Session. Command papers are in general restricted to matters of government policy likely to be the subject of debate or legislation or to reports of the work of government departments and committees. For example there are the reports of Royal Commissions or Committees of Inquiry, the Civil Estimates of departmental expenditure, and the Annual Reports of the eight or ten departments which publish them.[2] Some Parliamentary reports are prescribed by statute—for example it is now obligatory for the Home Secretary to report to Parliament on children's homes—most are not. Many papers are the texts of trade agreements and political or commercial treaties; some are statements of government policy like the Economic Survey or Defence White Paper; some are hardy annuals like the preliminary estimate of National Income and Expenditure which usually appears just before the budget; others may be solitary swallows—on Service Pay, on the Ballistic Early Missile Warning System, or a Mines Inspector's report on a Yorkshire pit explosion, to quote a few examples at random from one session. Similarly, the Factory Inspector, and the Chief Inspector of the Fire Services, the Prison Commissioner, the BBC and the Development Corporations of New Towns are among the many government and government sponsored authorities who lay annual reports before Parliament. All these form part of the enormous exercise of telling the governed what the government is doing.

---

[1] Papers laid before Parliament are sometimes known as Blue Books. A White Paper is something which is not big enough to be bound in a cover. Covers at one time were always blue, but cream is now more common, although sometimes other colours are used.

[2] Many of the major departments, such as the Foreign Office, Treasury and Board of Trade, do not publish annual reports.

The Minister's Relations with the Public outside Parliament

Through the Press, Radio and Television. Parliament, of course, is not the sole contact between Ministers and the outside world. Ministers can have direct access to the press—including radio and television—and provided they have something important or interesting to say, they will get reported. If a Minister wants to make an announcement of general interest outside the House of Commons, he can gain the attention of the press by making a speech to his constituents, or at a public luncheon or dinner, or at a party conference, or to a foreign trade delegation and hope the press will report him. He can also issue a press statement, hold a press conference, or he can appear on radio or television. All these press contacts will normally nowadays be arranged by the department's Information Division and the Minister's speeches will often owe something to their help. At a press conference, the Minister and the Chief Information Officer, together with other senior officials, will be present.

A press statement is appropriate when the news to be given is not thought to require elucidation by discussion—the number of deaths on the roads over the Christmas holiday, for example. A press conference is normally called when there is to be an important policy change which will need explanation—farm prices or slum clearance, for example. After the Minister's statement, journalists are free to ask questions, to have particular points clarified, or to get their own particular 'angle' on the general news release. Afterwards the Minister can be quoted as the source of information.

A Minister will also from time to time meet the Lobby correspondents of the various newspapers. The Lobby organization is a part of the Parliamentary Press Gallery. All the national and most of the important provincial British newspapers and the Commonwealth and foreign newspapers, agencies and broadcasting organizations have representatives who comprise the Press Gallery. To be admitted to the Press Gallery a newspaper representative must have his name approved by the Serjeant-at-Arms. Within the British section of the Press Gallery there are about fifty journalists who are Lobby correspondents. Every important British newspaper and agency has a Lobby correspondent and usually a deputy as well.[1] Lobby correspondents have the special privilege of access to the Member's Lobby just outside the debating Chamber. The Lobby organization also has its own Chairman, Committee and Officers, and its own

[1] The Overseas Press Services Division of the Central Office of Information also has its own Lobby correspondent.

room in the House. The difference between the Press Gallery journalists and the Lobby correspondents is that the former are concerned with reporting and describing debates and other proceedings in the House, while the latter provide political news, interpretation and comment and explain the background of political events.

The Lobby correspondents, having access to the Members' Lobby, are in daily contact with Ministers and MPs and have the opportunity of discussing with them the political topics of the day. Through their Lobby organization these political journalists also have collective conferences with Ministers and representatives of the Opposition. The Lobby correspondents guarantee the secrecy of such proceedings and write about such information as they may gather on their personal responsibility, without revealing the source. In their individual contacts with Ministers and MPs, Lobby correspondents are similarly scrupulous to keep confidential their sources of information. An informant is never named or quoted unless there is some exceptional reason for doing so and a special request is made that this should be done.[1]

The strict practice of Lobby journalists in maintaining confidential relations goes even further than the ordinary journalist's refusal to name the source of his information, about which there was trouble at the time of the Vassall inquiry. Lobby practice requires, for example, that no member shall reveal to anyone outside the professional circle even what collective meetings may have taken place.[2] As Lobby correspondents do not reveal the source of information given to them, Ministers can provide them with background information or reveal the way in which they intend to deal with a particular subject, and the reasons for their proposed actions. Lobby correspondents are then at liberty to make their own comments and predictions in the light of what the Minister has said, but without referring to the Minister as the source of information. There is also a well established procedure for liaison with the Lobby when important statements or White Papers, etc., are to be issued.

The existence of the body of Lobby correspondents is of enormous importance to the business of communication between government departments and the press. Firstly, because they are very influential.

[1] The only occasion on which a Lobby correspondent has revealed the source of his information was to a Parliamentary Committee of Inquiry.

[2] It is only comparatively recently that there have been references in public to the Lobby correspondents and their functions. Most books refer to them only in very general terms. For further details of the relations between the Lobby and the Information Services see Chapters IV and VI.

Lobby correspondents are usually men of great Parliamentary experience and judgement; some of them are paid as much as Cabinet Ministers. Secondly because the practice is so convenient. A Minister (or an Information Officer) can, if necessary, get in touch with all the British press that matters simply by arranging to go into the Lobby room.

Ministers have been heard on sound radio for some forty years or so, and nowadays most of them also appear from time to time on the television screen. Both the BBC and the Independent Television Authority have complete independence in the arrangement of their programmes, and the government does not have privileged access to either of them for presenting its policies, any more than it has to the other media of communication.[1] It is not relevant to this book to discuss party political broadcasts, which are governed by formal agreements between the BBC, ITA and the political parties, and in which Ministers appear in their capacity as politicians and not as heads of departments. As Ministerial heads, we mostly see or hear them when their activities are of news value—saying a few words at the airport on the way to international conferences, making speeches at dinners or party conferences, commenting to interviewers on some news item of the day, explaining the government's views in a programme on the Common Market. We can expect to see Ministers, from time to time urging us along various socially beneficial lines—adjuring us not to drink and drive, or to post early for Christmas.

It is normal practice nowadays for the Chancellor to be invited by the BBC and independent television companies to make a television appearance on the evening of Budget Day to explain the changes in taxation or the concessions made: he usually includes a review of the country's general economic situation with simpler explanations and couched in language more informal than the conventions of Parliamentary style allow: the Opposition nominates a spokesman, usually the 'Shadow' Chancellor to exercise his right of reply to the Budget speech on the following evening.

There are Ministerial broadcasts on sound radio—like the Foreign Secretary speaking about the United Nations on United Nations Day —which are on non-controversial subjects and to which the Opposition does not normally reply, although it has the right to do so if it thinks the Ministerial broadcast is not sufficiently impartial. The BBC and ITA are also under a legal obligation in their charters to make time available for government announcements—foot-and-

[1] The Postmaster-General is answerable to Parliament in broad matters of policy only.

mouth disease warnings and police messages, for example—which are usually given by their own news readers.[1]

As we have seen already, some Ministers and some departments prefer to announce policy changes first to the House of Commons. Some do not. But even when the particular change of a policy is first to be announced in the House of Commons, Ministers often refer to coming legislation, or drop hints about it, in other places beforehand—it is one way of testing the temperature of the water before jumping in. The Home Secretary, for instance, told the Conservative Party conference that the Government were thinking of restricting Commonwealth immigration before there was any announcement in the House of Commons. The Chancellor of the Exchequer introduced his 'little budget' in the House of Commons in July 1961— the budget that introduced the pay pause restriction on government spending, and other austerity measures—but in the previous June, a month earlier, he had already announced to the Association of British Chambers of Commerce that overseas military expenditure was to be cut and public sector spending restrained.

Nor is there any rule to say that only one of the various methods of communication can be used when an announcement is to be made. The handling of publicity for a Defence White Paper, for example, shows that although the White Paper was presented to the House of Commons, the Minister of Defence used every other medium of communication on the same day. Once the Defence White Paper had been circulated to the Cabinet and the final draft agreed on, the Director of Information of the Ministry of Defence prepared for his Minister a list of questions likely to be asked by the press and the Minister then decided what he would like to say to them. The White Paper was then laid in dummy in the House of Commons the night before its presentation and laid in full in the Vote Office on the following morning. On the day of the presentation to Parliament, the Minister saw the Lobby correspondents and answered their questions. He then recorded a statement in the Ministry for sound radio and for the BBC and ITV television and made special recordings for the United States, Australian, Canadian and Overseas Services of the BBC. After this, the Minister saw the United States and Commonwealth press representatives. Similar publicity is arranged for the other Ministers when they present important papers to Parliament.

Direct with the Citizen. Besides these public appearances, Ministers

---

[1] In an emergency, the BBC is also required to broadcast 'any matter' which the government asks it to do.

also have to deal directly with people. They visit factories—or hospitals or schools, whatever their particular interest may be—and deputations visit them. They have a large correspondence from members of the public, private firms, trade associations, local authorities, industrialists, trade unions and so on. In fact ministerial, post bags appear to be much bigger today than they were pre-war.[1] The Minister also gets a stream of letters from MPs on behalf of their constituents or organizations in which they are interested. The most usual way for a MP to appeal to a Minister nowadays is by private letter rather than by public Question in the House. Questions are 'the upper part of the iceberg, prominent, but much the smaller part of the whole'.[2] (It should perhaps be added here that although we speak of the Minister dealing with his correspondence and seeing the deputations, it is often the officials of the department who write or appear on his behalf.)

The Minister also spends time in the House, where his fellow members can and do approach him informally about any particular matter which concerns them; the grievance is aired or the view expressed on a personal level without going through any formal process. A Minister may maintain, with some justification, that by the close contact he has with MPs and his constituents he is the main source of information for his department on public opinion and the likely reactions of the public to any proposed measures.

OFFICIALS

Officials, always as representatives of their Minister, have a number of important relations with the public, other than through Information Divisions. Occasionally senior officials make public speeches on non-political subjects; or, on behalf of their Minister, explain the policy of their department at some public function. Officials write to individual members of the public, and answer a voluminous mass of their queries and requests. Officials appear before Parliamentary Committees and royal commissions, and have special publics with whom they correspond and whom they meet on committees.

Officials' Relations with the General Public
For most people, their main personal contact with the government is

[1] K. Couzens, 'A Minister's Correspondence', *Public Administration*, Vol. XXXIV, Autumn 1956.
[2] D. N. Chester and Nona Bowring, *Questions in Parliament*, Oxford University Press, 1962, p. 105.

through officials like the postman and the counter clerks at the Post Office—where on average everyone transacts business in stamps and allowances and so on, to the tune of £80 a year—and the Officials in the local offices of the Ministry of Labour and the Ministry of Pensions and National Insurance. These three departments whose officials are in close day-to-day contact with the general public go to considerable pains to train their staff to be efficient and courteous. Clearly, it is impossible to analyse the nature of this face-to-face relationship in any real sense, and it is governed quite as often by the manners of the public as by those of the civil servant.

All departments, and especially those which have to run local offices all over the country are conscious of the need for improvements; all make some effort to brighten their premises. But spacious, airy premises are not the only thing necessary to good relations with the general public at this level. The quality of the service rendered is dependent upon the attitudes of the individual officials. At the worst, officials deal with members of the public in loud voices, refuse to explain regulations in clear and simple language and generally behave as if they were in a position of authority over the individual concerned, rather than his or her 'humble servant'. At the best, the individual is dealt with courteously and quickly and made to feel that his problem is of real concern to the official dealing with it. What instruction the officials receive and what training is given to them for the job of dealing with individual members of the general public will be dealt with in a later chapter.

The public also has to deal with government departments by correspondence and has to fill in forms for the Census or for passports, for income tax, or, if they are farmers, for the Ministry of Agriculture. As citizens we may approve of income tax, labour exchanges, passports or national insurance; as human beings we resent having to pay for them or having to fill in the necessary particulars, declare our incomes, the colour of our eyes, or the acres we have under wheat. The officials whose job it is to make or persuade us to do these things should at least not exasperate us by badly designed forms, grubby acknowledgement slips, undue delay in answering our letters or our telephone calls or in dealing with us over the counter.

But officials at all levels are administering regulations of increasing complexity, so that it is increasingly difficult to explain them simply but accurately. One of the biggest problems is that of communication between the well educated administrator in the Civil Service who constructs the rules and writes the regulations and the ordinary man or woman in the street who has to understand them. Once upon a time this lack of communication may not have mattered so much. But when virtually all a state's citizens vote, are literate, earn enough to have a surplus to spend, and when the state accepts responsibility for their education, health, and welfare, failure to communicate becomes serious. If administration is to be not only efficient but fair, the citizen's contacts with it should leave him feeling neither resentful nor bewildered. Civil servants at all levels are required to remember that fostering good public relations in this sense is not just a frill to be added to administrative action, but an integral part of good administration.

Officials and their Public Relations through Committees
Civil servants have to appear in public before Parliamentary Committees such as the Public Accounts Committee, the Estimates Committee or the Select Committee on Nationalized Industries, mainly as defenders of their departments. To royal commissions and inter-departmental committees, they submit written and oral evidence as expert witnesses when the subject investigated comes within their department's purview. For example, the Home Office offered evidence to the Royal Commission on Capital Punishment, 1949–53, the Admiralty, Air Ministry, War Office and Home Office submitted evidence to the Wolfenden Committee on Homosexuality and Prostitution, 1957. The Treasury was a witness to the Royal Commission on the Press, 1947–9, and the three Service departments to the Royal Commission on Doctors' and Dentists' Pay, 1957–60. The Royal Commission on the Civil Service, 1953–5, took evidence from the Treasury, Ministry of Supply, Admiralty, Air Ministry, Ministry of Works, Post Office, Ministry of Food, Scottish Office and Ministry of Labour.

When they appear before committees or royal commissions, the civil servants concerned act not as individuals but as the representative of their department's views or interest. Their written evidence will have been agreed within the department before submission, and the line to be followed in oral evidence will also have been agreed beforehand—if the subject is important enough, by the Minister as well as the senior civil servants involved.

In addition to appearing as witnesses, civil servants are often present on the other side of the table as well. Royal commissions are usually set up as temporary bodies[1] to study long-term problems on which there is little existing information; inter-departmental or

[1] There are a few royal commissions—mainly on academic or aesthetic matters, like the Royal Fine Arts Commission—which are in permanent session.

departmental committees are usually intended to deal with questions of more limited interest—broadcasting in Wales, the employment of children for the potato harvest, the composition and nutritive value of flour, for example—when a policy decision needs to be taken within a relatively short time. (The Wolfenden Committee on Homosexuality and Prostitution was an exception in that it dealt with the kind of subject usually given to a royal commission.) The members of a royal commission are usually taken from outside the civil service; some committees are composed entirely of officials, although many are non-official or only partly official. The Plowden Committee on the Treasury Control of Expenditure was unusual in that officials and eminent outsiders sat on the committee, and both were given confidential information. Two reports were drawn up. The published report, which was more circumspect than the full report, was signed only by the outside members. The confidential report was signed by all the members.

But whatever the composition of the commission or committee, it is civil servants who act as secretariat and staff.

Officials and Relations with Special Publics
Each government department has its own special publics—the groups of people who are more closely concerned with its activities than are the public in general. Employers and trade unions are closely concerned with the Ministry of Labour; those who operate the railways and use the roads with the Ministry of Transport; one of the Treasury's special publics is the City. The Ministry of Education, for instance, has three special publics, the local education authorities who run the schools, the teachers and the consumers—that is, the parents and children.

Local authorities are the special public of some departments. Many government departments have to consult them regularly and frequently. It is often imposed on them by statute. In many cases it is the local authorities which carry out the administration of one field of work—like running old people's homes—while the Minister retains Parliamentary responsibility. Departments may communicate with them by meeting and writing to them, often by official circulars. These may give the local authorities, for example, information concerning some new regulation, advice on handling particular cases or they might be asked to increase their publicity about something like the local opportunities for further education.

By special publics, therefore, we mean the various groups or bodies of people with whom central government departments have to work.

C 33

They may be employees of the government, like members of the Association of Prison Officers; they may be autonomous professional groups individually in receipt of government money, like doctors and dentists in their varied associations; or they may be quite independent. Some special publics, like the hospital boards and advisory committees, are the administrative creations of the central government. Others, departments use for consultation, like the trade unions or the Federation of British Industries, over a fairly wide field; there are also organizations such as the British Legion or the Automobile Association set up to protect the interests of one particular section of the public. These special publics are not administrative creations; they exist separately in their own right and they cannot be abolished, even if their existence happens to be inconvenient.

As a means of securing co-operation, reaching the widest possible agreement and framing workable legislation and regulations, the central government has in recent years developed this complicated series of advisory and consultative committees, conferences and even less formal contacts and meetings between administrators and the people outside. This network of communications is a vital part of the public relations work of government.

The fact that a great deal of the contact between government and special publics is conducted at administrative level in Britain highlights one of the contrasts between this country and the United States. In America, the Senate and House of Representatives remain the happy hunting ground for pressure groups and lobbyists and public information is to a large extent channelled through elected representatives. American administration is publicly, personally and at times extremely visibly, responsible before a system of congressional committees; American senior civil servants are still often involved in politics, whilst in Britain they are not. For the most part contacts between civil servants and their special publics in Britain remain discreetly within the Whitehall corridors.

Special publics, then, are of two kinds—the advisory committees which are the creation of the central government and the special interest (or pressure) groups which are not. There is also a third kind of organization, which although not a special public in the way we have been discussing, fits most conveniently into this place in the chapter. It is the bodies which receive some financial aid from the government and which we have called a supported propaganda body. We will look at each type separately.

Advisory Committees. Advisory committees remain more or less permanently in commission as an adjunct to the machinery of government, unlike departmental or inter-departmental committees, which are set up to do a specific job and are then disbanded.

There are plenty of them. One of the most striking developments in administrative practice since the war has been this increasing use of outside advisers. Ministers and administrators do not rely so much on their own departmental resources as they used to. (Although there has been a parallel increase of expertise within government service, as well. The employment of scientists, economists and statisticians inside departments had greatly increased since the war.) When they were counted in 1958[1], there were over 480 advisory committees in existence, attached to twenty-six government departments, from the Ministry of Agriculture, Food and Fisheries with its fifty-four to the Scottish Education Department with only two. They vary in scope from the Bee Diseases Advisory Committee or the China Clay Council, to the University Grants Committee or the National Economic Development Council. There is also an Advisory Council on Child Care, the Central Advisory Council on Education, a National Insurance Advisory Committee and a host of local National Insurance Advisory Committees. (Most of the government departments which have regional and local organizations also have advisory bodies at these levels too.)

Some advisory committees are set up by statute. For instance, it has become common for Acts concerned with new social services to contain provision for a standing advisory committee. In 1958 about 100 of the 480 advisory committees had such a statutory basis. Others originate from Ministerial regulation, and some exist because of a recommendation by a royal commission or departmental committee of inquiry. Most advisory committees meet not more often than monthly or less than annually, the only common practice being round-the-table discussion. Only a few publish reports; most give their advice confidentially to their interested departments.

Advisory committees are of three kinds. The first and largest group of them are the committees of experts, on many of which civil servants do not sit. About two-thirds of advisory committees are of this kind. Their job is to provide expert and technical advice to a department. They range over the whole field of government activity. The Central Health Services Council, the National Advisory Council on the Training and Supply of Teachers, the Scientific Advisory Council, the Committee on Social Development in the Colonies, are all ex-

[1] PEP, *Advisory Committees in British Government*, George Allen & Unwin, 1960, p. 23.

35

pert committees of this type. The Council on Prices, Productivity and Incomes set up in 1957 and the National Economic Development Council set up in 1961 were slightly different kinds of expert committees in that they did not tender confidential advice to one government department, but published reports on the economic situation for the general public.

Then there are the administrative committees which—under the sanction of a Ministerial veto—decide matters themselves. They detach administrative work from the main government machine. Of such kind are the University Grants Committee, the Board of Trade Development Areas Committee, or the Central Training Council on Child Care.

Thirdly, and perhaps most important from the point of view of public relations, are the consultative committees. People from outside the government machine—sometimes nominees of interest groups and sometimes appointed by the government—meet for general discussion with civil servants or sometimes Ministers, as fellow members of the committee. The purpose of consultative committees is twofold. They can warn the officials in advance about the feelings or prejudices of the interested parties; in return they get a foreknowledge of what politicians and administrators have in mind. It is undoubtedly useful to both parties. Sir Geoffrey King, referring to the National Insurance Advisory Committee and the Industrial Injuries Advisory Council with which the Ministry of Pensions and National Insurance works, has said:

The procedure whereby the merits and reasons for proposed regulations are explained by civil servants to an independent but well-informed committee . . . seems to be a good answer to critics who complain that regulations are too often made behind closed doors . . . and there is no doubt that the necessity for going through this procedure is a very wholesome discipline for the department itself.[1]

Such consultative committees were the National Production Advisory Council on Industry, and the National Joint Advisory Council of the Ministry of Labour, the Engineering Advisory Committee and the various Consumer Committees.

Special Interest Groups. Special interest groups are those associations which are devoted to furthering some special cause, and are often

[1] Sir Geoffrey S. King, *The Ministry of Pensions and National Insurance*, New Whitehall Series, No. 6, George Allen & Unwin, 1958, p. 120.

called pressure groups, although they may not in reality put pressure on anybody.

British government rests traditionally upon consent and co-operation rather than coercion. The co-operation of special interest groups is not essential to administration—an industry could be nationalized against its will; farming subsidies could be abolished without the farmers' support. But in most cases a government department prefers an interest group's co-operation, if it can be obtained. Legislative proposals and changes in administrative regulations are commonly the subject of prolonged discussion and negotiation between a department and the interested bodies before they are introduced.

One prominent industrialist has complained,[1] however, that although new departures of a minor and non-controversial type often receive extremely detailed and adequate inquiry and consultation, really major changes like the setting up of the Restrictive Practices Court or entry into the Common Market are often announced publicly without much prior consultation. This is no doubt because the policy is often a political decision and there is a need for secrecy. Consultation will take place on the practical application of the policy when it has been decided.

Special interest groups are of two kinds. The first are those associations which represent the permanent interests of a group of people. They may be trade unions or the AA and RAC for motorists, St Dunstan's for the war-blinded, the National Farmers' Union or the various trade associations. The groups expect departments to consult them regularly, and regard relations with the department as part of their normal work. The civil servant finds himself dealing not so much with the individual firm, pensioner or trade unionist, but with the full-time staff of their representative bodies. It is official talking to official.[2] The position of the Federation of British Industries is one example of this regular contact. The TUC is another. They sit on official advisory committees—the TUC has representatives on the National Economic Development Council, for instance. They are called on to give evidence to inquiries, are asked for their views on draft bills, etc., and perform some administrative functions for government departments —for example the FBI and the policy of voluntary divided limitations.

The second type are those associations which set themselves some particular goal—to change government policy about capital punish-

---

[1] Sir Raymond Streat, 'Government Consultations with Industry', *Public Administration*, Vol. XXVII, Spring 1959, p. 5 and p. 7.
[2] The National Farmers' Union is reputed to have an exact hierarchy matching the sections of the Ministry of Agriculture with which it deals.

ment, licensing hours, Sunday observance or road improvement, for example. These special interest groups are normally most active in putting pressure on MPs and the government when legislation is contemplated which affects their own subject, but most of them are in permanent existence even if they remain in the background. A government department would normally take such a group's views into account except when the matter was one of minor importance or completely straightforward.

The Ministry of Education is an example of a department which has learnt in recent years the value of good public relations with one of the special interest groups concerned with education—the Church schools. The ease with which increased financial aid for Church schools was accepted virtually unremarked in 1959, can be contrasted with the controversy surrounding the financing of Church schools between 1943 and 1951. The administrative, political and public relations history of the Church schools question may in fact be taken as the pattern of development and lessons learnt in the handling of special publics since the end of the last war. During the period 1943 to 1951, the department found itself the prey of the opposed interest groups and made almost no headway in its search for an agreement between the bodies concerned; it frequently found its Minister under fire in the House for contradictory statements and undertakings made separately to individual groups and it was forced to make liberal use of the device of the planted question. By 1959 a system of joint consultation had been evolved and perfected, whereby although no interested group was perfectly satisfied, none of the bodies concerned made use of their 'retained' MPs to contest the Minister's decision.

Some people consider that the increasing development of good public relations between the administration and the special interest groups over the last ten or twenty years tends to diminish parliamentary responsibility. It also raises the question of what happens to the views of minority groups within a large pressure group. The Tomato Growers' Board, for example, did not always seem to be entirely representative of all its members' views. And on occasion the London Cab Drivers appear to have felt that the Transport and General Workers' Union has not pursued their case with the Minister of Transport (on the subject of banning U-turns, by which a cab is forbidden to turn round in a busy street, for example) with sufficient vigour. The department concerned, however, cannot put right such a state of affairs, but can only try to make sure, as far as possible, that all interests are consulted. Many professional bodies have splinter groups

38

and rival associations. The Medical Practitioners' Union, for example, is not consulted directly by the Minister of Health, but arranges for the British Medical Association to represent its views. There is a rival to the major dental practitioners' organization too, which at present the division concerned within the Ministry does not think is of sufficient importance to consult; but if this organization grew in membership, the division would have to consider whether present consultations with only one organization were enough.

Supported Propaganda Bodies. Within the broad definitions of public relations used in this chapter, mention must be made of those organizations which are in receipt of government grants. Out of the sixty or so listed in the Civil Estimates only a few bodies have a publicity content, i.e. perform propaganda functions which otherwise government departments might have to do for themselves: the British Council and the British Travel and Holidays Association, the Royal Society for the Prevention of Accidents, the Central Council for Health Education, the Council of Industrial Design and Design Centres, the British Standards Institute, the British Productivity Council, the National Federation of Young Farmers' Clubs, the International Red Cross Committee, and so on. These bodies get grants from the government because their function is to educate the public.

Among the voluntary welfare associations which qualify for government grants are some which undertake the education and persuasion of the public in controversial fields where the government may well feel that it cannot initiate publicity, though it may welcome the campaign as socially useful, for example: the National Marriage Guidance Council, the Family Welfare Association, the Prisoners' Aid Societies, and the Central After-Care Association (set up in 1949 to look after those discharged from prison or borstal, which is entirely financed by government grant).

Among the learned bodies and institutions which receive government grants or subscriptions are a number which supplement the technical information services of government departments, e.g. the Bureau of Hygiene and Tropical Diseases, the Medical Research Council and the National Institute of Oceanography. A further subgroup within this latter category consists of libraries and teaching institutions whose work supplements the national and local authority contributions to education and the arts in general, e.g. The Royal Academy of Music, the National Central Library, the British Film Institute, the Royal Academy of Dramatic Art, and the Arts Council of Great Britain. All these bodies, assisted as they are to varying extents by government financial aid, are another way in which the government seeks to 'maintain understanding' with its citizens.

GOVERNMENT PUBLICATIONS

There is a mass of instruction and technical information which pours out of government departments themselves but which is not laid before Parliament. A good deal of this material is statistical. The *Annual Abstract of Statistics*, kept up to date by the *Monthly Digest of Statistics*, *Economic Trends* and *Financial Statistics* give the specialist as well as the informed public a general picture of the economy. Individual departments issue, for example, the Colonial Office's *Quarterly Digest of Statistics*, weekly sheets of coal output and consumption, the Report on Overseas Trade, the Trade and Navigation Accounts, the Registrar-General's returns of Births, Marriages and Deaths, the Weather Reports, and so on. Nearly all of these figures are collected and prepared by the departments themselves, or by the Central Statistical Office; sometimes the Information Division of the department concerned publishes the figures, as in the *Board of Trade Journal*. There is also a good deal of educational material issued by departments. The Central Office of Information prepares for publication factual information on very varied subjects—the Official Handbook of Great Britain, a hundred booklets in the Choice of Careers Series or on such diverse matters as an ABC of Cookery, a series of reference pamphlets on Britain, Disarmament, the Commonwealth, Safety in Industry, the Hydrogen Bomb, and so on.

H.M. Stationery Office

When this material is printed, it is usually issued by the Stationery Office[1] which was founded in 1786 and has been the government publisher since 1883. The Ministerial head of the Stationery Office is the Chancellor, but Questions are usually answered in the House by the Financial Secretary. On behalf of Parliament and government departments and museums, it issues 5,000 publications a year and over sixty periodicals. They include *Hansard*, the *London Gazette* the *War Histories* and the *Highway Code*, and pamphlets giving

[1] Not all government printed material is issued by the Stationery Office. Patent specifications, Ordnance Survey maps and Admiralty charts are not. Nor do the Stationery Office undertake completely straightforward printing jobs, like Lost Property notices, which involve no problem of presentation or display.

technical advice for farmers on such things as mineral deficiency in plants, or pest infestation. HMSO issues guides to historic country houses, catalogues and guides to the London museums or hints on better handwriting; postcards of National Gallery masterpieces, information on lagging pipes in frosty weather, or a book on the Dynamics of Exploited Fish populations. The man who can find nothing to interest him in the Stationery Office's list of publications must be either very erudite or very dull. Its annual sales at home and abroad stand at about 20 million copies, two-thirds sold to the public and the rest issued to Parliament or government departments. The Stationery Office runs one wholesale and two retail bookshops in London, and six retail shops in the provinces.

INFORMATION DIVISIONS

These then are the main channels of communication between the government department and the public: the Minister in Parliament and outside it; the civil servants and their relations with the public whether they are the special publics or the ordinary citizen. The information services have been superimposed comparatively recently on these traditional relationships. On the whole it is true to say that the Information Division is that part of each Ministry which is professionally concerned with the press, radio and television; the rest of the department—that is the Minister and the administrators in the policy divisions—deal with Parliament and the public. There is a good deal of overlapping of course. Information Divisions are often intimately concerned with Parliament and the general public; Ministers and civil servants are also concerned with the press. But when the Minister deals with the press, radio or television, he will be advised by his Information Division. When, as frequently happens, the ordinary civil servant and the information officers work together for these media, the role of the civil servant is to deal with *what* to say; of the Information Division to deal with *how* to say it. In the last fifty years *how* has developed into a technique in industry and commerce and in public life generally; this, and the developments in radio and television have greatly increased the relative importance of communication through these professional organs of information and opinion—and hence the need for experts in these techniques within the government departments.

An Information Division is the branch of a Ministry which is expert in publicity techniques. Each Minister is responsible for the information activities of his department in exactly the same way as he is responsible for any other part of his department's administration. He has the final responsibility for deciding his department's public relations policy, and is answerable for it to Parliament. The Chief Information Officer[1] of the department serves his Minister as an adviser and an expert in public relations just as the legal adviser or a Chief Engineer or a Chief Scientific Officer are the expert heads of their branches. The Chief Information Officer's status is such—the equivalent of an Assistant Secretary or above—that he has direct access to the Minister and to the Permanent Secretary, and his special knowledge makes him consulted both as particular occasions arise and often also through being present at policy-forming meetings which are held by Ministers and by senior civil servants.

The Information Division is often shown as part of Establishments Branch because it has to be attached to the departmental organization somewhere; but the Chief Information Officer does not have to go through the head of Establishments to reach either the Minister or the Permanent Head of the department. The Information Division's attachment to Establishments does, however, emphasize the fact that it is not a policy-making division, but one which serves the rest of the department.

The size of the Information Division varies from one department to another as does the internal organization and the status of the senior officer. Some Ministries think they need big information staffs, some do not. Normally, Information Divisions are divided into three sections—the Press section, the Publicity section, and what is called an Intelligence section (or a Briefing section in some departments). The Chief Information Officer has responsibility over the whole Information Division, while his second-in-command is often, though not invariably, in charge of the Press section.

The government information services work under the same constitutional conventions as those which govern the behaviour of the older parts of the civil service, that is, they are non-political. Information officers are responsible for providing information about the activities of their department. They are precluded from discussing the merits of government policy with the press or public although they may repeat to enquirers the declared objectives and

[1] For purposes of convenience the head of the Information Division is referred to in this book as the Chief Information Officer. In some departments, such as the Ministry of Defence and the War Office, his title is the Director of Public Relations; in the Post Office and the Ministry of Health he is the Public Relations Officer, and their divisions are called Public Relations Divisions. The Foreign Office has a Head of the News Department. Whatever their titles, all these officials hold similar positions and perform similar functions.

ideas of their Ministers. The central position of Parliament is safe-guarded to the extent that there is a general ruling that matters which are subject to Parliamentary privilege are not proper questions for information officers to deal with. It is proper for information officers to argue the merits of announced government policy even before it is approved by Parliament but they do not, for example, anticipate a Ministerial answer to a Parliamentary Question, nor do they give information which would anticipate the contents of a White Paper when one is pending. They do, however, publicize the contents of Ministerial speeches delivered both in and outside Parliament on official occasions and the contents of a White Paper are usually publicized by information officers after it has been tabled, but before it has been debated in Parliament. The practice of supplying advance press statements and confidential information, or giving information to the press simultaneously with giving this information to Parliament has grown up because the press (including radio and television) need to have the facts and comments published as soon as possible after a statement has been made in the House. Unless they have this information beforehand, the delay would be too long by the standards of modern journalism.[1]

There are also an enormous number of things that government departments do which are not matters of political controversy, or only intermittently, and which are not 'hot' news releases. Government departments find you jobs and pay you pensions, arrange to educate your children, persuade you to drive carefully, be immunized, or volunteer for the army, and so on. These kinds of campaign too need special publicity skills. It is one of the jobs of the information services to break down the barriers which divide the 'we' and the 'they'—the people and the government. The way in which they do the job will be described in Chapter V below.

THE CENTRAL OFFICE OF INFORMATION

It would be uneconomical and indeed impractical for each division to have specialists in all branches of publicity, so for paid publicity of all kinds they rely on the Central Office of Information.

---

[1] Normally the Press keeps to the 'embargo' rules very strictly. On one or two occasions it has been broken. When the Wolfenden report on Homosexuality and Prostitution was published, for example, the evening papers carried special articles of comment immediately after publication of the report, which indicated that the contents of the report had been revealed to the writers of the articles before the embargo had been lifted. This was an exception to normal practice, however.

The Central Office of Information provides for the Information Divisions all the technical services which professional advertising and publicity agents give commercial clients. It does not publish anything on its own behalf, but acts always as the agent for a policy department or departments. The Ministerial department is responsible for the policy and contents of a publicity campaign while the Central Office of Information provides the expert and technical knowledge to translate the department's wishes into publicity material.

The Central Office of Information was set up to replace some of the functions of the wartime Ministry of Information, but it is not headed by a Minister. (The Financial Secretary to the Treasury is responsible to Parliament for the Central Office of Information's total vote and staffing.) It was not intended to be a Ministry of Propaganda; nor does it perform on the home side those policy co-ordinating functions which were a major part of the wartime Ministry of Information's job.

Apart from its overseas responsibilities—its chief activity being to provide material for publicizing Britain overseas, which is outside the scope of this book—the Central Office of Information either prepares material itself, or arranges for commercial agencies to produce material to its requirements and under its guidance. For example, press advertisements are commissioned from advertising agencies and films from independent production companies, while exhibitions, posters, leaflets, and books are produced by the Central Office of Information's own staff. It has ten production divisions, of which seven—the Publications, Advertising, Exhibitions, Films, Photographs, Reference and Social Survey Divisions—are relevant to information activities in the United Kingdom. The work of the Central Office of Information is described in Chapter VI below.

The Central Office of Information distributes all government press notices to London and provincial papers as a common service. Through its regional organization it provides a public relations and a common press service in the provinces for those government departments that need one. In Wales this is provided through the Welsh Office, and in Scotland and Northern Ireland through the agency of their Information Offices. In these two countries information and publicity is handled centrally by the Information Service, and not by separate departmental Information Officers. In Scotland, the Scottish Information Office is responsible for information for the Scottish administrative departments—Agriculture, Education, Home and Health—and for any other bodies the Secretary of State for Scotland is interested in. Northern Ireland has a Parliament and Government of its own to deal with Northern Ireland affairs, and as at Westminster, each Minister is responsible for all information or publicity policy relating to his Ministry. But the work is done centrally by the Northern Ireland Government Information Service, which is attached to the Cabinet Offices.

The information officers in Scotland and Northern Ireland act for the Central Office of Information in their own countries when necessary, organizing campaigns and exhibitions, and producing films and so on.

CO-ORDINATION OF THE INFORMATION SERVICES

The information services, split as they are between the Information Divisions in each department and the Central Office of Information, do not have a Ministerial head. Some co-ordination of information policy is necessary, however, and it is important to have someone who can speak in Parliament for government information generally.

The Minister responsible for co-ordinating government publicity for the home side is the Minister without Portfolio; the Secretary for Technical Co-operation is responsible for the co-ordination of overseas information services.

The co-ordinating Minister's duties do not affect the responsibility of each Minister for the information of his own department; he is not the head of the information services. His co-ordinating role is intended to help the Cabinet to get a broad picture of information activities as a whole, and meetings of the Chief Information Officers, held once a week under his chairmanship, are intended to encourage inter-departmental discussion of common information problems and to co-ordinate information policy as much as possible. The growth and development of the co-ordinating role, both at Ministerial and at official level, is described in Chapter VI.

SUMMARY

In these pages we have indicated some of the ways in which the government tries to tell the people what it is doing and why. No government can function in the long run without the consent and co-operation of the governed. In a democracy it is especially important, and the central government of this country spends a very great deal of time and effort explaining its actions to its citizens. In the rest of the book we will set out in more detail the contribution the information services make to this continuous process of explanation.

BIBLIOGRAPHY FOR CHAPTER I

Chester, D. N., and Nona Bowring. *Questions in Parliament*. Oxford University Press, 1962.

Finn, David. *Public Relations and Management*. Reinhold Publishing Corporation, New York, 1960.

Johnson, Nevil. 'Parliamentary Questions and the Conduct of Public Administration.' *Public Administration*, Vol. 39, Summer 1961, pp. 131–48.

King, Sir Geoffrey S. *Ministry of Pensions and National Insurance*. New Whitehall Series, No. 6. George Allen & Unwin, 1958.

PEP. *Advisory Committee in British Government*. George Allen & Unwin, 1960.

Streat, Sir Raymond. 'Government Consultations with Industry.' *Public Administration*, Spring 1959, pp. 1–8.

Williams, Francis. *Press, Parliament and People*. Heinemann, 1946.

Willson, F. M. G. Information and Advice: How they are obtained by the Central Government.

CHAPTER II

From the Beginning to 1945

It will be easier to understand the organization of the information services today and the way they carry out their task if we look first at the origins of a specialized government information service and its historical development.

The idea of having specialists employed by the government to report on its actions is no invention of the twentieth century. As long ago as 1030 when St Olaf, King of Norway, drew up his men in battle order, he arranged for his scalds to be present on the field, within a shield fence of the strongest and boldest warriors, so that 'ye shall remain here and see the events which may take place and then ye will not have to follow the reports of others in what ye afterwards tell or sing about it'.[1] Nor have men like John Milton or Daniel Defoe hesitated to use their pens to support the policies of the government of the day. Present day government information officers are neither reporters nor propagandists, but their office retains perhaps a little of the flavour of both.

BEFORE 1914

Different strands which make up the government information services as we know them today had different origins. If we consider that information includes putting forward the views and policies of the government and feeding back facts about the 'market' being reached, the origin of the overseas information service lies in our diplomatic representation abroad. If information means publicizing the departments' activities, the first government department to engage in advertising its wares to the public at large was the Post Office. Their first Annual Report, published in 1854, showed a lively concern for good public relations. In it the Postmaster General deplored the public's imperfect knowledge of the Post Office's activities and said, 'it could not be otherwise than satisfactory to Parliament if by means of a periodical Report the general scope and extent of the progress made

[1] Snorre Sturlason, *The Olaf Sagas*, translated by Samuel Laing, J. M. Dent & Sons, 1930, p. 358.

by the Department were brought under its notice'.[1] This report also contained a section on 'Suggestions to the Public' urging them to post early in the day, write the address legibly and provide a suitable letter box on their front doors—adjurations which have a familiar ring still in the 1960s.

In 1876 the Post Office embarked on the first government mass advertising campaign. On behalf of the Post Office Savings Bank they distributed 'a million handbills, setting forth in clear and simple language the advantages offered by the Government system of Savings Banks, Life Insurance and Annuities'.[2] No doubt the Post Office was a pioneer in this sphere because unlike most government departments, they had something to sell.

Before the First World War, some of the activities which fall to the Information Divisions today were carried out as part of the administrative machine. Official publications like the *Board of Trade Journal* (founded 1886) which aim at supplying factual information and statistics for the business community were originally published by ordinary divisions within the department: nowadays they are published by the information staff.

Information has to be collected as well as disseminated. In this sense, probably the first specialized information unit within a government department—although it was never called by such a name—was the Office of Special Inquiries and Reports set up under Sir Michael Sadler in 1895 within the Board of Education. This office served as an intelligence department to collect information on education from all sources, for the use of the Board of Education. The Bryce Commission,[3] set up to report on secondary education in special districts of the United Kingdom and also in other countries, had shown the necessity for having accurate and up-to-date information about education, which until then had not existed for the country as a whole. 'There is a large number of matters affecting education,' said one Minister,[4] 'as to which the Department lives merely from hand-to-mouth, failing to record the knowledge it obtains for future use, and unable to obtain information as to what is being done elsewhere, whether at home or abroad, in an efficient manner. There is now such a waste of power through this deficiency . . . the appoint-

[1] First Report of the Postmaster General on the Post Office, 1854. HMSO, 1955, p. 7.

[2] Raymond Nottage, 'The Post Office. A Pioneer of Big Business', *Public Administration*, Vol. XXXVII, Spring 1959, pp. 55–64.

[3] Royal Commission on Secondary Education, 1894. HMSO, 1895.

[4] Mr Arthur Acland, Vice-President of the Committee of Council (which was responsible for the Board of Education at that time).

ment of an officer with a limited amount of help whose duty it shall be to collect and supply information and to make occasional reports in special matters . . . has become essential if the Education Department . . . is to do its work efficiently.' Over the years numerous special reports were published on, for example, modern language teaching in Holland and Belgium, secondary education in Germany, the general education systems of America, most European countries and the Dominions and Colonies. There were memoranda, too, on the treatment of particular problems in Britain, such as the pre-school-age child, domestic and handicraft instruction in schools, school hygiene, and so on. The foundation of the national system of education in Britain was due in part to the work of the Office of Special Inquiries and Reports. The Office also came to function as foreign correspondent for the Board—assisting the Colonial and India Office in the selection of people to teach abroad, arranging exchanges of modern language teachers between England and France, answering letters from foreigners on British educational methods, and so forth. It was also responsible for the building up of the Board's library on education.

In 1912, too, the Post Office, wishing to give better service, set up Telephone and Telegraph Advisory Committees in the main provincial towns. All important local interests were represented on these committees to 'inform the Post Office of local conditions and requirements'—the first efforts at the regional organization of inward information.

Information, too, means explaining new enactments to the public. The first time this technique was practised was in 1912 when a corps of lecturers was organized by Mr Lloyd George to travel all over the country and explain to employers and members the provisions of his new Act—the first National Insurance scheme.

So before 1913, some information services existed, but they were carried out patchily and piece-meal in various odd corners of government departments.

THE 1914–18 WAR

The outbreak of war in 1914 presented the central government with entirely new problems. This was the first large-scale war for 100 years, and things had changed since Napoleon's day. Then private citizens could travel fairly freely on the continent to enemy countries, newspapers were only newsheets read by a few people, days or weeks after the events had occurred. By 1914 the invention of the telegraph meant

D   49

that news was received almost immediately, and the mass circulation of newspapers meant that it was read by everybody. Propaganda and news became important and public morale mattered. It was only surprising that it took so long, by modern standards, for the central government propaganda services to get under way. A Home Office Information Bureau and a War Propaganda Bureau were committees of outside experts set up in 1916 to advise on information and to organize propaganda respectively. There was an Information Advisory Committee consisting of leading journalists and newspaper proprietors, appointed in December 1916 to advise the government about publicity matters. But a Department of Information was not set up until early 1917, and not until a year later were the three main organizations which had to deal with publicity firmly established.

The first was the Department of Information, set up mainly to co-ordinate and extend the work of the Home Office Information Bureau and the War Propaganda Bureau. Its chief concern was publicity in the Dominions and in allied and neutral countries, and it was responsible partly to the Prime Minister and partly to the Foreign Office. The Commercial Propaganda Bureau in Madrid and the British War Mission—consisting of a group of prominent public men who visited America during 1917 to persuade them to enter the war— were also under its aegis. It was also responsible for setting up hospitality committees in the chief towns of the United Kingdom for looking after American troops after America had entered the war. In March 1918 it was made into a Ministry of Information under Lord Beaverbrook. The second body, the National War Aims Committee started out as a private organization to carry out patriotic propaganda in Britain. It was later taken over by the War Cabinet. The third body was the Crewe House Committee, started in 1917, under the Chairmanship of Lord Northcliffe, to organize pro-Allied publicity in enemy countries.

By the end of the war information and propaganda had become accepted features of central administration. The appalling losses at the Front and the U-boat campaigns in the Atlantic forced everybody to see the importance of press censorship of troop and ship movements. It had become clear that public morale on the home front mattered too. At first publicity campaigns, like the poster of Lord Kitchener saying 'Your country needs you', had been enough to recruit a volunteer army, but the introduction of conscription had needed explanation in principle and in detail. Similarly, food shortages and then the introduction of food rationing had had to be explained. It was considered important that the Allied case in neutral and enemy countries should not go by default. Gradually it had become acceptable for government organizations to provide explanatory information, although the acceptance of such an idea was a considerable psychological change for the British parliament and people.

1919–39, THE INTER-WAR YEARS

Peace saw the whole apparatus dismantled. A few of the functions of the wartime organizations were transferred to other departments; for instance, the Foreign Office News Department continued to operate the British Official Wireless Service which had been started during the war and was the forerunner of the London Press Service of the Ministry of Information and later of the present Central Office of Information.

A few departments, though, started press sections in the first years of peace. The Air Ministry had a press officer from its inception in 1919 and soon afterwards other Service departments started to employ press officers. The Ministry of Health started a Housing Information Office also in 1919. The next developments were on the overseas side. In 1920 the British Library of Information (the predecessor of the British Information Services) was set up in New York and press attachés were appointed to the British Embassies in Paris, Rome and Berlin. In 1921, Mr Winston Churchill left the War Office to become Secretary of State for the Colonies. The creation of a Middle East department in the Colonial Office had brought that office into unaccustomed press prominence. Mr Churchill therefore arranged for the War Office Press Officer to act also for the Colonial Office. The experiment of having a specialist as a link between the Colonial Office and the press proved a successful one.

During the General Strike in 1926, the government ran its own newspaper, *The British Gazette*, and the absence of the normal newspapers gave enormous importance to the BBC's radio news service; for six weeks government information had a virtual monopoly of the news media available. But little else happened during the twenties to develop departmental information services. Indeed there were complaints[1] that the government was lagging behind in the public relations field, both in home and overseas propaganda.

There was one exception to the generally slow development of official information services. The Empire Marketing Board, set up in 1926, marked a considerable advance in the application of publicity

[1] PEP, 'Government Public Relations', *Planning*, Vol. I, No. 14, November 21, 1933.

techniques in official service. The main function of this Board was to encourage the production and marketing of Empire goods, especially agricultural products. The genesis of the Empire Marketing Board had been the Imperial Conference of 1923, when the United Kingdom had promised a certain amount of preference for imported Commonwealth products. But the government found it could not persuade the British to accept this anti-free trade measure. In 1924, therefore, Mr Baldwin persuaded Parliament to grant £1 million a year to promote the sale of Commonwealth produce here. This sum represented the equivalent cash value of the advantages which it was thought would have accrued to Commonwealth countries if the preferences had been approved. In 1925 the Imperial Economic Committee recommended that the £1 million should be spent on maintaining a body which would undertake publicity and research for the marketing of Commonwealth produce in the United Kingdom. This was the Empire Marketing Board.

Much of the success of the Board was due to the animating genius of its secretary, Sir Stephen Tallents, who was convinced of the value of publicity to the government, excited by the possibilities of the new techniques and determined to introduce professionalism into the ranks of government public relations. He said, 'The skilled and judicious employment of publicity, is I am convinced, a subject of major importance in public administration. It enjoys at present some lip service, but little sound thought or practical experiment. It demands the most careful study and experiment and the application to both of first class brains and first class taste. Central government and local government must be weaned from the idea that publicity is a luxury, if not a folly. . . . Publicity should be recognized as a professional job demanding special training and special capacities, which incidentally do not include a flair for personal boosting but do include, in the broadest sense, artistic capacity.'[1] In the Board's Film Unit, which later became the Crown Film Unit of the Ministry of Information and then of the Central Office of Information and continued in existence until 1952, he employed directors like Grierson, Flaherty and Cavalcanti, pioneers in this country of the documentary film. They made outstanding films, like *Drifters*, for the Empire Marketing Board. This was an entirely new concept of publicity, not by direct exhortation or advertisement but by an attempt to excite the viewers' interest and imagination.[2]

[1] Sir Stephen G. Tallents, 'Salesmanship in the Public Service: Scope and Technique', *Public Administration*, Vol. XI, July 1933, pp. 265–6.
[2] John Grierson writing later of these pioneering days said, 'the basic thesis

The Empire Marketing Board also created a Central Film Library managed for them and later for the Post Office by the Imperial Institute. This Central Film Library is still in existence and is now a part of the Central Office of Information. The Empire Marketing Board also distributed popular articles illustrating scientific agricultural research to the press of the Empire, and the British Broadcasting Corporation arranged similar talks on its overseas service. The Board made a film, for example, of the work of the Welsh Plant Breeding Station.

In 1932 the United Kingdom ceased to be a free trade country and it became possible to give preferential tariffs to Commonwealth goods. Therefore it was no longer necessary to publicize Commonwealth imports and the main reason for having an Empire Marketing Board ceased; in 1933 it fell the victim of economy cuts[1] and its expert public relations staff dispersed. But if economy closed down the Empire Marketing Board, in another sense it marked the beginning of public relations inside government departments. The disbandment of the Board coincided with the expansion of the Post Office's publicity and advertising work. The Postmaster General, Sir Kingsley Wood, wanted to improve the relations of the Post Office with the public and develop its selling methods to increase the public's desire to write letters, telephone friends and send greetings telegrams. He secured the services of Sir Stephen Tallents. Thus the first full-scale government public relations division was formed. Sir Stephen continued to employ the same techniques as Public Relations Officer to the Post Office as he had in the Empire Marketing Board. (One of his first achievements was to conduct an inquiry into customer dissatisfaction which resulted in full ink wells and pens that actually wrote being put into ordinary post offices.) The Film Unit became the Post Offices' Film Unit. Their documentary film, *Night Mail* directed by John Grierson, with a commentary written by the poet Auden and music by Benjamin Britten, became one of the outstanding documentary films. Similar films, for the Post Office's internal consumption, for example on the telephone service, dramatized the work to help create proper pride in the department, on the grounds that a good film does for an organization what a 'new hat does for a woman'.

was that education for modern citizenship had to find new and dramatic forms.... In the great departments of state . . . we were at the heart of the matter—of technological and scientific progress, of new citizenship in the making.' *Public Relations*, Vol. 3, No. 1, September 1950.

[1] Certain of its functions were transferred to the Imperial Economic Committee and some to the Executive Council of the Imperial Agricultural Bureaux. Some lapsed.

Both the Empire Marketing Board and the Post Office had special problems quite unlike those of the ordinary Whitehall department. They were engaged in commercial activities like a private firm and entered the public relations field to do a similar thing—to sell more goods and services. In this they were very successful.

The years following the disbandment of the Empire Marketing Board saw piece-meal development of government information at departmental level—the initiative being left to individual departments. 'The Whitehall of 1933 represents specimens of publicity in all its stages from chrysalis to butterfly,'[1] said Sir Stephen Tallents. The thirties saw important developments in overseas information too. In 1932 the Empire Service was established by the British Broadcasting Corporation, which later became the Overseas service, and in 1934 the British Council came into being to foster educational and cultural relations with overseas countries. In 1932 a Chief Press Liaison Officer was attached to the Prime Minister's staff at 10 Downing Street. An addition was built to accommodate him—the first new building at No. 10 since Sir George Downing's day. The Press Liaison Officer combined the post with that of Press Officer at the Treasury, a dual position he held for over ten years. The first government departments to have Information Divisions were the social departments which had daily contact with the mass of the public, e.g. the Post Office, the Ministry of Health, the Ministry of Labour, the Home Office and also the Service departments who wanted recruits. The last were the departments concerned with trade and finance (the Treasury did not have a complete one until 1947).

In 1935 a joint public relations branch was set up for the Ministry of Health and the Board of Education—this was in addition to the Housing Information Service established at the Ministry of Health in 1919. It was designed, said the department, to 'help to overcome the lack of understanding which has handicapped their relations with the press and public while they were administering huge sums of public money yet had virtually no means of keeping in direct day-to-day touch with the reactions of those affected'. The Home Office started a public relations branch in 1936; and the British Industries Fair started in the same year to boost British goods.

When Sir Kingsley Wood became Minister of Health, he took with him to his new department his policy of positive public relations. In 1936, for example, he called a meeting of commercial advertising experts to help to plan a campaign to get a wider use of local authority

[1] Tallents, op. cit., p. 265.

health services—there was at that time no sufficient publicity expertise within government departments.

When these early information sections were set up, the approach
was negative rather than positive. Press Officers, sometimes with staffs
of assistants, were appointed mainly to deal with press inquiries—
to be a convenient channel for answering newspaper inquirers in
order to save the time of busy Ministers and administrators. Indeed,
the appointment of the press officer at the Home Office was a result of
pressure by press representatives themselves who said the Home
Office was coming more into the news and they found difficulty in
getting from it the information they wanted in the time they could
spare. The status of such press officers did not generally reflect within
the department much appreciation of the importance of public
relations.

Gradually departmental press officers developed in the thirties and
still more during the forties into public relations divisions, not only
meeting the needs of press and the British Broadcasting Corporation,
but stimulating them to use the news and views of their departments
and also making use of publicity as a means of implementing departmental policy. 'The tendency seems to be for public departments to
start publicity from motives of self-protection and then, realizing its
possibilities, to pass from the defensive to the initiative.'[1]

Lord Reith in his autobiography[2] describes what happened when
he went to the Ministry of Transport in 1940. He considered the
Ministry was suffering from a lack of proper public statements and
explanations. The Permanent Secretary argued civilly but strongly
that there was no work for a public relations officer to do. In spite of
this, a public relations officer was appointed. A few months later
when Lord Reith had moved to the Ministry of Works he asked for
this man to be released to him. 'Not on any account,' said the Ministry
of Transport, 'he was much too valuable.'

The development of public relations in this way was accelerated by
the growth of popular journalism; by the new media of the cinema
and radio; by a new social awareness of the responsibility of the
government to the governed; by the growing consciousness of the
success of the propaganda machines of the continental dictatorships.
At the outbreak of war in 1939 the need to take positive and considered steps to publicize departmental policies had obtained some
general degree of acceptance.

In the inter-war period the government had also made a tentative

[1] Tallents, op. cit., p. 265.
[2] Lord Reith, *Into the Wind*, Hodder & Stoughton, 1949, p. 394.

use of survey techniques to counter the age-long complaints that the 'measures of government, however well-intentioned, simply do not fit the habits of common life'.[1] The original data for the cost-of-living index had been started in 1904 by the Board of Trade and based on investigation into the spending habits of working class families. This investigation had been expanded in 1918. The much more substantial family budget study made in 1938 by the Ministry of Labour carried this a big step forward. The Post Office conducted surveys, too, of the potential telephone market, and the Ministry of Agriculture employed commercial agencies to study public reaction to the National Mark scheme.

By 1939, then, there were public relations divisions in almost all the social service departments and in the three Service departments. The head of the War Office press division was given the title of Director of Public Relations; this enhanced status reflected the importance of recruiting for the army. It was far from being generally accepted in Whitehall that government public relations were of central importance. It was the approach of war which speeded up the expansion of government information services still further. When it started, the new Air Raid Precautions branch of the Home Office had a public relations division, with staff borrowed from the Post Office, to instruct the public about air raid precautions. The Ministry of Food had a public relations division from the beginning which was working even before the appointment of Lord Woolton. The Dominions and Colonial Offices separated and enlarged their publicity branches and so did the Board of Education and the Ministry of Health. A Ministry of Information was set up in 1939, a few days after the outbreak of war. It had been planned beforehand as an essential part of wartime administrative machinery, to present the Allied case abroad, to meet the needs of press and public at home and to provide the necessary security censorship.

1939–45 WARTIME DEVELOPMENTS

The Second World War, unlike the First, did not spring on a nation accustomed to a century of peace. In the 1914–18 war, the Ministry of Information had not been set up until towards the end of hostilities: in the 1939–45 war it was set up when they began. Henceforward there was to be some sort of government information policy and some kind of central service unit to perform functions for the various

[1] PEP, 'The Social Use of Sample Surveys', *Planning*, Vol. XII, No. 250, May 24, 1946.

departmental public relations or information divisions; this structure in spite of some changes, has remained the basic one for the information services up to now.

The information services became particularly important after the fall of France, when it became clear that all our resources and the total mobilization of the population would be needed if we were going to win the war; this implied a multitude of special duties in the field of information. Total war in a democratic country can only be waged if people understand what the government is doing and can be persuaded to co-operate with it. It meant explanation and exposition to people who were unlikely to read Parliamentary debates or government White Papers.

There were two main kinds of function for the information machine. First, it was necessary to recruit volunteers for all the onerous, boring, unpleasant or dangerous jobs that had to be done. Men and women had to be persuaded to man the war factories, join the Home Guard and the fire fighting services; they were needed as bus conductresses and civil defence wardens. They must be induced to Dig for Victory and save waste paper; to ask themselves if their journey was really necessary; to take only five inches of hot water in their bath; to remember that 'careless talk costs lives'; to eat potatoes in their skins.[1] They had to be discouraged from black market dealings.

The other main information function was explanation. The vast network of rationing, price control, conscription and welfare services was unfamiliar and confusing. The public had to be told how they all worked, and have their rights and duties explained. In the process of explanation it was sometimes discovered that the regulations were too complex to understand, too difficult to carry out, or too unfair; in these cases they were often modified in the light of the information collected.

Such were the objects of government information during the war. By what means were they achieved?

The Organization

At the centre there was the Ministry of Information. Official war news came from the Service and other departments, but the Ministry of

---

[1] This was a typical piece of Food Facts propaganda. The whole verse ran:
'Those who have the will to win
Eat potatoes in their skin
Knowing that the sight of peelings
Deeply hurts Lord Woolton's feelings.'

Information was the centre from which it was issued, where liaison officers of the main news issuing departments were available for the press and British Broadcasting Corporation and where material intended for publication was submitted for censorship.

The Ministry of Information was also responsible for all press and British Broadcasting Corporation relations that went beyond the interests of any one department. It was also responsible for the provision of publicity services and materials for the information sections of the domestic departments. The Minister of Information was responsible in Parliament for general government information policy, but the departmental Ministers retained control over their own information policy. Overseas, except in enemy and enemy-occupied countries, the Ministry of Information was responsible for the policy as well as for the content and execution of government publicity. A unified political warfare plan was operated by the Overseas Planning Committee of the Ministry. At its peak the Ministry of Information had a staff of 2,950[1] in this country and another 3,600 working overseas.

In the service of information and explanation, the Ministry of Information used every technique of modern publicity—films, broadcasting, press advertisements, posters, exhibitions, illustrated booklets, public lectures—and allocated the services of a number of first class writers and publicists of widely different backgrounds to do the job.

Ministry of Information booklets—dealing with subjects of great dramatic interest, stories of heroism, arresting pictures, maps and charts—were meant to bring home to the most inexperienced the significance or the distant battles where husbands and sons were fighting. They were published for other government departments, especially the Service Ministries, for example, booklets like *Bomber Command, The British Coaster, Ocean Front, Front Line*. The sale of these official booklets totalled over 30 million copies in the United Kingdom. Photographers collected, distributed and took photographs of every phase of the war at home and abroad. Films Division and the Crown Film Unit produced first-class full-length documentaries like *Target for Tonight, Coastal Command*, and *Western Approaches* as well as about 100 shorter ones every year. There were other sections of the Ministry, too: Display and Exhibitions Division,

[1] Including Press censorship staffs and staff working in this country on overseas publicity, but excluding the substantial postal censorship staff. Select Committee on Estimates, Session 1950, 5th Report. Memorandum by Central Office of Information, Annex 21, Table IV.

General Productions (responsible for posters and advertisements), Campaigns Division (responsible for recruiting and other campaigns), the Photographs Division and so on.

The Ministry of Information also controlled a regional organization which had set up a series of local information committees. They were intended to be the connecting link between the Ministry of Information and the public. Their purpose was to prepare the public mind for new measures, spread instruction and appeals as widely as possible, and to disseminate instruction and news under 'conditions of emergency resulting from enemy action', i.e. invasion. They were staffed, usually voluntarily, by local people—representatives of the three political parties, the press, education, the Churches, Chambers of Commerce, trade unions, welfare societies, women's organizations and so on. Their object was 'to make sure that the national war effort at home and abroad is fully supported by a united nation'. They were expected to report back to the Ministry of Information on the state of public opinion, arrange meetings, films, lectures, displays and exhibitions, distribute leaflets and pamphlets and help in special publicity campaigns (e.g. salvage drives and recruiting for war workers), and act in co-operation with the Regional Commissioner and the Regional Controllers of other Ministries.

Government information services were not confined to the Ministry of Information. All the departments with established information divisions enlarged and expanded them during the war— for example, at the Ministry of Labour and Ministry of Agriculture— and new ones were established at the Ministries of Supply, War Transport, Production, Fuel and Power and the Board of Trade. They were all very active. The Ministry of Food and the National Savings Committees had their own publicity staffs as well as the more normal information sections. (The famous 'Food Facts' advertisements, for example, demonstrated the best use of available supplies and helped the housewife to improve nutritional standards; they were also intended to boost morale by showing that a besieged nation could feed itself adequately and sometimes even pleasantly.) Altogether by January 1944 there were about 1,700 people outside the Ministry of Information engaged in information work in this country.[1]

The war disclosed the need for government public relations efforts in the most unlikely places. For example, taxation changes and rising wages increased the number of income-tax payers from something

[1] Over 1,000 were employed by the three Service departments, including staff employed in psychological warfare in the RAF and War Office Film Production photographic units, and staff for the Allied Expeditionary Force.

59

under 4 million to about 12 million. Newcomers to income-tax had neither the leisure nor the capacity to master its rules. The first step towards securing their co-operation was to make them understand it. So in 1942 the Board of Inland Revenue appointed a Public Relations Officer charged with the task of making income-tax 'understanded of the people'—even though no publicity campaign could persuade them to like it. (It is perhaps significant that Sir Kingsley Wood was Chancellor of the Exchequer at this date.)

During the war, it became for the first time important for the government to find out about conditions in Britain. Before the war, the Board of Trade, for example, had not been called on to take much interest in the nation's living and working conditions. No one knew how many houses had no bathrooms or indoor sanitation, no gas or electricity. But when scarce resources had to be used to the best advantage, it became important for the Board of Trade to know that in some districts people had to have oil lamps, large heavy kettles and galvanized iron baths—in others it was not necessary. 'If in peacetime no soap-maker would dream of bringing out a new line without interviewing thousands of housewives and hundreds of shopkeepers ... so in wartime it was a million times more necessary that this great super-industry at the Board of Trade—which had no benefit of trading experience, which had to deal with an incredible multiplicity of goods ... should know the effect of what it did and calculate the effect of what it proposed to do.'[1]

The planning of Clothes Rationing was the most important instance of this need for consumer information at the Board of Trade. It was only by market research that a realistic scheme could be constructed. It was only by continuous market research that the scheme could be economically operated. Apart from social justice, the purpose of rationing was to ensure economy of labour and materials: market research, with its study of points spending, made possible the economical planning of production to meet the ration. The introduction of clothes rationing also posed new and difficult problems of communication with the retailers and the public. Since no census of distribution then existed, paid advertising in the press was the only available means of announcing the scheme and at the same time of explaining to retailers their duties, and to the public their rights and expectations. The announcement had to be made without possibility

[1] E. L. Hargreaves and M. M. Gowing, *Civil Industry and Trade*, History of the Second World War, UK Civil Series, HMSO & Longmans, Green, 1952, p. 296. Quotation of Sir Francis Meynell, the Board of Trade's Adviser on Consumer Needs.

of any prior leakage: a pre-ration run on the shops would have ruined the whole plan. Even the Ministry of Information which had to book the advertising spaces, was denied the knowledge of what these spaces were to be used for. The first announcement (under the conciliatory slogan 'Fair Shares') was made in the Whit-Sunday papers, to give the retailers Sunday and the Monday Bank Holiday in which to mark the 'points' value of the various items in their stocks before they were open to the public.

The Consumer Needs branch of the Board of Trade, too, was a most useful two-way channel between the Board of Trade and its distributing and consuming public. They had a network of distribution officers whose task was to report back on consumer goods shortages of all kinds from razor blades and teats for babies' bottles to matches and wedding rings. One of their methods was to conduct stock counts shop by shop in selected areas. The team could be employed to study shortages both locally and nationally and they were used to pinpoint shortages of essentials after bombing. They were necessary because they were the only unbiased information about local shortages the Board of Trade could get. The Board of Trade also had three wardrobe checks of the clothes owned by typical families in a 'clothing panel' and made a shortages survey (through Social Survey) every two months, when 3,000 consumers were asked to state which of thirty scarce items they had tried to buy and whether they were successful. They also carried out some fifty *ad hoc* inquiries on consumer goods shortages in specific places—on clothing needs, and why vitamin supplements were not taken up, and so on— and the functioning of various consumer services like laundries.

The Ministry of Information was also anxious to assess the impact of government advertising and to investigate morale. Its Home Intelligence Unit made an attempt to assess public morale by interviewing a panel of people at regular intervals.[1] In the first instance it was intended as an attempt to estimate the success of German psychological warfare and for the first year daily reports on the state of the nation's morale were issued. The men and women interviewing householders for this investigation, however, leapt into unwelcome fame as 'Cooper's Snoopers'[2] when some Fleet Street Editor—when there was no better news—discovered their existence and suggested they

[1] In a similar way the BBC's Audience Research department get audience reactions to sound and television programmes today.

[2] Mr Duff Cooper was Minister of Information at the time, but he had not started this method of investigation. He was, perhaps, not always successful in keeping editors 'in the picture', and this tended to get his Ministry a bad press.

were knocking at strangers' doors and trying to trap them into making incriminating remarks against the government which would be reported back to the Ministry of Information. This created a good deal of press stir, partly because it was said that newspapers were afraid that this was the beginning of a government news-collecting agency.

The panic died down eventually, and in May 1941 the Home Intelligence Unit was split into two sections. A Social Survey Division was set up—it had first started under the auspices of the National Institute of Economic and Social Research, and was then transferred to the Ministry of Information—to do factual surveys about the physical side of people's lives. The remaining part of Home Intelligence remained concerned with morale, and continued to report on people's reactions to the news or to new government regulations throughout the war, although the reports were made weekly and not daily. The value of this 'morale' survey was that censorship and the smallness of newspapers made the airing of grievances in the press difficult, and so it was one of the ways of finding out what regulations were causing distress.

During the war, not only Social Survey but all the private survey organizations were used to collect information for the government, for example, Mass Observation, British Market Research, the London Press Exchange and the British Institute of Public Opinion.

The Ministry of Food was one of the departments which sponsored a large number of surveys. The food rationing system was founded on research into the public's buying habits, as well as nutritional needs and food resources. A National Food Survey was carried out by the London Press Exchange during the war. Other surveys, mostly by Social Survey, were also made about reactions to the national loaf, individual diets and the use of vitamin supplements. There were also three continuous surveys on household food budgets. There were surveys on 'points'[1] expenditure and on body weights in relation to ration scales (mines and factories weighed their workers, and the British Institute of Public Opinion made surveys of housewives' weights). The consumption of cakes, dried milk and dried eggs was also studied.

Other departments, too, used surveys. The Ministry of Health undertook studies, through Social Survey, on colds, diphtheria im-

[1] Certain foods like sardines, oatmeal, prunes and most tinned foods were not available in sufficient quantities to be issued to everybody as a ration. The household therefore had a number of 'points' to spend each week and could choose how to spend them amongst these supplementary goods.

munization, and so on, and they also asked the public whether they would object to publicity about precautions against venereal disease. (The answer, to the surprise of many, was that people had no objection to the public discussion of VD.) The Ministry of Health initiated surveys by Social Survey on people's reactions to different heating systems, lighting, and noise, which provided 'a body of social data of considerable value in relating dwelling design to function'. The Ministry of Agriculture studied the impact of the Dig for Victory campaign. The Ministry of War Transport studied travel to work, bicycles and road safety. These were all carried out by Social Survey. The Ministry of Home Security made a Social Survey study of social dislocation as a result of different forms of air attack. There were also Ministry of Information studies of cinema-going and reactions to Ministry of Information films, the circulation and impact of Ministry of Information books and the effect of salvage campaigns.

We see the state here taking an interest in the doings and possessions of its citizens—getting them to declare the contents of their wardrobes, the size of their children's feet, their likes and dislikes in food and films, and the state of their health—'a passion for administrative detail reminiscent of the Elizabethan State'.[1] The result was that after six years of total war people were better clothed and fed than they had been before the war. Maternity and child welfare services, health precautions and industrial safety were carried to a far higher standard. The welfare benefits had been supported by large-scale government advertising and publicity which could reach captive audiences gathered together in canteens, in welfare clinics and at factory benches. The government information services could at least claim some of the credit for a nation which emerged from the years of siege better nourished and fed than it had been before it started.[2]

Not all information campaigns had the desired effect, however. In the early years of the war, a poster saying 'Your courage, your cheerfulness and your resolution will bring us victory' caused offence by its unfortunate contrast between 'you' and 'us' and had to be withdrawn. On one occasion, the government techniques of explanation and popularization boomeranged back at them. When the Beveridge Plan for social security was first issued, the Ministry of Information were instructed to do everything they could to make it widely known and appreciated. The plan was launched with a press conference, a

[1] Hargreaves and Gowing, op. cit., p. 338.
[2] It was during the war that deficiency diseases, like rickets in young children, finally disappeared.

popular version was issued in large numbers by the Ministry of Information before it was debated in Parliament; the BBC devoted considerable time to it. The British public were enthusiastic, not only because of the publicity but because the plan was just what people wanted at that time. Lord Beveridge himself was a national figure and did much to popularize the plan's provisions too. There had been a certain amount of editorial publicity in the newspapers even before the government campaign started. The Beveridge plan became a symbol of the Government's intention to create a brave new world after the war. Meanwhile, however, Treasury experts were reporting various objections to parts of the plan and the big insurance groups and others were mobilizing opposition; it became clear that the Beveridge Plan was going to be very controversial. The Government had second thoughts and produced an alternative scheme. But it was too late. The public had been 'sold' the Beveridge Plan so successfully that the Government's own proposals got a cold reception.

Criticism of Wartime Information Services
Information may have been a necessary adjunct to the war effort and the necessity for public relations accepted as a normal function of administration but there was plenty of very vocal criticism of the work of the Ministry of Information during the war from the press and public, from within the Civil Service and from Parliament. The public and press had a hearty dislike of any prying into public opinion and morale as the 'Cooper's Snoopers' row had shown. Nor did extensive advertising and explanation to the press stop public and press criticism of rationing allocations, direction of labour and so on.

The Ministry of Information's first days as a Ministry were unhappy. It started off with 1,000 members of staff at headquarters—most of them brilliant individualists; there was perhaps too much technical expertise and not enough administrative expertise within the new department. It was a difficult team to handle and the first Ministers, Lord MacMillan, Lord Reith, and Mr Duff Cooper held office for only a few months each. It was not until July 1941 that the Ministry settled down under Mr Brendan Bracken and a mostly new team of administrators.

One of the functions of a wartime Ministry of Information, when there is paper rationing and strict censorship of news, is to establish itself as a medium through which the government can communicate privately with the press in this country and overseas. The early Ministers of Information did not always have happy relationships with the press. But when Mr Brendan Bracken became Minister this relationship improved. He appeared to have been particularly successful in establishing friendly personal relationships with press proprietors; visiting Americans of note were swept into his circle of hospitality and he set himself to cultivate the friendship of overseas correspondents and visiting editors, radio commentators and so on from America and the Dominions. There were also monthly tea parties for British provincial editors, with Ministerial explanations of world events.

Especially in the early days, the Minister of Information was vigorously questioned in Parliament about his department's work. Much of the criticism came from MPs, who felt that the authority of Parliament was likely to be undermined, because what was described as information might, in fact, amount to one-sided explanation and persuasion. Ministers, they feared, might be able to appeal to the public over the head of Parliament, or get public support for a policy before Parliament had time to debate it. Many wartime measures proposed by the Government—although it was a coalition Government—were hotly opposed by considerable groups of MPs, who wanted to have them withdrawn or amended. Did not the government departments who employed men skilled in every publicity medium have thereby weapons denied to the other side? In the process of simplifying and expounding, the critics said, a public relations division working within a department could not help stressing the favourable aspects of the proposals.

The other criticism expressed during the war was that information officers might, at the public expense, become the personal publicity officers of their Ministers—especially in the case of one or two Ministers who, when they transferred to different departments, took their public relations officers—and some other officials—with them.[1]

There was one argument in the early days of the war which has had an important influence in the way in which the information services have developed since 1945. The Ministry of Information, which was responsible for overseas information policy, antagonized some of the home departments by assuming it had some special responsibility for the maintenance of morale and the conduct of government publicity as a whole. Other Ministers felt that the Ministry of Information was trespassing on their policy preserves. The argument was settled decisively against the Ministry of Information. Each Minister it was decided was to remain supreme in his own kingdom, for information as for other policy matters. It was laid down

---

[1] This was a wartime practice, by some Ministers, which was not carried over into peacetime, and this criticism has therefore not been heard since the end of the war.

that there was no subject for publicity in the home front that was exclusively the domain of the Minister of Information. All publicity which he handled was also the responsibility of some other individual Minister or group of Ministers.

The wartime experiences of the working of the Ministry of Information and the rest of the information machine, greatly influenced the kind of information services which were to develop after the war. For the future, the most important aspects of the wartime organization were not so much the co-ordinating functions of the Ministry of Information, as the build-up of personnel and experience at departmental level and the experience of providing common services and publicity materials for the use of departmental public relations divisions. The other valuable experience proved to be the habit of using government machinery to collect information on which policy and administrative action could be based.

CHAPTER III

1945 to the Present Day

ESTABLISHING THE PEACETIME INFORMATION SERVICE

At the end of the war, the Ministry of Information's duties on political warfare abroad and censorship and news releases at home came to an abrupt end. The Ministry's staff had been recruited as temporary and unestablished civil servants, and many of them had jobs to return to when the war was over. The peacetime structure of the information services had to be settled. There had been an official inquiry in 1944 on the future of the information services, held under the aegis of the Coalition Government. The Labour Government decided to accept its recommendations. In December 1945, the Prime Minister, Mr Attlee, said:

> The Government . . . are satisfied that . . . these services . . . have an important and permanent part in the machinery of government under modern conditions. It is essential to good administration under a democratic system that the public shall be adequately informed about the many matters in which Government action directly impinges on their daily lives, and it is in particular important that a true and adequate picture of British policy, British institutions and the British way of life should be presented overseas.[1]

In peacetime, then, the information services were to continue, but it was decided they should be on a reduced scale. On March 31, 1946, the Ministry of Information was abolished. Its responsibilities for overseas publicity reverted to the Foreign, Colonial and Dominions Offices; and the Overseas Planning Committee of the Ministry, which had operated a unified political warfare plan, disappeared with the end of the war. Some of the staff of the Empire, American and Foreign Divisions of the Ministry went over to the Information Divisions of the Foreign Office and the other departments. The Ministry of Information's production divisions became the nucleus of a new organization, the Central Office of Information.

[1] H. C. Deb (1945–6), 417, c. 916.

It was thought economical and sensible that there should be a central pool of technical services and production functions to supply specialist publicity services for all departments. Some wartime departments, like the Ministry of Food, had built up large public relations divisions complete with their own experts in the different publicity media, and had not made much use of the common services provided by the Ministry of Information. The Central Office of Information was to serve all departments.

The Central Office of Information was thus conceived, and has remained, a common service department, just as the Stationery Office is a common service department.[1] There was no longer to be a Minister exclusively concerned with information matters at the head of the new Central Office of Information, and each departmental Minister retained responsibility for his own information policy, as before.

The existence of a Minister of Information has tended to be regarded by the British public as a wartime emergency, and his disappearance at the end of the war was in line with the basic principle of the British constitution that individual departmental Ministers retain complete responsibility for everything which is done by and on behalf of their departments, in the public relations field as in all other. The same Minister is thus answerable to Parliament both for his department's policy and for the publicity for that policy.

But this disappearance of the Minister of Information left unresolved the problem of co-ordinating different departments' information policies; it was found convenient, for example, to have a single person able to speak in Parliament for information policy generally. In 1946 therefore, the 'higher policy' of the Central Office of Information was brought within the purview of Mr Herbert Morrison (now Lord Morrison of Lambeth), Lord President of the Council, who was also responsible for co-ordinating information policy generally. The changing position and responsibilities of the co-ordinating Minister will be discussed in Chapter VI below. Here it is sufficient to note that with two brief exceptions—1951 to 1952, when the Conservative Government first came back to power, and April 1955 to January 1957 when Sir Anthony Eden first became Prime Minister—there has always been a co-ordinating Minister for the information services.

The tasks of the information services in the immediate post-war

[1] The cost of publicity arranged by the Central Office of Information for other departments appears in the Central Office of Information financial Estimates, but the individual Ministers are responsible to Parliament for the whole of their expenditure on information. (See Chapter VI, Appendix A below.)

period were very different from those before or during the war. The Labour Government were facing a period of economic reconstruction and were inaugurating a programme of social legislation and the nationalization of industry. From 1945 the emphasis in government information work was on publicity for these tasks.

The Films and Publications Divisions of the Central Office of Information give a good illustration of the kind of work the new information services were intended to do in these early years. They were expected to explain economic problems, encourage exports, explain the details of the new social security measures, or boost confidence in Britain's heritage and achievements.

In the financial year 1947–8, for example, the Central Office of Information was responsible for producing eighty-eight films, about one-third made by the Crown Film Unit and the rest carried out by contractors in the documentary side of the film industry. There were films on the economy—*Report on Coal* and *The Balance*, a film about Britain's dependence on imports to show the seriousness of the economic crisis. There were films designed to make vivid both in the British and overseas markets, a record of our permanent way of life —films like *The Cumberland Story*, or *Five Towns*. Thirdly, there were films of national achievement, aimed primarily at the overseas markets, like *Down to the Sea*, which was about British ships and ship-building, or *Precisely Yours* which dealt with British scientific instruments. They also made films on world affairs like *The World is Rich* (food problems and the work of the Food and Agriculture Organization), or accounts of colonial stewardship like *Voices of Malaya*. There were also purely instructional films on agricultural and industrial techniques, on housekeeping and housing, on road safety; films for doctors showing methods of diagnosis and operations, and for parents and teachers on the spiritual and physical care of children. Finally, there was a group of teaching films for schools— a series on Crete, and on the history of writing.

The Publications Division was also concerned with the national economic crisis. They produced, for example, a text and diagram pamphlet for the Board of Trade, *We Live by Exports*, and *Something Done*, an illustrated account of post-war national achievements. These low-priced pamphlets, sold to the general public as a means of explanation and instruction, were something new in peacetime for a government department to publish.

Several important pamphlets explaining new social legislation were distributed free to each household. For example, at the start of the new National Insurance scheme and the Health Service in the summer of 1948, a 32-page booklet, *The Family Guide to National Insurance*, and a 4-page leaflet asking every citizen to choose his National Health doctor were issued: 14 million copies of each were printed and pushed through the nation's doors by the Post Office.

There was another important new development in the immediate post-war period in the field of government information—the setting up of the Economic Information Unit of the Treasury. For about eighteen months after the end of the war, there had seemed to be a reasonable chance—with the help of the American loan—that the British economy would return to normality without too much difficulty. But by the winter of 1946–7 it became clear that we were faced with an immediate and serious economic crisis and a continuing long-term balance of payments problem which would require fundamental adjustments in the economy. The bad weather and the coal crisis of the winter—when for a few weeks over $2\frac{1}{2}$ million people were unemployed—could easily be observed and understood by the man in the street; but it was less easy to understand why Britain's economic position had fundamentally changed nor why the apparently vigorous recovery of activity as manpower was demobilized was accompanied by 'too much money chasing too few goods'.

There was a general demand from Members of Parliament, the press and other sources, that the nation as a whole should be told 'the facts', and that the economy ought to be planned. But no one government department was responsible for economic policy, and no one Information Division was therefore equipped to deal with the problem. It was no one's responsibility to help Ministers 'to convey to the country the meaning of the economic problem as a whole and to focus together all its many and superficially diverse elements'.[1] So Mr Herbert Morrison, Lord President of the Council, who was generally responsible for economic matters, set up the Central Economic Planning staff and in June 1947 an Economic Information Unit was associated with it.

The Economic Information Unit was at first part of the office of the Lord President, then together with the planning staff it went to the newly-created Ministry of Economic Affairs, and finally in November 1947 to the Treasury, where it absorbed the existing Treasury press office. Sir Stafford Cripps, the Chancellor of the Exchequer, asked the Treasury staff to think of information work as 'much more than a hobby or a frill to smooth and protect the administration' but as a 'fundamental part of our great experiment

[1] S. C. Leslie, 'Work of the Economic Information Unit', *Public Administration*, Vol. XXVII, Spring 1950, p. 17.

upon which a considerable part of its success or failure will depend'.[1]

The Government's policy at the time was 'austerity'—to reduce imports and consumption, and to see that the resources thus saved went into exports. They also tried to increase production as fast as possible by tackling bottlenecks and by encouraging the redeployment of labour. The Economic Information Unit became the spearhead for educating the public—and Ministers—about these complicated problems. Sir Stafford Cripps called it 'an almost indecent economic striptease performance . . . which may probably make a few of the older inhabitants of Treasury Chambers shudder'. He added, 'we are bringing out into the open a great deal of material that hitherto was considered most secret and confidential'. The Economic Information Unit was a general briefing unit on economic affairs, that is it took official papers, committees' minutes, memoranda, statistics, reports on economic and financial themes, 'boiled them down, took them apart and recombined them' into a basic speech or an information bulletin or a film script, or an advertisement—depending on what use was to be made of it. The Economic Information Unit also took over responsibility for an inter-departmental committee of information officers from economic departments concerned with economic matters. There were special sections in the Economic Information Unit concerned with special needs, for example, the women's section whose job was to explain to housewives how economic problems were affected by what housewives did. *Bulletin for Industry*, published regularly with charts and diagrams, explained topics like agriculture or exports for the industrialist. The Unit also inaugurated a system of regular fortnightly or monthly press conferences on economic affairs with a news communiqué on current economic topics circulated to the press.

The Economic Information Unit also started a new idea in economic explanation—a popular version of the White Paper Economic Survey of 1947, produced for them by the Central Office of Information. This told the same story as the White Paper, but in it the economic problems were seen from the viewpoint of the ordinary citizen paying his bills, buying his food and clothes or his amusements. The experiment was repeated with even greater success in the following years. On each occasion the simplified version sold about six times as many copies as the White Paper.

The value of the kind of economic education the Economic Information Unit of the Treasury achieved is that the educated public became far better informed about the economic issues that it was,

[1] Quoted by S. C. Leslie, 'Their Lordships Inform Us', *The Times*, June 6, 1959.

say, when Britain went off the Gold Standard in 1931. In the post-war world, probably the general body of citizens has a good deal of power to frustrate the intentions of its elected representatives by peaceful means. This can be helped by systematic efforts to uncover the crucial facts and highlight them so that ordinary men and women can understand them.

The work of the Economic Information Unit was not without its critics. Much of the Opposition's attacks on the government information services in the post-war period particularly applied to the kind of work the Economic Information Unit was trying to do. In 1950 a Parliamentary Select Committee proposed that it be disbanded; this proposal was based on a failure to understand why the specialized work of the Unit could not be carried out by the Central Office of Information. In fact, it was not disbanded but the Economic Information Unit's name was changed to the Information Division of the Treasury; its title changed, but not its functions. It became a departmental Information Division, and has remained so. Nevertheless, the Treasury remains an extraordinary department, having kept its old financial responsibilities and added new ones, like the co-ordination of economic planning, and having a general responsibility for production and growth in which other departments have their particular interests. To that extent, the Treasury Information Division has different functions and wider responsibilities for economic explanation than other Information Divisions.

INQUIRIES INTO THE HOME INFORMATION SERVICES[1]

Although the basic system set up by the Labour Government in April 1946 has remained unchanged, there were a number of official inquiries made into the information services in the post-war period. The first was an official committee appointed by the Treasury in November 1946 under the Chairmanship of Mr J. I. C. Crombie (later Sir James Crombie) to consider the best methods of staffing Information Divisions and recruiting information officers; how they should be paid and what should be their conditions of service. The Crombie Committee reported in 1947. In August 1949, as a result of their findings, an established class of Information Officers was

[1] The overseas information services were also investigated from time to time. In 1952–3 an independent committee under the chairmanship of Lord Drogheda testified to their 'important and indeed essential role' in support of UK policies, and in 1957 expenditure on these services was appreciably increased, after a series of detailed studies carried out under Dr Charles Hill (see Chapter IV).

formed. Some 250 men and women—press officers, artists, book editors, etc.—were established.[1]

The Crombie Report defined the functions of the Information Divisions as being wider than public relations. Their job was 'to create and maintain an informed public opinion: to use methods of publicity to help a department to achieve its purpose, e.g. the Ministry of Food to lead people to eat foods readily available and dietetically beneficial; to advise departments on the reaction of the public to a policy present or contemplated and to assist and advise in all matters bearing on the relationship between Department and the public'. Only the last, in the view of the Crombie Committee, was a public relations function.

But not all Committees were to take the view that the information services should accept wider responsibilities. The policy of economic education which the government was pursuing in the early post-war years proved expensive in paid-for publicity—unprecedentally so for peacetime. During 1948–9 an inquiry was set up by Sir Stafford Cripps as Chancellor of the Exchequer into the cost of the home information services. Its Chairman was Sir Henry French, who had had wide experience of public relations in the Ministry of Food. Most of the other members[2] were serving civil servants, with Mr A. P. Ryan, a member of *The Times* staff, as an outside voice. The Committee's report,[3] published in November 1949, had very important results for the future development of the information services.

The French Committee made a number of general recommendations as well as some particular proposals. They considered that the 1949–50 Estimates figure of over £5 million[4] for spending on information in this country was too high and recommended that departments should take steps to see that expenditure in that year should be kept as far as possible below the Estimates figure. Spending on and spending by the information services they said, should be cut. The most important general recommendation was that 'particular attention should be paid to the correct choice and use of the

[1] This report is discussed more fully in Chapter VII on Staffing the Information Services.
[2] The members were: Sir Henry French, Messrs S. A. Bailey, J. I. C. Crombie, E. M. Nicholson, and A. P. Ryan. Mr Ryan had had experience in the public service during the war.
[3] Report of the Committee on the cost of the Home Information Services, Cmd. 7836, HMSO, 1949.
[4] This figure covers expenditure on the home information services by the Central Office of Information, Stationery Office and the departmental information divisions. (The latter is mostly for salaries.)

various publicity media available', and that even when the right medium had been selected, consideration should be given to whether the expense or manpower involved could be afforded. Paid publicity, the Committee considered, should be used only as a last resort. They looked especially at the economic information campaign and the Economic Information Unit at the Treasury, on which a great deal of money had been spent since the end of the war. This campaign, the Committee recommended, should rely much more on Ministerial speeches and press conferences, on the provision of information and material for discussion, and on helping interested groups to educate their own members; press and poster advertising should be used only for the purpose of enlisting 'some specific action which can reasonably be expected from the public to which they are addressed or when it is of urgent importance to communicate factual information'. More concentration on 'selective advertising in local, regional or specialized publications' was preferred, rather than national advertising campaigns.

The Committee also said: 'A general conclusion to which we have come as the result of our review is that there is need for individual proposals to be put more clearly in perspective in relation to information services as a whole. We would emphasize the need for a clear appreciation by all concerned of the potential uses and disadvantages of each of the main media of information. These media may be compared to the instruments of an orchestra and care is needed in the choice of the correct instrument. It would be unfortunate if the Government information services became accustomed to relying too much on the "brass" and too little on the "strings". Cost as well as appropriateness for the particular purpose needs critical consideration.'

In the financial crises of the late forties, their ideas for economy seemed attractive; information expenditure was one of those non-essentials which is often treated harshly in budgeting cuts. The Conservative Party, who were returned to office two years after the French report was published, were certainly in no mood to increase spending on home information.

From 1949 onwards, therefore, the emphasis in the work of the information services shifted from paid-for publicity to the utilization of the free media, by the provision of background information and facilities for journalists, reporters, photographers, film makers and so on. The immediate reason for the change-over was the French Committee's report, but it was also because it was now possible to get more space or time in the free media.

Immediately after the war, shortage of newsprint, the smallness of the film industry and the embryonic state of television had meant that the information services had had to rely a good deal on paid-for publicity, posters, leaflets, advertisements and campaigns. As the mass-media recovered from the limitations of wartime, they could absorb editorially, and in news and feature columns, much more of what the government information services could put out. It now seemed reasonable to depend on them for much more 'free' publicity, and consequently to cut down 'paid-for' publicity.

Secondly, the welfare state was now in being; the new education, health and national insurance schemes had all been in existence for a year or two and needed much less explanation as fundamental legislative changes, or increased regulations. Henceforth, the success of the information services was to rest largely on the initiative of departmental information officers whose task was to create an interest in government affairs and to provide the means for other people to satisfy that interest. Success rested ultimately, that is to say, on the responses of communications organizations which were in no sense under government control. The information officers' chief concern in future was to get information into the news columns, and to spend less on buying space for advertising.

The French Committee certainly succeeded in cutting back expenditure on the home information services. In the financial year 1948–9, and 1949–50, before the French Committee reported, the estimates had been about £5 million; in the 1950s the estimates were half this figure—about £2 million a year. And the pattern of spending changed, also, as the French Committee had recommended. The Treasury, whose economic education programme had made it the biggest spender of all the home information departments—over £500,000 in the estimates for 1949–50, became one of the smaller spenders, and has remained so. The Central Office of Information, which in the earlier year spent over £2½ million on advertising publications and films, spent only about three-quarters of a million pounds in the post-French period.[1]

Since the early 1950s, however, home information expenditure has crept up again. First the Korean war, and later the 1957 decision to abolish conscription, both involved the Service departments in increased recruiting campaigns and therefore increased spending on advertising and publicity campaigns. In the latest financial year (1963–4) estimated expenditure on the home information services—

[1] For detailed figures of departmental spending see Appendix A, below, Tables 4 and 5.

at £5·2 million was as high as the pre-French Committee figure; and of this total half was for the three Service departments, mainly for recruiting campaigns for the armed forces. Since the value of money has fallen, however, £5 million in 1950 would be about £8½ million in 1964.

In spite of the radical nature of the French Committee's proposals, the Report explicitly accepted the need for the continuation of the government information services, and made no fundamental alteration in the nature of the organization. They said, 'The justification for some government information services is beyond question. The citizen has a right to be told, and the government has a plain duty to tell him, what it is doing in his name and with his money, and why.' In fact the French Committee report was published almost simultaneously with the implementation of the Crombie Committee's recommendations to set up an Information Officer class.

There were some cuts in information services after the French Committee's report. For instance, in 1952 the Crown Film Unit of the Central Office of Information, which had over the years made so many outstanding films was disbanded. The reason given was that the widely differing film techniques demanded by different government departments could not be provided by one small film unit (although this argument could have been used to justify expanding the Film Unit instead of abolishing it). The Central Office of Information now has no film unit of its own, but commissions films from independent companies. The convoy of mobile film vans attached to the regional offices of the Central Office of Information were also abolished, partly on the grounds of economy and partly because increased activity by organizations outside government control—local newspapers for example—were in future to be used to spread government information.

POST-WAR CRITICISMS OF THE INFORMATION SERVICES

The information services had largely grown up during the war on an *ad hoc* basis, and although there had been some dissatisfaction and some criticism of them in Parliament, they had been accepted, if only as a necessary evil. After the war, there was distrust in the Conservative Party and the anti-government press of the whole idea of peacetime government information services;[1] a feeling that govern-

[1] The most significant press controversy about the government information services does not directly concern us. It was a campaign in the Beaverbrook Press against the British Council in particular and the Overseas Information Services in general.

ment public relations meant government political propaganda and the suppression of information unfavourable to the government.

How far could government publicity go without becoming an instrument employed by the government of the day to influence public opinion in its favour for party political purposes? This subject remained contentious in the post-war period and was raised constantly by the Opposition in Parliament between 1945 and 1951.

From 1945 to 1949, the Labour Government, whose general economic policies were bitterly opposed not only by the Opposition, but by the City and most of the press, were also pushing through vast schemes of social reform, some of it equally controversial. The nationalization of industry and the socialization of medicine, for instance, were matters of deep disagreement between the parties. When government information services issued popular explanations about their benefits, however much the information officers concerned leaned over backwards to be dispassionate, they were open to the suspicion that they were making a political case for the Labour Government's own views.

As one Conservative speaker, Mr Boyd-Carpenter, said in a debate in 1948 on the Central Office of Information's Estimates: 'If you carry as far as (the Lord President) has done the issuing of statements on broad general matters of importance to the public, these officials cannot conduct their affairs without giving to the public an impression favourable or adverse to the Government.'[1]

What the Conservative Opposition was saying was that any necessary government publicity—urging people to have their children immunized against diptheria for instance, could be performed by departmental information officers through the free media, and that the Central Office of Information was expensive and unnecessary. It 'has become the organ of a vast machine of Government information' they said 'which can with difficulty be distinguished from political propaganda'.[2]

In fact the two political parties were completely at odds in the role they thought government information services ought to play. Under the economic conditions of the post-war years, the Labour Government considered that it was necessary to pursue a policy of economic education. This included the frequent publication of newspaper advertisements informing the general public of the state of various sectors of the economy and explaining the reasons for such exhortations as 'Work or Want'. They claimed that such economic informa-

[1] H.C. Deb (1947–8), 450, c. 2288–2406.
[2] Ibid.

tion was a necessary part of the effort to increase productivity and exports and control private spending. The public must be able to understand the mechanics of the situation in order to play its part in the post-war recovery. The Opposition view was that it was unfair to use government machinery for this purpose. They said the reason for the difficult economic situation was not the facts which the Government publicized but the incompetence and mistaken policies of the Government itself. There were, they said, two distinct economic theories and the government machine and public money were being used to propagate one at the expense of the other.

The way in which the information services were used were 'inseparable from, and the main instrument for, the sapping away of individual judgement and the substitution of the state machine'.[1] This was a fundamental difference of opinion about the role of the information services in peacetime. Whereas one party believed that the government should be a leader and educator of the public, the other put forward the contrary doctrine that freedom of individual judgement was incompatible with expenditure on government 'educational' information.

The 1948 debate was not the only time the information services in general, and the Central Office of Information in particular, were attacked in Parliament on the grounds of political bias. The attacks, especially from the back benches, were pretty continuous. If one looks at the index to Hansard under 'Information' and the 'Central Office of Information' during the six years 1945–51 when the Conservative Party was in Opposition, one finds four major debates and an average of twenty other references a year.

Many of the criticisms levelled in the House of Commons were not particularly serious, in the sense that they were debating points rather than informed and reasoned criticism. In fact, the information services, though accused, were not convicted of any serious political bias. They did undoubtedly make mistakes in those early days which an information officer today would not commit. It must be remembered, also, that the newly appointed Labour Ministers had also new information officers to advise them; it was like the raw recruit and the unbroken horse—they had to learn together, and some mistakes were inevitable. For example, some information officers in the early days accompanied their Ministers to Party Conferences; on one occasion Central Office of Information government speakers were briefed with a handout from the Labour Party Headquarters. There was sometimes exuberance too in publicity which pointed out the

[1] Mr Macmillan, in the same Debate.

delights of the brave new post-war world, and which could hardly fail to displease the political party which had been in office during the 1930s and was out of office in the 1940s.[1] The Opposition did not fail to point out these errors.

When the Conservative Party itself took Office in 1951, it might have been expected that the structure of the information service as set up by the Labour Government would have been dismantled and that heads might have rolled. After six years of attack, one might have expected to see drastic changes made in the information services, especially as Mr Boyd Carpenter, one of the most persistent critics in Parliament of government publicity, was given special responsibility for the information services. But in fact, no basic changes were made. What happened was that the Central Office of Information was allowed to remain, after a period of uncertainty; so too was the Economic Information Unit of the Treasury, although it became an ordinary Information Division. It is true that there were cuts in the information staff and spending, and that for instance, the Crown Film Unit was disbanded, but these followed the recommendations of the French Committee which had been set up by the Labour Government. By and large, the information services remained fundamentally the same. Individual information officers, who had been identified with Labour policy in critics' minds, remained to do their jobs with the Conservatives and to demonstrate that Information Divisions were staffed by professionals, who were interested in the job of information and not in playing politics. No posts were abolished; Ministerial responsibility and a Central Office of Information remained the same; and although expenditure on paid publicity was cut, and more emphasis put on the free media, the Conservative Ministers found the information services as useful as their predecessors had.

As the Conservative administration continued, the information services did not become less important or less used. Nor did the Labour Opposition take on the Conservative Opposition's role of snipers at the information services on all possible occasions. To compare with the four debates and twenty annual references in *Hansard*, quoted above, in the first six years of the Conservative Party's office, there were no debates and an average of only five other references a year in *Hansard*.

Since 1951, the information services appear to have been accepted

---

[1] E.g. a film called *Ours is the Land* about new housing schemes, which said roughly 'They promised us new houses in 1935—but look at Paisley and Dunfermline. Now we are at last beginning to get new houses.'

by both sides as a part of normal government administration. This is partly because the information services were established[1] as a result of the Crombie Committee's report, and therefore information officers were no longer temporary birds of passage in a Ministry, but were part of the civil service structure; and partly because since 1953,[2] the impartiality of the information services has never seriously been called in question in Parliament.

Today, it appears that the government information services have settled down. There is an Information Division in every major department, relying for the most part on getting its news into the editorial columns of the press, and on the radio and television news services, and relying less on advertisements and paid for publicity than it had done in the immediate post-war period. There is the Central Office of Information providing common publicity services for the individual departments: and a Minister of Cabinet rank with a general, if vague, responsibility for the government's information policy as a whole. We can now turn to look in some detail at the functioning of each of these pieces of the machine.

BIBLIOGRAPHY FOR HISTORICAL CHAPTERS

Brebner, J. H. *Public Relations and Publicity*. National Council of Social Services for Royal Institute of Public Administration, 1949.

Coatman, John. *The British Family of Nations*, Harrap, 1950.

Curtis, S. J. *History of Education in Great Britain*. 5th edition, University Tutorial Press, 1963.

Dearle, N. B. *Dictionary of Official Wartime Organizations*. Economic and Social History of the War, British Series. Oxford University Press for Carnegie Endowment for International Peace, 1928.

Hargreaves, E. L., and Gowing, M. M. *Civil Industry and Trade*. History of the Second World War. United Kingdom Civil Series. HMSO and Longmans, Green, 1952.

Harvey, Heather J. *Consultation and Co-operation in the Commonwealth*. A Handbook on Methods and Practice. Oxford University Press for Royal Institute of International Affairs, 1952.

Leslie, S. C. 'The Economic Information Unit.' *Public Administration*, Vol. XXVIII, Spring 1950, pp. 17–26.

Nottage, Raymond. 'The Post Office: A Pioneer of Big Business.' *Public Administration*, Vol. XXXVII, Spring 1959, pp. 55–64.

PEP. 'Government Information Services.' *Planning*, No. 230, February 1945.

Selby-Bigge, Sir Lewis Amherst. *The Board of Education*. The Whitehall Series. Putnam, 1927.

Tallents, Sir Stephen. 'Salesmanship in the Public Service: Scope and Technique.' *Public Administration*, Vol. XI, July 1933, pp. 259–66.

Williams, Francis. *Parliament, Press and People*. Heinemann, 1946.

[1] 'Established' in Civil Service sense means offered a permanent pensionable post.

[2] When the Conservative Government were sharply criticized for their pamphlet *Operation Rescue*. See Chapter IX.

CHAPTER IV

The Apex Organization: Co-ordination of Information

THE EMERGENCE OF THE CO-ORDINATING POSTS—AT MINISTERIAL AND AT OFFICIAL LEVEL 1946–62

During the post-war period, various attempts were made to settle the problem of Ministerial responsibility and the co-ordination of information policy. The basic principle has always been that individual departmental Ministers retain complete responsibility for everything which is done by and on behalf of their departments in the public relations field as in all else. It fits conveniently into the British constitution to have one Minister speaking both for his department's policy and for the publicity for that policy. Separate Ministers of Publicity or Propaganda do not sound attractive to a British ear. Even when there was a Minister of Information during the war, he was not solely responsible for information policy; he had a direct responsibility for civilian morale, but apart from that he was always associated with another Minister or Ministers whose departments were concerned with that particular policy.

The Central Office of Information, set up at the end of the war with no ministerial head, left information policy divided into a multiplicity of separate departmental channels. It was necessary, however, for a single person to be able to speak in Parliament for information policy generally, and to be able to answer for the information services as a whole; it was useful, too, to have someone who could speak to the press on information matters generally. If we look at the growth of the two co-ordinating roles from 1945 onwards, we see that various expedients have been tried at various times. For most of the post-war period there has been a Minister or Ministers, usually in the Cabinet, with some kind of responsibility for the information services. At official level, the emergence of a Public Relations Adviser to the Prime Minister at No. 10 Downing Street has supplied a central point and a secretariat for the co-ordinating Minister—something which can almost be called the focal point of

Date	Co-ordination at Ministerial level	Comments
1945 Labour Government Prime Minister–Mr Attlee	Ministry of Information abolished. The Lord President of the Council (Mr Herbert Morrison) made responsible for the 'higher policy' of the Central Office of Information and co-ordination generally.	Mr Morrison was respo for co-ordination of hor formation policy only.
May 1951	The Secretary of State for Commonwealth Relations (Mr Patrick Gordon Walker) took over responsibility for information from the Lord President of the Council.	
October 1951 Conservative Government. Prime Minister–Mr Churchill	No Minister appointed to co-ordinate.	The Government inf tion services generally scrutiny by new admi tion.
May 1952–April 1955	Chancellor of the Duchy of Lancaster, Lord Swinton, given responsibility for the information services. Lord Swinton kept this responsibility when he became Secretary of State for Commonwealth Relations.	Lord Swinton co-ord home information policy He restored the conta tween Ministers and the and the information se and the Lobby.
Prime Minister—Sir Anthony Eden, April 1955 to January 1957	No Minister generally responsible.	Co-ordinating post abo when Lord Swinton from politics (April 19
November 1956	The Paymaster-General, Sir Walter Monckton.	Appointed to co-ordina Service departments' in tion policy during the crisis only.

Prime Minister's Adviser on c Relations at No. 10	*Comments*
ancis Williams 1945–7	A political appointment. Mr Williams was a prominent journalist, a known Labour sympathizer and a personal friend of Mr Attlee.
hilip Jordan 1947–51	A personal appointment. A journalist but not specifically a Labour supporter.
eginald Bacon, appointed on death of ordan.	A civil servant from the information service.
acon continued until May 1952	Mr Bacon remained in office for a short time under the new administration. Links with the Lobby were broken.
e Clark, appointed Adviser on Govern- Public Relations.	An established civil servant from the information services appointed Adviser on Government Public Relations generally and attached to Lord Swinton. He also acted as Press Officer to the Prime Minister; therefore for the first time the same man was adviser to the co-ordinating Minister and to the Prime Minister.
e Clark continued.	
illiam Clark appointed October 1955. ark resigned in November 1956 because agreed of information during the Suez e new appointed as Adviser to No. 10. aties covered by Mr Alfred Richardson, puty Adviser, alone for a few months.	An appointment from outside the Civil Service again. This was again a personal rather than a political appointment. Mr Clark was a journalist from a politically 'neutral' paper. He was responsible only to the Prime Minister—no responsibility to a co-ordinating Minister.

Date	Co-ordination at Ministerial level	Comments
November 23, 1956	Dr Charles Hill, Postmaster-General, took charge of all government information. Dr Hill made responsible for co-ordination of all government information as Chancellor of the Duchy of Lancaster, with a seat in the Cabinet.	Mr Fife Clark tempo seconded from COI a adviser. A new approach the first time a Cabinet ster with no departm responsibilities was in c of both overseas and information policy.
October 1961	The co-ordination of overseas information policy was given to the Secretary for Technical Co-operation (Mr Denis Vosper). Co-ordination of home information policy remained with Dr Hill who became Minister of Housing and Local Government.	The co-ordination of ov policy was now wi Minister not in the Ca Dr Hill had now departr responsibility and coul less attention to inforn affairs.
July 1962	Mr William Deedes, Minister without Portfolio, became responsible for the home information services. Overseas information policy remained with the Secretary for Technical Co-operation.	A Cabinet Minister w departmental responsi took over the home s information affairs as a time job.
October 1963. Mr Macmillan resigned. Prime Minister–Sir Alec Douglas-Home	Mr William Deedes continued.	

Prime Minister's Adviser on c Relations at No. 10	*Comments*
Harold Evans appointed to No. 10. ıary 1957.	An established civil servant from the information services. Like Mr Fife Clark he become Adviser to the co-ordinating Minister as well as to the Prime Minister.
arold Evans continued.	Mr Evans continued as adviser to Dr Hill as well as the Prime Minister on home affairs, but not to Mr Vosper on overseas matters (although he continued to deal with the overseas side of the Prime Minister's office).
arold Evans continued.	
arold Evans created a baronet, and ıed as Adviser until January 1964, he left the Government Service. No ∆dviser was appointed and the deputy ∵r covered the post for a few months.	This honour is one usually reserved for non-civil servants.

the information services. But these two co-ordinating roles have only emerged gradually. The chart on pp. 82-85 sets out the various people who have filled these posts and their differing responsibilities at different periods.

In 1946, Mr Herbert Morrison, Lord President of the Council, was given responsibility for the oversight of the 'higher policy' of the new Central Office of Information and for home information policy generally. He had no concern with overseas information. The co-ordination of home information was only one of Mr Morrison's many functions as co-ordinator in the Labour Government, expecially on the economic side of home affairs.[1] Mr Morrison was a busy Minister and was also the manager of the Labour Party; he had not the time to concern himself with day-to-day inter-departmental co-ordination of information. Instead there were Ministerial and official inter-departmental committees dealing with specific information problems; for example there was a Home Information Committee under the official head of the Central Office of Information and a committee on economic information under the chairmanship of the head of the Treasury Economic Information Unit; but these committees were not much concerned with the co-ordination of policy. The Lord President answered criticisms in the House about the information services in general and the Central Office of Information in particular: Mr Patrick Gordon Walker, the Secretary of State for Commonwealth Relations, sometimes deputized for him. In May 1951, in the last few months of the Labour administration, Mr Gordon Walker became the Minister formally responsible for home information instead of the Lord President.

On the official side, the Labour Government made another important innovation. Mr Attlee appointed Mr Francis Williams to be his Public Relations Adviser in the Prime Minister's office. Until then there had only been a press liaison officer at No. 10 who had combined this post with that of press officer to the Treasury. His function had been to keep the press at bay. Mr Williams's appointment was quite different. The No. 10 job was separated from the Treasury Press Office and became a much more important job than that of mere press liaison. Mr Williams was a prominent journalist who had been a wartime civil servant in the Ministry of Information, and he was known to be a Labour party supporter and a personal friend of Mr Attlee's. The appointment was a political one—the only purely political appointment made to the No. 10 job. Mr Francis

[1] It will be remembered from Chapter III above that he set up a new Economic Information Unit in the Treasury.

Williams had a good deal of influence with the Prime Minister, but his position was always quite clear to the press—he was a government spokesman, speaking with sympathy for the party line and with expert knowledge of the party's views.

After two years as Prime Minister's adviser, Mr Williams decided to return to his career as a journalist; he was succeeded by Mr Philip Jordan who was a journalist from the *News Chronicle*, although he had also seen government service as a press attaché in Washington. Mr Jordan was not so identified with the Labour Party as Mr Williams had been; his personal position also became less strong as the General Election approached. When Mr Jordan died, the post at No. 10 was filled by Mr Bacon, who was an established civil servant from the Treasury Information Division, although he had also had experience as a journalist. The Lobby journalists had been asked informally whether they would prefer a journalist or a civil servant as Public Relations Adviser—and, perhaps surprisingly, they had indicated that they preferred a civil servant; equally informally, Fleet Street editors had confirmed this preference. It was thus the Labour Government which made the change away from a political or a personal appointment as the Prime Minister's adviser and spokesman to an information officer appointed from within the Civil Service.

When the Conservatives came to power in 1951, no co-ordinating Minister was appointed. This was possibly because the information services were during this time the subject of searching official and Ministerial inquiries—the French Committee had recently reported, recommending cuts in expenditure on information generally and there were Ministerial committees inquiring into the *raison d'être* of the Central Office of Information and the Treasury Economic Information Unit. Mr Bacon remained at the No. 10 job for a few months, but Mr Churchill did not find a Public Relations Adviser necessary, and Mr Bacon was not encouraged, for example, to talk to the Lobby.

When the Conservative Government decided that the information services should be kept basically unchanged, they too appointed a co-ordinating Cabinet Minister for them. Lord Swinton, Chancellor of the Duchy of Lancaster, was made co-ordinator, with instructions from Mr Churchill that 'more information was to be made available in a form suitable to the press'. There is evidence that the Lobby correspondents, for example, had been pressing for the restoration of a spokesman on government affairs generally. Lord Swinton succeeded in restoring the broken links between Ministers and the Lobby, and between the information services and the Lobby. He saw the Lobby frequently himself and persuaded other Ministers to see them, too.

Mr Fife Clark, an established civil servant from the information services (although he had been a journalist originally) was made Adviser on Government Public Relations generally. He and his deputy were not housed in No. 10 however, but were made responsible directly to the co-ordinating Minister, Lord Swinton. At the same time, Mr Fife Clark acted as Press Officer to the Prime Minister as well, and this double position gave him a very central position in the information field. Also, as an established civil servant he was in a stronger position *vis-à-vis* his political masters than one whose appointment was personal to one Prime Minister. It was at this time (1952) that the Weekly Diary was started in which every department stated its information 'plans' for the following week.

Lord Swinton kept his responsibility for the information services when he moved to the Commonwealth Relations Office, and in fact remained co-ordinating Minister until he retired from politics in April 1955 and Sir Anthony Eden succeeded Mr Churchill as Prime Minister.

When Sir Anthony Eden became Prime Minister, Mr Fife Clark was appointed his Public Relations Adviser, but no Minister was given any special responsibility for information—at Ministerial level the co-ordinating post was again vacant. A few months afterwards Mr Fife Clark became fulltime Director-General of the Central Office of Information, a post to which he had been appointed in October 1954 while remaining the Government's Public Relations Adviser. The post of Prime Minister's Adviser on Public Relations was given to Mr William Clark, a journalist from a politically 'neutral' newspaper, the *Observer*, although again he had had experience in the British information services in the United States. This again was a personal appointment to the Prime Minister. There was no co-ordinating Minister, so Mr William Clark's position was somewhat different from the one Mr Fife Clark had had under Mr Winston Churchill.

The Suez crisis in the autumn of 1956 precipitated a considerable change in the handling of British information policy generally. Whatever the merits or demerits of the British position at the time of Suez, it was clear that there was a failure to present British policy favourably to the rest of the world. Ministers kept civil servants in the dark about their intentions, and communication with the press broke down. For four days there was an 'information silence' on the British side. In November the Prime Minister's Adviser, Mr William Clark, resigned because, it is understood, he disagreed with the Government's handling of information matters over Suez; for a few weeks no one was appointed to succeed him—Mr Clark's deputy, Mr Alfred Richardson, covered the position as acting Adviser, and Sir Walter Monckton, the Paymaster-General was made responsible for co-ordinating the three Service departments' information policy.

The Suez crisis demonstrated three things; that the information services cannot do their job unless they themselves are informed; that government information work must be co-ordinated so that, especially on the overseas side, it speaks with one voice and not with a separate one for each department concerned; and thirdly, that if the Prime Minister is the only co-ordinating Minister who can speak for government policy as a whole, in a period of international crisis he is too occupied to deal fully with the press, and there is no one at Ministerial level who can brief the press after, for example, a Cabinet meeting on the subject.

In the last phase of Sir Anthony Eden's premiership, Dr Charles Hill,[1] the Postmaster-General, was asked to take over responsibility for the information services generally. The Suez crisis was not over, and when Dr Hill came into the picture his first task was to see that the information that *was* available was given first to the information officers and through them to the press. In other words, to co-ordinate 'spokesmanship'; to look at the existing organization of both home and overseas services in order to see what needed to be co-ordinated. But after the immediate crisis was over, Dr Hill was asked to re-organize all the British information services. Taking advantage of the after-Suez mood he and the head of the Central Office of Information, Mr Fife Clark, worked out a scheme to improve the overseas information services[2] and, almost incidentally, they overhauled the co-ordination of the home information services at the same time. Dr Hill had started off by arranging for all the Chief Information Officers, including the heads of the Information Divisions of the overseas departments, to meet daily under his chairmanship. These meetings were intended to give information officers a general picture of what was going on, even when they were not personally involved.

[1] Now Lord Hill of Luton, but referred to in these pages as Dr Hill because he was so well known by this name.

[2] Dr Hill subsequently undertook a series of tours abroad, aimed both at identifying points of need and at strengthening the morale of overseas information officers; he was also instrumental in obtaining more money for overseas information generally and also for the British Council. See White Paper on Information Services, 1957.

After a time they were held only twice a week, and finally settled down to being weekly meetings, and they have remained as weekly meetings of Chief Information Officers ever since.[1]

When Mr Macmillan became Prime Minister, Dr Hill was appointed Chancellor of the Duchy of Lancaster with a seat in the Cabinet and no departmental responsibilities. This represented a considerable change. For the first time a Cabinet Minister, looking over the whole field of home and overseas information policy, was able to devote all his time to thinking about information. He could think about the information content of government policy *before* the event—something that busy Ministers had previously never been able to do. The effect of Dr Hill's appointment was quite different from any of his predecessors. From the first he acted as a real co-ordinator. Whereas previously the departmental Chief Information Officers had observed very little difference whether there was a co-ordinating Minister functioning or not, the change was very noticeable as soon as Dr Hill took over. Because of the background to his taking over the job, Dr Hill gave about two-thirds of his time to overseas information, and about one-third to the home side. Meanwhile the vacant post at No. 10 had been filled by Mr Harold Evans when Mr Macmillan became Prime Minister. Mr Evans's appointment was similar to Mr Fife Clark's. He was an established civil servant, again with journalistic experience in his background, and he was Adviser to the new co-ordinating Minister, Dr Hill, as well as to the Prime Minister.

This particular arrangement, with Dr Hill as co-ordinating Minister and Mr Evans at No. 10 lasted for nearly five years, until in October 1961, Dr Hill was made Minister of Housing and Local Government. The Prime Minister asked Dr Hill to continue to take responsibility for the co-ordination of the information services at home, but in view of the heavy departmental responsibility he had now assumed, it was decided that the overseas information services should be hived off. This part of the job then passed to the Secretary for Technical Co-operation. Mr Evans continued to advise Dr Hill in his work of co-ordinating the home information services, but did not become adviser to the Secretary for Technical Co-operation on the overseas information side.

To the extent that the Prime Minister is involved in foreign affairs

[1] One of the side results of the setting up of the machinery of co-ordination in the information services generally, resulted in closer co-operation between the two Foreign Office departments dealing with information—the News Department and the Information Policies Department, especially in overseas work.

his Adviser acts as a spokesman on foreign affairs, and this part of his duties was quite unaffected by the changes in October 1961. In fact, the Public Relations Adviser estimated he still spent more time on the overseas information side than on the home information side.

This situation continued until the Cabinet reshuffle of July 1962, when Dr Hill left the government and co-ordination of the home information services was given to Mr William Deedes who, as Minister without Portfolio, took over the home information services as a full-time job with Mr Evans continuing as Adviser at No. 10. Overseas information remained with the Secretary for Technical Co-operation. This was the first time home information policy alone had been given to a Minister without any other responsibilities—possibly because in the summer of 1962 it was thought that the Common Market might prove to be a big information job.

So, gradually and spasmodically, over the last seventeen years, we have moved from Mr Morrison's position, when the co-ordination of information services was a sparetime activity for a busy Minister, to Mr Deedes, who is the wholetime co-ordinator of the home information side only; from Mr Francis Williams, a personal and temporary appointment as Public Relations Adviser to an individual Prime Minister, to an established civil servant in the No. 10 job who is a vital link in the information services.[1]

THE FUNCTIONS OF THE CO-ORDINATING MINISTER

The co-ordinating Minister is the custodian of government interests on information in the Cabinet, in Parliament and in dealing with the press. It has been found useful to have a Minister to speak in Parliament for information policy generally (or sometimes two, one for home and one for overseas); to have someone who can stand back from departmental problems and look at information problems in the round. The press, and especially the corps of Parliamentary correspondents, need frequent briefing and guidance from a central source; and they have complained when they did not get it.

Perhaps more important, the co-ordinating Minister can un-officially advise other Ministers on matters of public relations. He cannot dictate to his Ministerial colleagues; nevertheless we are told it has proved useful to Chief Information Officers to have someone outside the department who can if necessary have a word with their own Minister at his level about specific problems. Not all Chief

[1] The Adviser's post is not however established as a prerogative of the Civil Service. See p. 95.

Information Officers, it must be remembered, have an easy access to their own Ministers.

The co-ordinating Minister is not the head of the information services, and he has not, at least since 1951, had any responsibility for the Central Office of Information. He is not expected to interfere in any department's internal affairs, but he is someone who can co-ordinate, through influence and persuasion, the work of information officials. This is mainly done through the regular weekly meetings under his chairmanship.

The weekly meeting under the co-ordinating Minister has also proved of great value to the Chief Information Officers. For one thing, they get to know each other. Secondly, information officers have found it valuable to meet and exchange views with their opposite number in other departments—the individual Chief Information Officer with a new problem nearly always finds, if he can discuss it round the table, that someone else has been there before. Thirdly, at these meetings, a diary of forthcoming events is tabled. Obvious clashes of dates can be avoided—it would be a mistake for two important news items to be released to the press on the same day, so that neither got their fair share of space. Information officers can look at their own problem against the general background—for example is it wise to suggest Russian should replace some French lessons in schools during the very week the Prime Minister is to visit France? The co-ordinating Minister, too, will voice problems of his own—did *The Times* article on restrictive practices give a fair picture of the position from the Board of Trade's point of view? Was there anything in a story another newspaper picked up? Then, on any specific problem, an *ad hoc* committee of interested information officers can be set up. The value of these special committees is very great. The three or four departments involved can get together with the co-ordinating Minister to thrash out informally some particular information policy or problem which cuts across one or more departmental interests. There are nearly always one or two such *ad hoc* committees in existence.

The co-ordinating Minister also sees the Lobby when information questions arise which are wider than one Minister's responsibilities. He will take up any general problems, e.g. if there are difficulties with a particular newspaper; if departments are treating embargoes differently; or if the Lobby correspondents are complaining about some procedure which affects more than one department.

It is important for the co-ordinating Minister to be of Cabinet rank—only Cabinet Ministers have that picture of the whole field of government intention which is essential for dealing with the Lobby, and the co-ordinator ought to be influential enough to carry weight with other Ministers. It is also helpful if the co-ordinating Minister is a man of stature in the party, as well as in the government. The line between party policy and government information is a delicate one to draw, and Chief Information Officers have said that if the co-ordinator is influential in the party, it is much easier for him to prevent any attempt to use the government information services improperly for party political purposes.

The other point to be emphasized is the great importance of the Lobby to the information services and, in reverse, the first-class service the Lobby gets from the information services and the enormous amount of work that is normally done for the Lobby. When Dr Hill was the co-ordinating Minister, he considered one of his most important and difficult tasks was to persuade other Ministers—not always successfully—to talk to the Lobby as often as possible. He himself saw the Lobby regularly, at least once a week, talking to them and letting them ask him questions ranging over the whole information field. The Prime Minister's Public Relations Adviser sees the Lobby at least once a day. Not all co-ordinating Ministers would necessarily tackle the job in the same way. One co-ordinating Minister or Adviser at No. 10 might concentrate on keeping the Lobby satisfied; another might think it more useful to spend more time with newspaper editors and have a less close relationship with the Lobby.

The position of the co-ordinating Minister is an odd one, possibly for two reasons. First, the changing responsibility for the co-ordination of information policy reflects to some degree the difficulty of reconciling the public relations of government with the conventions of Parliamentary democracy. The entrenched distrust of anything called propaganda is reflected in the lack of a centralized government organization for government publicity. It appears that the necessity for propaganda overseas is more acceptable to public opinion than the idea of a policy for government publicity on the home side. On the other hand, the need for government information to speak with one voice makes some co-ordination essential, as the Suez crisis showed, and the two occasions since the war when the government has tried to do without a co-ordinating Minister only lasted for a few months in each case.

Secondly, there is the difficulty of maintaining the traditional constitutional function of the Prime Minister as supreme co-ordinator of government policy in an era of increasing complexity and greatly extended government activity. On both the occasions when the co-ordinating post was abolished, a new Prime Minister appears to have been trying to act as his own co-ordinator of information. The need for co-ordinating Ministers other than the Prime Minister has however now been accepted in other fields as well as in information. But the precise powers of such Ministers in policy formulation and co-ordination have been left vague and undefined; the way in which the job is tackled depends very much on the personality of the Minister doing it.

THE VALUE OF CO-ORDINATION AT OFFICIAL LEVEL

Constitutionally, the Prime Minister is the supreme co-ordinator of government policy, and his Adviser on public relations has therefore a very central position in the government information services. The No. 10 Adviser sees the Lobby and the overseas correspondents on matters involving the Prime Minister and also on all matters of general government policy, as well as keeping in touch with the individual departments concerned. The chart shows that the job has varied in scope and function from time to time and also in the kind of person who has held the post. Of the six men who have held the post since 1945, Mr Francis Williams, Mr Philip Jordan and Mr William Clark had been career journalists, although they all three had also had experience in the government information services. The other three have been established civil servants, members of the regular information services seconded to No. 10 for a tour of duty,[1] although all three had also been working journalists before they became civil servants. All six, therefore, have had experience both as journalists and as civil servants.

It obviously makes some difference whether the holder of the No. 10 post is a personal appointee of the Prime Minister and has an outside job to go back to, or whether he is a career civil servant. The tendency in recent years has been towards appointing civil servants, and there is evidence that the press, when asked what kind of person they preferred at No. 10 came down very plainly on the side of having an established civil servant in the post—perhaps because a civil

[1] It is for this reason interesting that Mr Harold Evans, a career civil servant, was given a baronetcy when Mr Macmillan resigned his premiership. Baronetcies are normally reserved for non-civil servants—for Members of Parliament for example. It is unusual for a career civil servant to be given an hereditary title. Sir Harold Evans did not go back to the normal information services, however. After a few months with Sir Alec Douglas-Home, he left to take up an appointment outside the government service.

servant is more likely to give the government's views and not party political views or his own personal ones. But there is no tradition about this. It would be open to a Prime Minister to appoint a journalist again, or indeed anyone else, as an Adviser if he wished to do so, although it would perhaps be difficult if the Adviser was not acceptable to the press and also to the civil servants with whom he had to deal.[1] The advantages of having a civil servant information officer in the job are that he is more likely to get full co-operation from the civil servants with whom he has to deal. With someone whom they felt to be an outsider and a temporary, there might be a tendency to withhold complete confidence. It has been suggested, too, that an ordinary civil servant can afford to be more independent of political pressure than a Prime Minister's personal appointee. On the other hand, it is only fair to say that Mr William Clark, one of the three personal appointments, resigned on a disagreement over a matter of principle at the time of Suez which shows independence rather than anything else. This is something a career civil servant would have been unlikely to do (although he could, of course, have requested a transfer).

The No. 10 spokesman handles all the press relations of the Prime Minister and advises him generally on public relations. He customarily accompanies the Prime Minister on major journeys abroad. The institution of the Lobby is of great importance and convenience to him—nearly all his press contacts on the home side are on a non-attributable basis—because through the Lobby he can get in touch with all the home press that matters very quickly; and he sees the Lobby at least once a day. When there was no co-ordinating Minister during 1955–6, the position of the Adviser at No. 10 was correspondingly more responsible. It was he who indicated to journalists when there was debate within the government about a particular policy and why the government had to take a particular line. Nowadays it would be more likely to be the co-ordinating Minister who would do this, rather than the Prime Minister's Adviser.

The Adviser has no departmental responsibilities. There is also a Deputy Adviser, but between them the two men have to provide a round-the-clock cover for the Prime Minister. The nature of the job varies a good deal with the personality of the particular Prime Minister—whether he is a good organizer of his own time and effort and whether he is temperamentally capable of leaving his subordinates

---

[1] There is evidence that on one occasion at least, senior civil servants have voiced objection to a particular political appointment to the No. 10 post, and that their view was respected.

to do their job without undue interference. The atmosphere in the Prime Minister's office is informal. Much of the business is transacted by discussion rather than by minute. The relationship is an intimate one—the office is after all the Prime Minister's residence and children's balloons sometimes come floating down the stairs at Christmas—and so far it has been customary for a new Prime Minister to appoint a new Adviser within a few months of taking office. It has been stressed several times both by those who have held the No. 10 post and by Chief Information Officers, how useful it proved to have one person as adviser both to the Prime Minister and to the co-ordinating Minister. This triple arrangement—the Prime Minister, the co-ordinating Minister, and the Adviser in between acting for them both—supplies a very necessary focal point for all information policy.

The relationship between the co-ordinating Minister and the Adviser at No. 10 can be very close. During the five years when Dr Hill was co-ordinating Minister, they met ever day and the Adviser accompanied Dr Hill, for example, when he went overseas and co-operated with him in writing the subsequent reports. He provides the secretariat for the weekly meetings of Chief Information Officers, and takes the chair if the co-ordinating Minister is absent. The Prime Minister's Adviser was the co-ordinating Minister's departmental link—the point at which the co-ordinating Minister 'hitched on' to the departmental information machine. With another Minister and another Adviser, the link might not be so close.

INFORMAL CO-OPERATION BETWEEN DEPARTMENTS

Each Information Division cannot operate within its own department in a watertight compartment. There is and always has been, a complex network of interdepartmental liaison, often by telephone, between information officers. Some information departments—such as the Foreign Office and Ministry of Defence or the Ministry of Defence and the Service departments co-operate very closely, and may be in touch daily on a purely personal 'old chap' basis. The co-ordinating machinery described above was superimposed on this informal co-operation, and is a very valuable addition to it; but the informal co-operation naturally continues all the time.

If a statement is to be made to the press about a subject like the Common Market, for example, the Treasury, Foreign Office, Board of Trade and Commonwealth Relations Office are all involved. The Foreign Office, Ministry of Defence, and Ministry of Aviation and the three Service Ministries will all be concerned with disarmament. When the future of the cotton industry is to be discussed, the Board of Trade and Ministry of Labour are both involved. The departments may issue agreed press statements or hold joint press conferences. In cases of joint departmental interest with subjects of fairly long standing, it is customary to make one department the leader and let it act as spokesman. This is frequently the Foreign Office in international affairs, but it could be the Treasury on other occasions.

CHAPTER V

The Departmental Information Divisions at Work

The way in which the Information Divisions fit into the departmental organization of their Ministries has already been described in Chapter I. Here we are concerned to see how the divisions set about their work.

Generalizations are difficult to make; each Information Division's task reflects the diversity of the various government departments, and the way they tackle it depends to some extent on the personality of the Chief Information Officer and his relations at any one time with his Minister and with the civil servants in his department. The Information Division in the Ministry of Defence, which is almost entirely concerned with defence policy, has very different problems from that of the Post Office which is largely concerned with 'selling' the postal and telephone services; the main function of Ministry of Pensions and National Insurance's Division is issuing simple explanations of complicated pension and insurance legislation to the general public; the Foreign Office News Department is entirely concerned with press releases and press conferences. A department like the Treasury is very much on the political battlefield, with an active interest in the country's general economic problems and in international negotiations like those for the Common Market. By comparison much of the Ministry of Labour's work is carried out by a network of local offices whose staffs are in direct contact with the communities they serve; and much of their work, that concerned with training schemes or industrial safety, for example, has no political implications for most of the time.

Information Divisions aim their message at very different publics, too. The Ministry of Labour, the Ministry of Pensions and National Insurance, and the Post Office are very much concerned with the general public and contacts with individuals: the Ministry of Education, the Ministry of Health, and the Ministry of Transport on the other hand, although their activities affect the public very directly, deal very little with the general public because their departments' functions are largely delegated to other bodies—to the local authorities, for example. Most of the Ministry of Education's information material, for instance, is not issued until it has been discussed with bodies like the local education authorities, teachers' organizations, and so on; the Ministry's proposals may be seen by as many as 1,000 people before they are crystallized into a final scheme to be laid before Parliament. Again, the Ministry of Agriculture, Fisheries and Food is concerned with the general public as food consumers but, in addition, they have a considerable number of special publics to cater for. The most obvious is that of farmers, but the activities of the Ministry are also of considerable interest to the food industry, the fishing industry, and the nature conservationists, reflecting the fact that the department has a wide range of responsibilities, from animal health to the Royal Botanic Gardens at Kew.

Most departments site their Information Divisions in a central place in the main building. The Chief Information Officer's room is often on the same floor as the Minister's: but in some Ministries, especially those where there is a busy public inquiry room, as at the Ministry of Labour and the Ministry of Education, the Information Division is on the ground or first floor, near to the public inquiry point. Where a Ministry is divided between several buildings, the Information Division is often—in the case of the Home Office, for example—in the same building as the Minister.

The Information Division of each government department visited in the course of research for this book[1] reflected a different picture, a different atmosphere, a different mode of work, different physical conditions; they were trying to reach different publics. The Chief Information Officers differed, too, in their approach to their work, in their attitude to Ministers and to departmental colleagues, and the emphasis they placed on different media of communication.

But in spite of this diversity, they have similar functions, some common problems and most of them are organized in the same way. It is possible to describe them as a common information service.

What sort of organization has been developed to perform their functions and how does it operate?

---

[1] The twelve Information Divisions visited were: Treasury, Board of Trade, Foreign Office, Post Office, Home Office, War Office and the Ministries of Health, Education, Transport, Labour, Defence and Pensions and National Insurance. The Central Office of Information, including the Social Survey and the Prime Minister's Adviser were also interviewed. The Information Divisions of the other Ministries were also asked whether their activities differed from those described here, and their comments have been incorporated in the Chapter. Evidence has therefore been collected from twenty-five departments and the Information Offices in Scotland and Northern Ireland.

THE CHIEF INFORMATION OFFICER

First we will consider the position of the Chief Information Officer himself, and then the various sections which work under him.

The Chief Information Officer has two kinds of problem: those he chooses, such as youth employment, and those forced on him by circumstances, like industrial disputes. He has two types of activity: on the one hand, advising his department of the public relations implications of their policies, and on the other, carrying out his own executive functions as an expert in press and public relations. The Chief Information Officer does not make policy; but the fact that he has to explain a course of action to outsiders shows up any lack of clear thinking or incoherence on the part of the department. To that extent his activities contribute to policy making.

Finally, he has three kinds of duty towards the public. First, the duty to tell them what the government is doing in their name, and how their money is being spent—to explain to them the general activities and policy of his department. Second, the duty to make clear to the citizen his, the citizen's, rights and obligations as set out in law, government regulations and so on—this is essential for efficient and fair administration, as well as for the citizen's own convenience. Third, the duty to persuade the citizen into some course of action which is not a matter of political controversy, for his own or for the community's good, e.g. to have his children immunized, not to drink and drive, to enrol in the army or to return to a teaching career.[1] On the whole, the Information Division performs these duties to the public not in direct correspondence with them, but through the mass media.

[1] It is interesting to compare these functions of the Chief Information Officer with the purposes of government 'salesmanship' which Sir Stephen Tallents listed as long ago as 1932.
  (i)   To interest the public in work done in their name and create an intelligent criticism of the public services.
  (ii) To justify to the public action based on considerations too technical, too complicated or too secret to be comprehended by the public.
  (iii) To encourage the public to make the best use of the facilities which they have caused to be provided.
  (iv) To make known to the public the results of scientific research, e.g. agricultural progress, etc.
  (v)   To carry out by modern publicity methods special functions of public administration, e.g. the value of films and posters, as aids to teachers, for promoting trade, for vocational guidance for school leavers, etc. 'Education for desirable ends.'
  (vi) To create an *esprit de corps* between different branches of scattered or multifarious public services.

In carrying out these functions, various difficulties arise. The main ones are the question of impartiality, and how to make the department's public relations effective. The Chief Information Officer, like the other civil servants in the department, is under an obligation to give unbiased factual information to inquirers; but, at the same time, his job is to serve his Minister to the best of his ability, and to explain and, if necessary, justify his department's policies.

The whole question of impartiality in government information is discussed in Chapter IX below. Here it is sufficient to differentiate between the press statements and paid-for publicity put out by Information Divisions, which should be confined strictly to facts, with comment conspicuous by its absence, and interviews with the press where the Chief Information Officer is clearly putting his department's viewpoint, not usually for quotation, but as a background to impending or recently passed government legislation. The press would not expect this background to be impartial. The information officer is acting as a spokesman for his department and they can always go to the opposition—Parliamentary or other—for another point of view. But they have a right to expect impartiality in the press statements and in government publicity.

Chief Information Officers are not always successful in acting as a link between the department and the public or special publics for whom the publicity is intended. It is not necessarily their fault. The Director-General of the Central Office of Information has said:

> The theory is accepted that every civil servant whatever his functions has important responsibilities in the context of public relations. . . . Whether in practice any government department becomes a really good department for public relations depends partly on the Chief Information Officer's skill as an executant in outward communication but just as much on his abilities and the use made of him as an adviser over the full range of direct dealings between staff and public. Far too few officials are both equipped and permitted to perform this internal educational function.[1]

These are the Chief Information Officer's problems. What in fact does he do all day? To take an example from the Ministry of Labour, a morning chosen at random from the Chief Information Officer's diary starts with the preparation of an internal memorandum about

---

[1] Mr Fife Clark, Director-General, Central Office of Information, speaking on 'Public Relations and the Civil Service' at an International Conference in Brussels, November 1962.

the considerations which arise when a member of the staff is invited to address an outside body on a subject which concerns his official responsibilities. A vacancy on his own staff has to be filled, and this involves discussions with the Establishments Department. Can it be filled by promotion or transfer from the Information Division of another department, or should the field be widened by inviting applications from outside the Civil Service? A newspaper correspondent, who is known personally, looks in for a few minutes—and stays half-an-hour. The Minister has to be consulted about staff participation in closed-circuit broadcasts arranged by the BBC as part of their plan for setting up local broadcasting stations. A major technical difficulty has presented itself in connection with illustrations intended for an advisory booklet in the Safety, Health and Welfare series, and this must be resolved as a matter of urgency. Or in another Information Division, their Minister may be due to speak in Rome at the Commonwealth Education Conference on the place of English as a world language and must be briefed about it; a committee has reported in favour of increased grants to university students, so the newspapers must have explained to them why the increase is necessary, why it is not bigger, and how it fits into the two other increases given in the last twelve months. The anti-smoking campaign in schools—a joint undertaking by the Ministries of Health and Education—must be launched. A film has to be distributed, and poster material too; 4,000 envelopes with material for local education authorities and youth organizations must be sent off. Or in another Public Relations Division, the head must make a trip to Germany; the British Army of the Rhine has been getting some unfortunate publicity in the more sensational press. There must be some informal talks with the men on the spot, and the newspapers convinced that the incidents involve only a few men. Or the Foreign Secretary and the Minister of Defence are going abroad to a Disarmament Conference, and their public relations officers must go with them.[1]

Chief Information Officers also have to receive foreign visitors who come to look at our Health Service or blind schools or prison system or whatever it may be; they have to arrange some of the details of royal visits when the Queen Mother opens the new Ministry of Pensions and National Insurance computer at Newcastle, or Princess Margaret visits the Leicester National College for training youth leaders. They take a good deal of interest in the press coverage

[1] The Head of the News Department in the Foreign Office spent more than a third of his working days out of the country in 1961.

of local events which affect the Ministry. For example, when the Minister of Transport opens a new road, the Information Division trys to hold press conferences which will interest the local press not only in that particular new road but in all the other, and often duller, road improvement schemes in the neighbourhood; the Ministry of Labour encourages the managers of their thousand or so employment exchanges to take an active part in local life, lecturing to local societies, giving facilities to local press and television interests and so on; the Information Division also publishes a broadsheet for local exchange managers three times a year setting out the rules of simple publicity techniques—how to use the material provided by head-quarters—how to make employment exchange notice boards and displays tidy and bright and attractive, what are good vacancy display techniques, and so forth. Similarly the Post Office Information Division makes a regular review of stock letters and forms, the design and colour of buildings, typography and advertisements, and issues background booklets and shows films to the staff about good public relations.

Such are the day-to-day events which may make up a Chief Information Officers' life. There are also major problems which may crop up and occupy all his time over a long period to the exclusion of all else. The Ministry has an important Bill coming up this session; it would be helpful if press articles and television programmes could discuss the problem in general terms, and must be helped to do so. Later, the Lobby must be seen, the Minister's speech drafted and the embargoed press release issued; perhaps a pamphlet of explanation will have to be prepared for publication when the Act has become law. Or the Chief Information Officer at the Ministry of Labour may be faced with a threatened rail strike; at the Treasury the Chief Information Officer may have to deal with the publicity problems created by the breakdown in the Common Market negotiations.

Several information officers have stressed that, whatever the size of the problem, the job they have to do has two aspects. An Information Division has a dual personality. On the one hand, it must look internally to its relations with the Minister and the department of which it is a part; the first qualification of an Information Division is that it must be informed. On the other hand it must look outwards to the delicate balance of its relations with the press, the public and with Parliament—it is the department's window and transmitter to the outside world.

The Information Division and the Minister[1]

The Chief Information Officer must obviously be able to get on well with his Minister. Public relations is a subject on which the Minister will consider himself an expert—in fact, in his frequent contact with his constituents and Members of Parliament he probably is very knowledgeable about the state of public opinion on most topics. He may well have strong views about public relations. It is probably particularly important for the Minister to have a sympathetic head of his Information Division simply because public relations is an intangible subject, open to individual interpretation and hunch, and depending on the personalities involved. It could be very difficult if the personalities conflicted.

Some Chief Information Officers see their Minister daily—the Chief Information Officer at the Board of Trade and the Director of Public Relations at the Ministry of Defence do so, for example. Others will see him rarely unless there is legislation pending, or some important piece of the department's work is in the news or likely to be. They all have freedom of access to the Minister, without an intervening hierarchy. Some do not cultivate this freedom, others do. It is very much a question of the individuals concerned.

Again, on Ministerial speeches, practice varies a good deal. In some departments the Information Division expects to write or draft or revise or comment on almost every speech the Minister makes. In others they only write those parts directly concerned with information matters, and rarely see speeches before they are delivered. Similarly with the drafting of White Papers. The Public Relations Division at the Post Office help with the drafting of all the Department's White Papers, and usually also produce a simplified version for the guidance of the press at the same time; the Home Office Information Division had a finger in the pie when the White Paper on Prison Reform was written. On the other hand, the Information Divisions at the Ministry of Labour and the Ministry of Pensions and National Insurance rarely come into the picture when a White Paper is produced—the administrative divisions concerned with the subject write it, although the Information Division would be consulted about its presentation.

The Chief Information Officer usually takes part in high level

[1] Minister or Ministers. The Foreign Office in 1963 had six Ministers and the Treasury and Board of Trade had four each. Customs and Excise, on the other hand, has no resident Minister, but is responsible to the Chancellor of the Exchequer and the other Treasury Ministers, who have their own Information Division in the Treasury.

meetings within his Ministry at which current questions of policy are discussed between the Minister and heads of divisions. Thus he is put in the picture on present activities and approaching events. In the Board of Trade, for example, the Chief Information Officer meets the President, the other Ministers, the Permanent Secretary and heads of divisions once a week. He is thus able to get a programme of all future Ministerial appearances and is able to discuss any points of difficulty on topics likely to arise during the coming week; this ensures that he has enough of the confidential background to what is being planned to avoid embarrassing his department when talking to the press. He in his turn looks ahead and warns his Ministers that, for example, consumer protection may be much more of a live issue in the future than it has been in the past, and that Board of Trade public relations must take this possibility into account.

In the Ministry of Education, there is a programme meeting, similarly attended, which looks at the whole field of education, and which until 1962 also reviewed all the Department's forthcoming Answers to Parliamentary Questions, looking at them particularly from the 'good public relations' angle. In the Ministry of Labour, the Chief Information Officer attends meetings of the principal consultative bodies appointed by the Minister—for example the National Joint Advisory Council over which the Minister of Labour himself presides and various internal meetings where policy questions are discussed, notably the monthly meeting of Controllers which is normally chaired by the Permanent Secretary. In this and other ways he is able to keep abreast of developments and to form a clear picture of the Ministry's methods and objectives.

The more important announcements, such as the introduction of a White Paper, Ministerial speeches in important debates, the introduction of legislation and so on, are normally the subjects of fairly formal consultation on the public relations aspect between the Minister, the heads of policy divisions and the Chief Information Officer. Similarly, the decision to launch a publicity campaign involves initiative from the Minister and the administrative divisions concerned and then departmental conferences before the matter is handed over to the Chief Information Officer for him to carry it out. He and his division will then normally consult the Central Office of Information and the professional agents employed by the Central Office of Information before deciding on the form of the campaign.

The Information Division and the Department
Clearly, the extent to which the Information Division is kept in-

formed of what is going on in the department depends on the attitudes of administrators, as well as the attitude of Ministers, and the relations the Chief Information Officer has with his administrative colleagues.

Although the Information Division is there to serve the Minister, most of the Chief Information Officer's time is in fact taken up with advising his colleagues.

The Information Division exists as a service division to the rest of the department. Just as a public relations firm in the outside world has a number of 'accounts' it deals with, so each administrative branch of a Ministry is an 'account' for the Information Division to look after—for example, the teachers branch, overseas branch, youth service branch, schools branch and further education branch in the Ministry of Education, or the advisory, planning, local government, water and minerals divisions in the Ministry of Housing and Local Government.

Contact is personal or by telephone rather than formal. An official on his way to a meeting of an important advisory committee might, say, drop in for a chat with the Chief Information Officer beforehand. Some, though by no means all, departments have a standing order that any internal papers with a possible bearing on public relations should be forwarded to the Information Division at an early stage. There are, however, understandably enough, differences of opinion among administrators as to what parts of their work are germane to the work of the Information Division.

All departments admit that the Information Division should be consulted at an early stage in policy-forming discussions, and the Chief Information Officer is also usually at liberty to attend other meetings within the department either by invitation, or at his request, when the agenda includes matters having a possible bearing on public relations. But there are many departmental internal meetings and the Chief Information Officer would find it difficult to attend more than a small proportion of them. In any case, it is not always a matter of course that the Chief Information Officer is advised of the times and agenda of internal meetings; nor is it widely regarded as necessary that the minutes of meetings should be sent for information to him. The process of communication within the department may well be something of a hit or miss procedure. It depends on information officers having free and speedy access to their colleagues and on the principal officers of policy divisions having formed the habit of keeping information officers informally briefed on decisions and actions taken or expected. It is from somewhere within this informal consultation process that what might be termed routine information policy decisions are made. Such decisions—about the right kind of publicity which will get the maximum co-operation, the handling of announcements of alterations in regulations, the timing of press statements and the form which they are to take—are made in the light of advice which the Chief Information Officer gives his colleagues. The ultimate decision, for example to issue a press statement or not, is the responsibility of the head of the policy division concerned. What factors he takes into account and what weight he gives to the advice of the Chief Information Officer are governed in great part by the standing of the Chief Information Officer and the attitude of the administrative division to the business of public relations.

Information officers who have been for some time in the service have noticed how much more 'information minded' civil servants have grown in the last dozen years or so, especially as the older generation have retired and younger administrators have taken their place.[1] Most Chief Information Officers have said they consider their relations with their civil service colleagues to be 'first class' and that in any case of difficulty with their Minister or with outside bodies, they feel they can rely on the support of their administrative colleagues, including the Permanent Secretary.

THE THREE SECTIONS OF AN INFORMATION DIVISION

The report of the Crombie Committee[2] on the staffing of the government information services recommended that Information Divisions should have three sections, split according to the subjects the division was concerned with. The three standard sections were to be Press, Publicity and Intelligence. Most, but not all, Information Divisions conform to this pattern.

All Information Divisions have a press section—contact with the press was after all their original *raison d'être*—but not all have publicity sections dealing with paid publicity. The Ministry of Defence, for instance, does not have one. It is a co-ordinating Ministry for the three service Departments, and is only concerned with press relations; any publicity campaigns are the responsibility of the individual service departments. Nor do all Information Divisions have an Intelligence (or Briefing) section.

---

[1] Of the present civil servants at the top of the Foreign Office, for example, three have themselves been in the News Department. They are therefore more likely to be aware of the problems of press relations than the older generation of Foreign Office officials.

[2] See Chapter VII below.

107

The Post Office is unusual in that its own staff is so big that one of their problems is keeping in touch with them, and the three sections of the Post Office Public Relations department are therefore Press, Publicity and Internal Relations. The Board of Trade, at the time of writing, have an unusual organization. The Chief Information Officer in charge of News Branch deals with press relations only. There is an Export Publicity and Fairs Officer of equal rank who is the head of a parallel organization dealing with trade exhibitions and fairs and paid publicity in general. In the Customs and Excise Department the normal position is reversed—the Information and Press Sections are part of a large and important Intelligence Branch which collects information, prepares revenue estimates, advises on taxation proposals and prepares the Annual Report.

Where the three sections do exist, the compartments are not water-tight, although work in the different sections calls for different types of expertise. When one subject is particularly in the news, for example, members of all sections of the Information Division will act as a team to cope with it; or all the members of the Information Division can be called in if necessary to do research for an important speech.

The standard hierarchy for an Information Division is that the Chief Information Officer has responsibility for the whole division, whilst his second-in-command (a Chief Information Officer or Principal Information Officer) is in charge of the Press Section. But in some departments—the Treasury, for instance—the Press Officer is not the second-in-command.

The Press Section

The Information Division is the main contact between a department and the press. If the Minister talks to the press he will normally tell the Information Division what he has said unless they have previously briefed him, or were present at the interview. Civil servants, too, tend to be very wary of press contacts without expert help in dealing with them. Officials do not normally talk to the press or broadcast or write anything for them without consulting the Information Division or asking them to be present.

But the Press Section's duties are considerably more than that. Press relations for a government department can be of two kinds. There are the continuous relationships which a department builds up with the different groups of journalists—the Lobby, the industrial correspondents, the defence correspondents, the education correspondents, the city editors and financial journalists. In the Ministry of Labour, for example, a press room is set aside for the industrial correspondents to use: in the Foreign Office the diplomatic correspondents are free to walk into the news room at any time; nor is it only Ministers who see the Lobby—most Chief Information Officers spend a good deal of time in the House, and talk to the Lobby fairly freely. It must not be forgotten that 'Press' in this context includes radio and television, who also have their correspondents belonging to the industrial group or the diplomatic group, and so on. The Press Officer has to be geared to their special needs and the tyranny of their news times as much as for those of the ordinary press.[1] Then there is the answering of isolated questions about current events; these can range from 'What arrangements are being made for a gun salute to celebrate the arrival of the Queen's baby?' to 'What explanation has the Ministry to offer for the subsidence of the Preston by-pass road . . . the cancellation of the latest missile . . . the escape of prisoners from Dartmoor?' Journalists who ask questions about particular events are answered as fully as the constitutional convention that matters tabled in either House are subject to Parliamentary privilege, allows. A well run Press Office can usually answer most queries without reference to any other division in the department; their function is to lift the burden of routine inquiries from the shoulders of administrative officers. If the press officer is unable to answer a query, he will normally ask if he can ring back the inquirer when he has obtained the information from the relevant division. The press officer does not himself perform the research which the journalist avoids by relying on him. It is the administrator who supplies the facts. Some departments, do, however, follow the practice of passing on an inquirer, whether a journalist or a member of the general public, direct to the division which can answer his question. This is the usual practice, for example, in the Ministry of Housing and Local Government.

The Ministry of Housing and Local Government, for instance, has an officer in each section, known to the Press Office, who has files of the kind of detailed information that members of local authorities, the press and general public are continually demanding. This means that in every section there is someone capable of answering telephone queries quickly and intelligibly, and providing background information. This method is used from time to time by all departments when a particularly complicated subject is 'hot news' and can be most

---

[1] In the Home Office, at one time, the Chief Information Officer himself concentrated on liaison work with sound radio and television, leaving the Press Office to concentrate on direct press relations.

efficiently dealt with by a member of the policy division concerned. The War Office, for example, when the Forces' pay was increased, appointed one member of the staff to deal direct with all press inquiries on the subject. In addition, journalists who are writing articles or preparing broadcast programmes do have facilities arranged for them by the Information Division, which include opportunities to talk to members of policy divisions.

There is, in fact, no hard and fast rule whether an inquirer deals only with the press officer or deals directly with the administrator concerned. Journalists, on the whole, prefer to deal with the press officer, who is someone known to them and capable of assessing their needs in terms of news, quotes, timing and so on. On the other hand, where a matter is complicated and where an answer is apt to give rise to a further question, it seems advisable that he should be passed on to the appropriate policy division.

Much press work is done very informally. The Chief Press Officer at the Ministry of Labour, for instance, may be talking casually in the press room to a representative of one of the popular Sunday papers and might suggest that there was material for a 'human story' about the growing total of accidents to young people in industry. The Ministry would be glad to see this presented in a graphic and forceful way, more especially as the paper's mass circulation would ensure that a substantial part of the working population would have the facts brought home to them; the paper's editor might like the idea and then the article would appear. Seed can also fall upon stony ground, but much of this informal suggestion is successful because most press officers have worked on Fleet Street themselves and know how to get a story over; many of them are well known to editors and journalists. (But the press also appears to maintain happy relations with information officers who have never seen a newspaper office from the inside—the soldiers in public relations jobs in the Service departments for instance, or the career diplomats in the Foreign Office New Department.)

There are subtle variations of temper and temperament between the various press officers which are well recognized by experienced journalists; some give only the minimum of information, only answering the questions put to them. More often, however, they are willing to fill in background information unsolicited and give a little local colour to be used unattributed and at the discretion of the press. But especially when important issues are at stake, a good press officer will go much further than this. The public cannot be expected to understand, for example, the Board of Trade's suggested solutions for present-day unemployment in the old depressed areas unless they have a clear understanding of the problem. Therefore it is worthwhile for the Chief Information Officer or his Press Officer to talk to the press about the special difficulties of unemployment before the Department's proposals become a 'live' issue; it is hoped this will trigger off a spate of articles and possibly television items, so that the solution, when produced, can be understood against a background of informed opinion about the nature of the problem. This applies equally well whether it is a new motorway network, teacher recruitment, increased health insurance contributions, the housing programme or an international crisis.

The normal day of the Press Section starts with preparing and circulating daily press cuttings. By 11 a.m. (10 a.m. in the Ministry of Defence) the Minister and the top civil servants get a news summary or the press cuttings relevant to the Ministry's affairs, culled by the Press Section from all the national newspapers and half-a-dozen provincial papers, or the leading foreign newspapers as the case may be. A duplicate set is circulated at a lower level, and in some places—the Ministry of Labour for example—a direct alert is sent out to any section of the Ministry that is figuring in the news.

Then there are queries to answer, mostly over the telephone, from journalists and also from members of the general public where there is not a separate general inquiry point; facilities have to be arranged for research and visits made in the preparation of articles and radio and television programmes about the department's work; journalists have to be seen either individually or in groups, in those departments which hold regular daily press conferences about the news of the day; background information has to be given to Lobby correspondents after the Minister has made a speech or answered questions in Parliament; press handouts have to be prepared[1] and statements for Ministerial speeches and appearances; government speakers have to be briefed before personal appearances; the 'agreed' press statement after a deputation has been received by a Minister has to be drafted; and visits for overseas dignitaries have to be arranged. When there is a Ministerial press conference, the Press Officer (and

---

[1] The Ministry of Agriculture, Fisheries and Food for example, regard this activity as very important. They issue about 400 press notices every year, covering Parliamentary statements and important speeches and policy decisions of Ministers; advice and exhortation to farmers, information about rates of guarantee payments, and statistics about such things as the stocks of agricultural commodities and the production of butter and margarine. Considerable trouble is taken over both the drafting and the timing of these notices so as to secure the maximum publicity effect.

the Chief Information Officer) have to arrange it, and brief the Minister and officials involved, foreseeing the kind of questions the press are likely to ask and providing the answers; they will both be present at the conference.

At the Foreign Office, whose News Department headed by a Foreign Office official is really a high powered Press Section, the day is probably more formalized than in other Press Sections. There the morning is spent in gathering information—first reading the newspapers and the telegrams, and then making the rounds of the department to discuss the news with the heads of divisions. At 12 o'clock there is an internal meeting, and by 12.30 p.m. the officer concerned is ready to brief the British and foreign press at the daily press conference. The afternoon is spent in giving out the day's news. From the briefing until 5 p.m. different members of the News Department see on average a dozen different groups of diplomatic correspondents —or in the case of certain newspapers, individual correspondents —every day of the week.

Similarly, the Ministry of Defence's work is almost all press work, and there too, the defence correspondents are seen every day. The work of the Ministry of Defence is, however, highly complicated and technical, and is also subject to security regulations. Therefore, their public relations staff have some technical knowledge, and a wide range of contacts in the Service Ministries as well as their own department in order to be able to get a quick answer to technical questions they cannot deal with themselves. They must also possess the ability to take evasive action when faced with a question to which the answer might involve security. With defence matters, a refusal to answer on the grounds of secur ty might, in itself, be revealing and contravene that security.

In many departments, for example, the Foreign Office and the Ministry of Defence, relations with the foreign press mean that there has to be a duty officer available all round the clock—some newspaper is going to press somewhere in the world all through the twenty-four hours. The press branch therefore have to anticipate what might happen during the night and see that the duty officer or resident clerk is briefed with exactly what to say, and who to refer to on any subject which is expected to crop up. (There are off-duty rosters in most of the home departments too—press officers take turns to be on call in their homes.)

The Foreign Office and Ministry of Defence are particularly concerned with briefing the press about specific items of news. Other press sections follow similar procedures when their departments are in the news, but they are also concerned to build up continuous, day-by-day press relations about the work of their departments.

Most information officers would agree that if you can get it, space in the free media is much more effective than paid-for publicity. It is the review rather than the advertisement that sells the book. A reference to foot and mouth disease precautions on *The Archers* or an exhortation to 'Mind how you go' from *Dixon of Dock Green* are considered to be far more effective than posters and leaflets. Inspiring the press and broadcasting to such 'editorial' comment is an important part of the work of the press section.

We might look in some detail at the work of the press section of one department, the Ministry of Health, which has relations with the press very different from those of the Foreign Office.

The division has evolved over the years a technique for gaining the maximum possible attention and maximum number of column inches for its health education programme, remembering that the free media really are free both in the sense that they don't cost anything and in the sense that they are free to use what information they choose and discard the rest. But an item in a newspaper or magazine has far more impact on the public than a plain announcement from a government department, so it is worth ensuring that what the department wants said gets used.

The popular myth of the press officer, with the limitless expense account, murmuring sweet nothings into the ears of a friendly editor over an expensive liqueur is very far from the Treasury-imposed reality. Members of public relations divisions vary in the amount of hospitality they give. Those at the Ministry of Health fairly frequently exchange hospitality with their opposite numbers in the free media of press, radio and television, usually at their own expense and in their own time. They think the establishment of closer personal contacts pays off because they are frequently successful when they take the initiative in suggesting subjects for articles and programmes. To mention only one example among many—*Emergency Ward 10* is to the Ministry of Health what *The Archers* is to the Ministry of Agriculture,[1] that is to say its planners have frequently consented to put into the programme items suggested by the Ministry of Health, such as mention of a shortage of radiographers, a short visual reference to the blood donor scheme, and so on.

One member of the Press Office staff at the Ministry of Health

[1] The Ministry of Agriculture, Fisheries and Food also have a ten-minute programme for farmers six mornings a week on sound radio, and five hours of television a week on agricultural subjects—an exceptionally large coverage.

works in the special field of women's publications, with a particular responsibility for nursing and midwifery, maternity and child welfare, geriatrics, mental disorders, health education and nutrition. She is also responsible for maintaining contact with the various women's organizations, and for liaison work with television and radio producers and script-writers preparing scripts in her particular field, especially when these are programmes for women. She issues regular notes and circulars to women's publications, drawing attention to anything and everything from the availability of polio vaccine for the over-25s, to the health-giving properties of green salads, the necessity for fresh air in winter and the increase in venereal disease among teenagers. The audience for this kind of education is to be reached mainly through women's magazines and women's pages in newspapers. These, unlike the newspapers of the daily press, do not need a story-line' or 'human interest peg' on which to hang their articles.

Such routine information as the Ministry of Health's Summer and Winter Health Notes and the printed details of maternity and child welfare foods and services are used as background information for these articles. The Ministry of Health's Notes give the information; the magazine writers and layout experts provide the glamour—the sugar-coating on the pill. There is also a never-failing demand from their female readership for advice and information. It is therefore fairly easy to get the women's editors to use this type of material, and to make sure it is not consigned to the waste-paper basket. Occasionally emergencies arise, such as the danger to infants of plastic bibs and to children of polythene bags. A circular from the Ministry of Health to all magazines and newspapers resulted in immediate national publicity being given to the dangers and, subsequently, considerable prominence was given to coroners' warnings at inquests on deaths from suffocation by polythene bags.

In some departments—at the Ministry of Labour, for example—the general inquiry room is under the supervision of the Press Officer. It deals with about 30,000 inquiries a year, and acts as a filter for incoming telephone calls as well as for personal callers at the Ministry headquarters. Often inquiries can be dealt with on the spot by the inquiry room, but if not they are routed to the correct branch of the Ministry. At the Board of Trade, on the other hand, telephone and personal inquiries are dealt with at a reception desk staffed by Establishments Division, and there is a separate Exports Services Branch which is responsible for detailed information about export opportunities; other inquiries from individual members of the public or private firms go straight to the policy divisions concerned and do not pass through the Information Division.

The Publicity Section
The Publicity Section of the Information Division is charged with all work on behalf of the department in the field of paid publicity. Paid publicity includes press and television advertising, and the production of books, posters and films. Most information officers would agree that if you can get it, space in the free media is much more effective than paid-for-publicity. But posters and leaflets are a necessary 'support'. A Ministerial speech will get a much more widespread reading, particularly if it is the subject of a press statement, than a brochure. The brochure must, however, be available for further information when this is requested. Nor could the free media do the job of public instruction without the supporting programme of government information. What body, for instance, would undertake the unprofitable enterprise of publishing booklets on career opportunities which have to be constantly available and constantly revised? Which newspaper or periodical would keep its readership constantly briefed on National Assistance or National Insurance regulations? Who would give regular space in the press and on the hoardings to exhortations to 'Mind that child' or 'Give a Pinta Blood a Year'?

The officials in the Publicity Section need both editorial and publicity skills. The Ministry of Agriculture, Fisheries and Food, for example, publishes about 200 major works a year, covering a range of subjects in agriculture, horticulture and food science and about 700 leaflets of practical advice to farmers; they also stage exhibits at more than fifty agricultural shows a year. In a department like the Post Office, the Publicity Section is mostly concerned with selling Post Office services like Telex or persuading the public to co-operate by packing parcels carefully, posting early in the day, addressing its envelopes correctly and so on.[1]

Money will be wasted unless the right publicity or information gets into the right hands at the right time. This is also something the Publicity Section must consider. The Ministry of Labour, for in-

[1] The results of some of these Post Office campaigns are quantifiable. After a campaign on correct addressing, they found there was a 3 per cent improvement—and as the Post Office deal with 28 million letters a day this is a daily improvement on over 800,000 letters. It costs 3d in the £ less to sell stamps in books than the same number of stamps loose. The advertising campaign for buying stamp books sent sales up from 30 million books a year to 33½ million, which represents an appreciable saving to the Department.

stance, may decide that the most effective way of reaching a particular audience at a particular time—say 15-year-olds on the point of leaving school—might be by making a film which shows the work of the youth employment officer in a lively and entertaining way, against a background of real children in a real secondary modern school. Or the Ministry of Pensions and National Insurance has to get information about welfare benefits into the hands of those who need it when they need it. The citizen cannot be issued once and for all with a complete statement of his or her welfare benefits and entitlements; but the widow must be told about death grants and pensions when her husband dies—so the Registrar of Deaths must have suitable leaflets to give to her: the expectant mother must be given information about maternity benefits when she visits her doctor or the clinic; the old age pensioner must see in the places he visits—the Post Office, or the local library—the information he needs about services to help old people. Publicity helps the administrator, as well as the public. For instance, there have always been time-limits for claiming sick benefit. A sick man who claims his benefit within the time limit gets his money without any difficulty to himself or complication to the department. If he leaves his claim too late, he gets his benefit only if he can show that he had good cause for the delay. He has a right of appeal to a local tribunal if his claim is refused and a further right of appeal to the National Insurance Commissioner if the tribunal does not find for him. There is, therefore, an appreciable saving in time and in administrative costs, quite apart from the inconvenience caused to the man, if he is aware of the time limit and claims at the right time and therefore gets his money without complication or difficulty. Publicizing the time limits through the press, broadcasts, leaflets, films and posters as well as on the medical certificate itself, therefore serves the dual purpose of reducing administrative costs and ensuring that the sick man receives his benefit at the time he needs it.

All these things are part of the work of the Publicity Sections, but there are also the big-scale publicity campaigns which departments require from time to time.

Once a decision has been made to launch a publicity campaign, the Publicity Section takes over the planning of the operation in consultation with the Central Office of Information and their professional agents. From the process of consultation there emerges a fully integrated campaign on behalf of anything from recruitment for civil defence to immunization against diphtheria or warnings against smoking. This, however, is only the routine work. Only a limited amount of money is available for direct spending on advertising and exhibitions. Therefore, the scope and success of most government publicity campaigns depends on the co-operation of outside organizations, like the local authorities or the Royal Society for the Prevention of Accidents, who are invited to take part and spend their own money within the themes of a proposed campaign. Success depends also on the attention given to the campaign in its various aspects by the free media. Arranging co-operation with outside organizations, and creating news for the free media is the responsibility of the Publicity Section and, more particularly, of the Chief Information Officer himself. We can sub-divide publicity campaigns into two kinds, those for recruitment and those for the education of the public.

Recruitment Campaigns. These are not confined to the armed forces. Most Publicity Sections undertake regular recruiting campaigns. The Home Office, for example, runs three more or less continuous major campaigns—recruiting for civil defence, for the police, and for the prison service. Recruitment for the teaching and nursing professions is undertaken by the Ministries of Education and Health, respectively.

The production of posters and advertising material, exhibitions and films are an important part of recruitment campaigns. But the cultivation of editorial publicity is also vital in the building up of long term continuous interest in the problem. Also, the best and most attractively mounted campaign will be worthless if it is preceded by a series of press attacks or unfavourable news items. This the Publicity Section usually prevents. The press gave a good deal of editorial space to support the Ministry of Education's campaign to encourage married women to return to teaching, for example.

Recruiting for the Army is a long term business. A description of what is done at the War Office gives a good idea of how Publicity Sections tackle recruiting campaigns. Recruiting for the Army has become very important since the abolition of National Service. It is recognized at the War Office that good public relations are the key to recruitment. The Army must be popularized as a career and it must be seen to be attractive. The 'image' must be right. The Army has something to sell by way of news and what might be termed visual entertainment, e.g. the pageantry of parades. It is easy to make attractive short TV films—'fillers'—showing how good life in the modern army is. The problem is to discover how best it can be sold throughout the year. A campaign can only last a limited time, but recruitment has to go on all the year round.

In addition to the Public Relations Department at the War Office, the Army commands have officers in charge of public relations. The local and national press is served with advance notices of all Army events and press; radio and television are granted all possible facilities for reporting them. In addition, and possibly of greater importance, the War Office takes the initiative in providing two or three hundred 'local boy' stories a month, that is providing news stories and pictures about the activities of individual servicemen abroad, which are sent to the local newspaper in the serviceman's home town plus an additional photograph to his wife or mother. The War Office also arranges for local newspaper editors or their staff to visit units which recruit in their circulation areas to get stories about the soldiers and their activities. These visits go on regularly throughout the year, extending to places as far away as Aden, Singapore and Hong Kong. As a result, full page illustrated feature articles showing the men at work and at play, often appear in one or even a whole group of provincial newspapers. Articles augment the handouts and features which are produced at the War Office and by the public relations officers in Home and Overseas Commands.

The annual recruiting campaign itself is mounted, as far as possible, round one particular theme or motif. The means used in this field include commercial television, with supporting television and press advertising, advertisements in national and provincial newspapers (display and classified), magazines and periodicals, sound radio announcements, films ranging from paid advertising shorts and recruiting films for use in schools, etc., to those with entertainment value which are accepted by commercial distributors for normal bookings. Other means employed are posters and participation in exhibitions. Although the whole campaign is integrated under the heading 'Army Recruiting', it falls into three major categories—officers, soldiers and women's services, the middle one being much the most important. Each major category covers further subdivisions, for example technicians and nurses, which each require a specialized approach in recruiting.

The publicity material, which is produced jointly by the War Office, Central Office of Information and the commercial advertising agents, reinforces the activities of those using the more personal approach—recruiting officers speaking in schools and at rallies and mobile exhibitions, and the additional efforts of particular regiments with local affiliations. Up to the end of 1962, the War Office recruiting campaigns appear to have been very successful. By the end of the year, when the last National Serviceman had left, the Army was over its target—165,000 officers and men.

Clearly, the armed services are at a considerable advantage in the publicity field. In many ways, 'selling' the army is easy—it is full of human interest stories. Army recruitment can aim, too, at a much wider public than can the social services, nursing or teaching professions, and the range of media from which they can select is, therefore, less circumscribed. With built-in and widespread training facilities the Army would seem to be immune from the stresses of the academic year's demands and the strictly limited accommodation at, for instance, teacher's training colleges. Apparently, too, they can absorb as many recruits as are likely to turn up. In other recruiting fields—the police, for instance—a national campaign is not always useful because some local authorities which are up to strength at the time of such a campaign, may find themselves inundated with offers and lose goodwill for the future by being forced to turn them down.[1]

Educational Campaigns. Educational or persuasive campaigns can range from the large national 'Keep Death off the Roads' and 'Mind that Child' road safety efforts to the smaller and more selective 'Export Drive'. Successful campaigns can be and are run centrally, but the central department also often needs co-operation from bodies outside its immediate jurisdiction—local authorities and voluntary bodies, and selected groups of individuals who have their own forms of association. Again, the best way to show the kind of work that is done is to describe one actual campaign.

The idea of the Ministry of Transport's *Mind that Child* campaign was first conceived by the Royal Society for the Prevention of Accidents (ROSPA). It was communicated to the Chief Information Officer, who passed it on to the Minister. When the Minister had approved the idea of the campaign, planning went ahead. The first task was to obtain the co-operation of interested bodies which the Department was likely to want to use in some way during the campaign. Support had to be obtained from other government departments, from the free media, and from private undertakings. These included the Ministry of Education, local education authorities and police forces, radio and television authorities, the Home Office, the Scottish Home and Health and Scottish Education Departments, the Post Office, and also commercial undertakings, women's organizations, trade unions,

[1] The War Office Public Relations Division points out that recruiting for some parts of the Army suffers from some of these disadvantages too. The Army has to recruit and train its nurses and its teachers, for example, and its advertising to meet these needs is just as circumscribed as it is for other departments. Sandhurst and Welbeck College also have the problem of periodical academic intakes. Equally, some recruiting categories are full, and for others national advertising is unsuitable.

and motorists', pedestrians' and cyclists' organizations. It might well be described as persuading a large number of people and organizations to do something not only for nothing, but often at considerable cost to themselves.

Possibly the most difficult task, and this is so of the majority of campaigns run by central government departments, was that of securing active and worthwhile co-operation from local authorities. Local authorities are supreme in their own sphere; they cannot be directed by the department; they can only be advised and persuaded and provided with campaign material at low cost and in the most attractive and easily usable forms.

The central work of organization and planning was undertaken by a Publicity Progress Committee convened at the Ministry of Transport by the Chief Information Officer. This committee consisted of representatives of the Royal Society for the Prevention of Accidents, the Central Office of Information, the Road Safety and Information Divisions of the Ministry of Transport, the Scottish Office and BBC television. Its work was defined under four heads: co-ordinating the various forms of effort to promote the campaign; enlisting the interest of radio and television authorities; ensuring co-ordination between Divisional Accident Prevention Organizers of the Royal Society for the Prevention of Accidents and the respective Chief Regional Officers of the Central Office of Information; and co-opting motoring and other road organizations to the committee.

The campaign was conceived as having three targets: to extend and publicize training schemes for child cyclists and to step up road safety training generally; to impress parents with their responsibility for bringing up children to behave sensibly on the roads; to persuade road users to show consideration for children. The work of the central bodies consisted of the preparation of publicity material for use throughout the country.

The campaign also had to be phased properly to ensure that, while the advertising campaign was under way and local authorities were publicizing their training schemes for children, there would not be a glut of news stories one day and nothing for the next four or five. The time of the Minister and Parliamentary Secretary also had to be apportioned so that their public appearances would be spread over the country and over the whole period of the campaign.

The campaign had also to be geared to the administrative machine. It would be no use enrolling children for cycling proficiency if training and testing facilities were not available in the right places at the right time.

In the event, this particular campaign did have some measurable results. In terms of press coverage and co-operation it was successful—a large number of column inches appeared in both the national and local press. The *Evening Standard* ran a special poster painting competition and the *Daily Sketch* ran overhead banners and the campaign slogan on every page throughout the duration of the campaign. The work of the regional officials resulted in small exhibitions in many parts of the country, shop-window displays, road safety rallies, road safety church services and so on. Statistically, the results could also be deemed satisfactory. Fifteen thousand children passed cycling tests during the three months of the campaign; fourteen new permanent local road safety committees were set up and thirty-six restarted. As compared with the corresponding months of the previous year, there were forty-one fewer deaths and 700 fewer injuries due to cycling accidents involving children.[1]

Even as far as this particular campaign was concerned, the effect may have worn off rapidly. Local road safety committees may again have ceased to function and enrolments for road safety training dropped. Some road safety campaigns have left a lasting impact— 'Keep Death Off the Roads', or 'Mind How you Go', for example— but most educational campaigns are expected to catch the imagination and attention only for a brief period. They must be supported or upheld by continuous efforts at local level to maintain the interest aroused. It is the vigour and imagination of individual officers and organizations—local councillors, police forces, education authorities, and so on—which finally make the difference.[2]

The Intelligence Section
Some Information Divisions contain a third section, normally called the Intelligence Section or the Briefing Section, whose function is to collect information for the use of their own or other government departments, rather than to communicate through press or publicity organs. A good deal of their work lies outside the scale of this study because they supply material for the Central Office of Information which is used in COI publications intended for countries overseas. (It should be noted, however, that many of these publications do

---

[1] It is seldom that the results of a campaign are quantifiable in this way and even more seldom that the machinery exists to measure results. In this case the divisional officers of ROSPA were able to collect statistics and other information about various local initiatives.

[2] This also applies to publicity, for the National Savings movement. The central organization advises and plans the broad outlines, but it is the fulltime man on the spot locally who keeps the campaign going.

have a sale in this country, particularly in schools and colleges.) Practice varies from department to department: sometimes the Intelligence Section actually writes up the material itself; sometimes it leaves this task to the Central Office of Information writers.

The Intelligence Section of an Information Division may also be responsible, as at the Ministry of Health, for editing notes of a technical nature for use either within the department or by its officers and agents in the field. The Ministry of Pensions and National Insurance Intelligence Section also produces general background briefing material on, for example, social security in Great Britain, the graduated pension scheme or the industrial injuries scheme. They are intended for the use of Members of Parliament, lecturers, trade union officials, personnel managers or Citizens' Advice Bureaux—all the people who may find themselves having to explain these matters to the general public.

The Intelligence Section also normally edits the department's annual report, where there is one.[1] These annual reports are an account in general terms of the department's work during the year, together with statistics of general interest—the number of children passing GCE, or of hospital in-patients, or the number of letters delivered and telephones installed by the Post Office, or the health of the school child over the last twenty years. At the Post Office, the Public Relations Division is completely responsible for their annual report from the first draft to the final editing. In others the policy divisions write a good deal of it.

Some Ministries, especially those with large numbers of staff scattered about the country, like the Ministry of Labour, the Post Office and the Ministry of Pensions and National Insurance, think it important to keep in touch with them by house journals and internal magazines which tell the staff what is happening in the rest of the Ministry from high policy decisions down to pictures and articles about staff weddings, and who won the most recent sporting events. The house journal or magazine, where it exists, is normally produced by the Intelligence Section. In the Post Office, whose staff is very large, the Internal Relations Section of the Information Division produces for example, a Post Office magazine with a circulation of

[1] Several major government departments—the Treasury, Board of Trade and Foreign Office, for example, publish no annual reports. At the Ministry of Labour, the Information Division produced the Annual Report until 1962, when publication was discontinued because it was felt that the *Ministry of Labour Gazette*, which appears monthly, could be more up to date than an Annual Report. The *Gazette* is produced by the Statistics Department of the Ministry of Labour but the Information Division will, in future, be concerned in widening its scope.

130,000, a technical telecommunications journal, and a wall news-paper; they also produce news and information sheets, in the ratio of one to every six members of staff, explaining the reasons, for example, why post has to go triangularly instead of direct between two towns. Ministries whose staff are almost all in headquarters buildings do not need internal house journals so much. The Ministry of Education is, however, starting one.

Much of the Intelligence Section's work is collecting information from departmental and outside sources for the use of their own department; in some Ministries this type of work is not performed by the Information Division at all but by the Library or Establishments Division or the Statistical Section. Recently two Ministries, the Home Office and the Ministry of Education, have set up specific research units which are outside their Information Divisions. They are mainly concerned to institute research into crime and education, respectively, and to collect information in a similar way to the Board of Education's original Office of Special Inquiries and Reports under Sir Michael Sadler in 1895. In other Ministries the Intelligence Section in the Information Division may do this kind of work.

The Briefing Section at the Treasury, however, is a special case. No other Information Division has one exactly like it. The reason for this is partly historical (see Chapter III above). The Treasury Information Division started off as the Economic Information Unit which on the one hand informed the public directly on economic affairs, and on the other made sure that non-economic Ministers and their senior civil servants had access to official data and judgement on these matters. This function has been retained. Unlike most other Intelligence Sections, the Treasury Briefing Section is manned neither by journalists nor administrators but mostly by graduates with economics degrees.[1] They publish *Broadsheets on Britain* and the *Bulletin for Industry*, which has a circulation of 200,000, half to businessmen. They write speeches and briefs on economic subjects, giving the general background to economic problems of the day mainly for the Treasury Ministers, but also for other Ministers who may require to make speeches about the United Kingdom economy or who ask for background material. They were given, for example, specific responsibility for briefing any Minister who required economic facts about the Common Market. They prepare a quarterly bulletin for circulation to the National Joint Advisory Council

---

[1] This creates career problems. Members of the Treasury Briefing Section tend to find themselves in a dead-end job. They cannot move easily to other parts of the Information Services, nor into the administrative sections of the Treasury.

which serves as a background to their discussions; this is also sent for information to the National Production Advisory Council on Industry.

OTHER FUNCTIONS OF INFORMATION DIVISIONS

The normal structure of an Information Division, then, is the Chief Information Officer with a Press and Publicity Section under him, and an Intelligence Section as well. This division of labour does not cover all the work of Information Divisions.

Complaints about government departments do occur, and although they should be addressed to the head of the department, they often come first to the Information Division, usually on press initiative. Individual citizens rarely know exactly where and to whom they should write when they have a complaint or a query. Various newspaper bureaux, however, have been developed, among the largest being those attached to the *Daily Mirror* and the *News of the World*, and they play a part in bringing complaints and queries to the attention of Information Divisions in government departments. They supplement the work of Members of Parliament in taking up individual cases with the relevant departments.

The Information Divisions usually pass such correspondence to the appropriate division for information and possible action. For the most part, however, complaints arise either from a misunderstanding of the regulations in force, or the failure of a local official or the complainant himself to explain the facts. It is the task of the Information Division to explain both the regulations in force and the reasons for the official's actions in as clear and as 'human' a way as possible. This side of public relations work is that of humanizing the workings of the bureaucratic system.

Some Information Divisions also undertake publicity for allied bodies outside the Ministry itself. The Charity Commission's press inquiries are automatically switched through to the Home Office press officer, for example. The Ministry of Education looks after the press relations of the Arts Council, on a fee basis, and publicity in this country for the United Nations Educational, Scientific and Cultural Organization without charge.

The Ministry of Housing and Local Government's Information Division is in a rather special position in the government information service in that it has a special relationship with the provincial press which is quite separate from its relationship with the national newspapers. Because it is the authority which forms the link between the central government and all the 1,500 local authorities of the country, and because it is the planning Ministry for England and Wales, dispensing among other things, some 8,000 decisions a year on local planning appeals into which there were local inquiries, the Ministry has both a unique responsibility and opportunity amongst the hundreds of smaller papers up and down the country, quite apart from the comparatively simple job of informing Fleet Street. In the matter of planning appeals, for example, every one of the 14,000 appeals a year made to the Ministry is individually scrutinized, and every newspaper which has asked at the public inquiry for details of the result is sent an individual letter when the decision is announced. This is something quite separate from the sorting out of items of national importance from planning decisions, which are obvious cases for national press notices.

The Information Division of the Ministry of Public Building and Works does two unusual jobs. It arranges press, radio and television facilities at state ceremonials, state visits, the opening of Parliament, and functions in Westminster Hall. This is partly because the Ministry carries out the rest of the work entailed by these occasions, and partly because it controls most of the vantage points on processional routes from which filming, photography and television can take place. The Ministry's Information Division is also responsible for the commercial management of ancient monuments. This job includes getting people to go to monuments and catering for them when they get there. They produce guidebooks and postcards, set up sales points and see that they are adequately staffed, and keep attendance and sales figures. They also look after signposting, catering, and all the other things which are associated with a large business.

The Ministry of Aviation's Information Division has a special task to disseminate, through the various technical and scientific journals, as much information about unclassified government sponsored research as possible. The government, directly or indirectly, sponsors the great majority of technological research and development in this country and, especially in the case of aeronautics, electronics, and space, undertakes much of it in government establishments. The taxpayer has to be shown how his money is being spent; and such publicity also helps to demonstrate to the rest of the world that we can 'keep up with the technological Joneses'. The Department of Scientific and Industrial Research is also concerned to put out a good deal of similar highly specialized technical information to the appropriate technical journals.

The second aspect of information work which is peculiar to the

Ministries of Aviation, Defence and the Service Ministries, is that of
controlling security on defence matters. Their Information Divisions
help to deal with the D-notice system[1] and act as the clearing house
for press releases, advertisements, exhibition material, etc., from
defence contractors, to see that they do not conflict with security
regulations.

These are some of the tasks Information Divisions tackle. Much
of it is routine; some of it is exciting. When all goes well, departments take the good public relations their Information Divisions have
created very much for granted. If things go wrong, the Information
Division is often blamed. But policy and the presentation of that
policy are linked—the right policy is no good unless people know
about it. It is the Information Division's job to make the facts
known, to make sure that the government explains itself to the
meanest citizen.

---

[1] The D-notice system is operated by the Services Press and Broadcasting
Committee set up in 1912 to deal with the issuing of information on matters involving security. There is no press censorship in peacetime in this country, but
there is some defence information, especially about new weapons, which must be
safeguarded. This is done by voluntary agreement through this Committee which
has Press, Broadcasting and Defence Ministry representatives on it.

CHAPTER VI

The Common Service Departments: The Central Office of Information and Her Majesty's Stationery Office

THE CENTRAL OFFICE OF INFORMATION

The Central Office of Information[1] is a common service department, acting as a central publicity agency for the government Information Divisions as they need one, in much the same way as advertising and public relations firms act for their clients. Most of its work is concerned with overseas publicity, which is outside the scope of this book. On the home side, the Central Office of Information acts only on the initiative of a policy department; it advises on and produces publicity material only when commissioned to do so, although it is responsible for co-ordinating departments at working level, that is for making sure that other departments are brought into a campaign if they are not already informed.

The Central Office of Information is concerned almost exclusively with publicity. Unlike the departmental Information Divisions, it has very little direct contact with the press, and does not employ press officers, except in the regions. Any press inquiries made to the Central Office of Information would be referred to the department concerned—it would only deal direct with questions referring to its own headquarters building or staff.

The Central Office of Information does, however, operate a central News Distribution Service; it would not be economical for each government department to have its own dispatch riders to send out notices to the press. Each government department is responsible for the content and form of a press notice, and for deciding who is to get it. The Central Office of Information's News Distribution Service is responsible for its physical distribution by teleprinter, dispatch rider

[1] A description of how the Central Office of Information fits into the general public relations picture has been given in Chapter I. Its beginning as an inheritor of some of the functions of the wartime Ministry of Information has been described in Chapter III.

or post to the press, BBC, and Independent Television News in London; and regionally to those provincial papers, particularly weeklies, which have no London editorial representation.

As we have seen above, the Central Office of Information has no Ministerial head; Treasury Ministers are responsible for it in Parliament and the Treasury controls its expenditure.[1] The administrative head and Accounting Officer of the Central Office of Information is the Director-General, assisted by two Controllers, one co-ordinating the home and the other the overseas information services. It is quite a big organization—there are about 1,300 staff on its payroll. The Treasury is responsible for fixing overall staff ceilings, but the Central Office of Information deals with smaller staff matters and individual problems.

There are ten production divisions in the Central Office of Information, each specializing in a particular kind of material or service, two administrative divisions for staff and finance matters, and a regional organization consisting of a regional unit at headquarters, nine regional offices, and a Welsh Office. The following are those divisions which are concerned with publicity campaigns in the United Kingdom.

Advertising Division

This division is responsible for the management and presentation of press advertising. About eighty campaigns will be conducted in a a typical year. It handles all press, poster and Independent Television advertising campaigns for all departments (except the National Savings Committee and the Scottish Savings Committee). The Advertising Division is also responsible for the allocation of advertising space in the national newspapers between departments, and the co-ordination of those announcements broadcast by the BBC for ten minutes before the one o'clock news bulletin on Fridays.

The Advertising Division does not create the material, but is responsible for the planning of campaigns, the briefing and supervision of the advertising agents employed and the style and standard of the material they produce. By using different advertising agents instead of its own staff for its campaigns, the Central Office of Information considers that it avoids the staleness inevitable when the same people work year after year on the same campaign. Many campaigns have lasted for six years or more, for example, teacher recruitment, the services of the Public Trustee and graduate recruit-

[1] See below, p. 140 and Appendix A, for details of Central Office of Information budgeting and expenditure.

ment for the Post Office. Some, like diphtheria immunization, the search for blood donors and the recruitment of nurses, have continued since the Central Office of Information started eighteen years ago. Advertising agencies are not chosen by competitive tendering, but are appointed for a year at a time on the advice of an independent Advisory Committee on the Appointment of Advertising Agents. It is the responsibility of the Central Office of Information to keep itself informed of the technical resources of advertising agents (and also film producers) and of the talents of their creative staffs.

Exhibitions Division
Exhibitions and displays are designed by the Exhibitions Division of the Central Office of Information or by commercial designers and are constructed under contract by firms specializing in the work. Exhibitions Division is responsible for the planning, design and supervision of the production of all information and prestige exhibits. Much of their work is for exhibiting in fairs overseas, but stands are also prepared for government departments exhibiting in this country, at, for example the Building Trades Exhibition at Olympia, and for touring exhibitions made up of easily transportable units, like the Commonwealth Exhibition, which went on tour for a series of Commonwealth Weeks held at centres throughout Britain.

The division also designs and produces small exhibits for special events and mobile exhibitions such as those used in support of the nursing recruitment campaign. Other divisions of the Central Office of Information collaborate with Exhibitions Division by providing pamphlets, films, photographs and press publicity for the exhibitions.

Films Division
The Central Office of Information has not since 1952 operated a film unit of its own; it employs documentary film companies.[1] A staff of Production Control Officers who are well acquainted with the techniques and costs of film production, particularly in the documentary and factual fields, provides the link between the sponsoring government departments and the film companies during the production period. A Production Control Officer is appointed to each film or series of films and he discusses with the sponsoring department the precise nature of its needs and the audience it wishes to reach. With this information a rough idea of treatment for the subject and the cost is worked out and final approval is sought. After a contractor has been appointed to make the film, the Production Control

[1] The commercial film producers employed are selected from an approved list.

Officer is responsible for briefing him, scrutinizing the treatment and script, giving advice and supervising the film through its shooting and editing stages.

A large number of short information films are distributed every week on television. These items, ranging in length from fifteen seconds to three minutes, are known as television 'fillers'. They are concerned with subjects like recruiting, road safety, industrial safety, foster parents, and youth training. They are supplied to independent television companies[1] to fill gaps in programmes, and are used by the BBC in a weekly period of five minutes on Saturdays. A small number of longer films are distributed through cinemas, or to special audiences. For instance *Mr Marsh comes to School* is a lighthearted film for secondary modern school leavers to encourage them to consult the youth employment service; or there are more serious films about the work of industrial rehabilitation. These films were made through the Central Office of Information for the Ministry of Labour. Films are also made on technical subjects, such as the training of nurses, new farming techniques and so on; Films Division are responsible for some of the films used in Civil Service training courses.

The Central Film Library hires out a large number of films on specialized subjects, either produced by the Central Office of Information or acquired from other sponsors, for non-commercial distribution. There are over 2,000 titles and 35,000 prints of films in the Library. On average they make about 5,000 issues a month to schools, institutes, industrial firms and other technical groups.

Photographs Division
The Photographs Division has its own press photographers and editors, and a research staff who deal not only with official photographs but material produced by commercial agencies and industry. It has a dark-room and a Photographs Library. The division takes or finds photographs for other divisions of the Central Office of Information who need them for the illustration of books, magazines, feature articles, etc., for display in exhibitions and for use in connection with the tours of the United Kingdom arranged by the Central Office of Information for overseas visitors. Photographs Division provides for all departments a common service for the distribution of official photographs to the home and overseas press. This is a service to departments similar to the News Distribution

[1] Contrary to what might be expected, the independent television companies make far greater use of these government sponsored television 'fillers' than do the BBC.

Service, but it is separately organized and works differently.[1] Normal trade charges are made for the use of official pictures. The Photographs Library contains over half a million photographs covering most aspects of British life and activities. The portrait files contain pictures of a large number of prominent British personalities and there are well stocked sections on the colonial territories, the social services, and industry, including atomic energy.

Publications Division

Publications Division is responsible, in consultation with the government departments concerned, for the preparation of information publications for issue both overseas and at home.[2] Publications range from bound books for sale, to single sheet leaflets for free distribution at an exhibition stand. This material is written (or edited) and designed in the division, finished art-work being provided where required by the Tours and Production Services Division Studio. All printing is arranged through H.M. Stationery Office. The division, as a rule, prepares the sales-promotion publicity for the material which it produces, and in a number of instances, distributes it.

Reference Division

Reference Division runs a library and provides two main services. One is the provision of material for the other divisions of the Central Office of Information. It supplies on request factual briefing, especially at the early stages of a project, and circulates also a weekly annotated list of articles selected from British periodicals. The second is the provision of a planned reference information service primarily for use and distribution by British Information Services overseas, but also distributed in the United Kingdom to over 500 recipients, such as Members of Parliament and the press. One of its more important regular publications is the annual *Britain: An Official Handbook*.

[1] The Central Office of Information does not distribute official news pictures directly to individual newspapers but has an arrangement with the agency groups that one of them, by rotation, accepts and handles official pictures; to this 'rota' agency the negatives and captions and release instructions are sent. When an official picture is issued through the Central Office of Information to the British press, the agency concerned automatically makes prints available to all other photographic news agencies for their overseas services. This means that official photographs reach all important newspapers overseas soon after their release in Britain, at no extra cost.

[2] Some of the types of publications issued were listed in Chapter I, in the section on government publications.

The compartments of the Central Office of Information are not, however, watertight divisions. When a campaign is planned, Advertising Division will call on Films Division for the production of advertising films for showing on television or in cinemas; Photographs Division will supply photographs to use in the press advertising campaign; Publications Division will design booklets and brochures (and provide the text as well where the department concerned has not provided it); the posters for the campaign may well be designed by their own studio section.

In addition to these production divisions, there are two other sections of the Central Office of Information of interest to this study —the Regional Organization and the Social Survey.

The Regional Organization

The Regional Organization provides a common information service for government departments in the regions and supplies material collected in the regions for use by the Central Office of Information, particularly for its overseas information services. The regional offices play a large part in the distribution of publicity material and in providing contacts with the press, local authorities and industries in their areas.

A Chief Regional Officer, responsible to the Controller (Administration) is in charge of information in each of the nine regions of England and Wales. Under him, there are normally two officers, one specializing in the press side of the work and the other in general publicity. The regional offices are responsible for the distribution of official press material and information, whether originating centrally from the headquarters of departments or locally, through the regional organization of other government departments,[1] to provincial newspapers and the regional services of the BBC, and Independent Television. They co-ordinate press, newsreel and broadcasting arrangements for royal visits and for official visits by Ministers; they make arrangements in conjunction with local authorities for publicity campaigns; and through their local contacts they increase the supply of articles, photographs, and so on, often about local industry, mainly for the Central Office of Information's overseas services. The Welsh Office has special responsibilities for advising the Minister of Housing and Local Government and Minister for Welsh Affairs, and the Minister

[1] The Board of Trade and Ministry of Labour, for example have Regional Controllers and Regional Officers in each of the nine regions of England and Wales, and other government departments also have regional representation.

of State for Welsh Affairs; it is also responsible for the Central Film Library of Wales.[1]

The Regional Unit at Central Office of Information headquarters assists the Controller (Administration) in co-ordinating the regional services and advises on publicity campaigns involving the regional organization. It directs and co-ordinates press relations and information work in the regions in consultation with other government departments, and also deals with Parliamentary questions. In addition, the Regional Unit is responsible for the News Distribution Service.

Social Survey Division
Social Survey Division is a social and economic research unit providing other government departments with those social facts and statistics which are not already available to them and which can only be obtained by asking the public direct. It is attached to the Central Office of Information for administrative convenience, but it is a central service organization available for the use of all government departments, and performs few special functions for the Central Office of Information itself. It is of course fundamentally different from any other part of the Central Office of Information, since its business is to *obtain* information for the government, not to disseminate it. But it has remained part of the Central Office of Information presumably because it happened originally to be placed in the wartime Ministry of Information.

We have seen in Chapter III that during the war it had become clear to the government that they did not know enough about the population, its habits, needs and possessions and that, in a period when the government had made itself responsible for the supply of food, clothing, furniture, pots and pans, etc., by rationing and similar schemes, it was essential to know a great many facts about ordinary people. Wartime surveys were carried out not only by the government's own Social Survey organization, but also by private market research agencies. Moreover, during the war the Home Intelligence side of the Ministry of Information had also occupied itself with surveys of public morale. At the end of the hostilities, the interest in morale vanished, but it was decided to continue the factual surveys and in September 1946 the Social Survey was set up on a permanent basis and has operated ever since.

[1] Information work in Scotland and Northern Ireland is carried out by their own information offices, which also act, when necessary, as agents for the Central Office of Information. See Chapter I.

Social Survey expenditure and staff were considerably affected by the economy campaign following the French Committee report. But only one year after the cuts, they were asked to undertake for the first time a big Household Budget Survey, and the continuing Food Survey was also given to them. Thereafter, Social Survey expenditure has increased from £89,000 in 1953–4 to £410,000 in 1963–4;[1] and their staff, which had been 58 in 1954, totalled 112 by 1964.

Social Survey research is used where it would be helpful to have first hand knowledge of the day-to-day habits and activities of the population; when policy decisions have to be taken, but there are not enough facts available. Social research can help to describe what exists so that the policy-makers can decide what should be changed and can choose between alternative lines of action. It can also show the results of past decisions. For example, the changing pattern of consumer expenditure can help to assess the effect of changes in purchase tax on various items; a special survey can be made, as it was in 1960, on the effects on tenants of the working of the 1957 Rent Act.[2]

Surveys can be made for government statisticians interested in economic development; inquiries can be made into health and social problems—crime, accidents or housing; or the operational problems of public services can be studied, for example nursing procedure in hospital wards or code-addressing of envelopes for the Post Office. The biggest customers of Social Survey change from year to year, but the Post Office, Board of Trade, Ministry of Labour, Ministry of Agriculture, Fisheries and Food, the Home Office and the Department of Scientific and Industrial Research are all regular users.

The surveys already carried out have been very varied. Social Survey ask at frequent intervals what the public thinks of the postal and telephone services so that those who run them do so against a background of the needs and views of the public. In the past they have asked grassland farmers how they learned improvement techniques; their White Fish inquiry looked into middleman's profits; they found out the types of domestic heating in use, and the number of caravans used as homes; they conducted a 'Survey of Sickness' to find out the level of incapacity and range of illnesses in the population as a whole and to provide a picture of the use made of

[1] These figures of expenditure include the salaries of headquarters staff, as well as operational expenditure, i.e. field work. They are therefore bigger than the figures shown in Appendix A, Table 2.

[2] Rent Act, 1957. Report of Inquiry by P. G. Gray and E. Parr. Cmnd. 1246. July 1960.

different parts of the medical service. There was an inquiry into the frequency of use of the London telephone directory; an investigation into the records of a number of Borstal cases—length of stay at first job, occupation of parents, age when convicted, and so on—from which a simple formula was worked out which could be used to predict whether the boys were likely to come back to Borstal a second time. There have been dozens of other surveys. Most reports of Social Survey are published; if they are not, they are made available on request, for example, to Members of Parliament and other interested bodies or individuals.

Some surveys are continuing; others are 'once only' jobs. For example, the Central Statistical Office publishes annually a picture of the whole national economic activity in the form of national income and expenditure accounts and other statistics. A great deal of the information on which this is based comes from economic censuses and other returns collected under statutory powers. Consumers' expenditure forms a major part of this picture and it is for this information that sample survey techniques are used continuously, either to check existing data or sometimes as the only source of information. Sometimes samples of all the households in the country are asked about spending in a particular field, e.g. consumer durables; or a picture of all household expenditure is produced by the continuing Household Budget inquiry;[1] the National Food survey provides continuing information about spending on all forms of food. The importance of this kind of continuing inquiry lies in showing the change of spending over the years—whether we eat more chicken and less fish, or buy more television sets, but have fewer holidays.

Royal commissions and departmental committees often investigate social problems, but they do not always have the facilities to conduct extensive research. Nor are all problems important enough to justify setting up a special body to investigate them. On these occasions, a properly equipped sample survey can produce answers quite quickly. In fact, Social Survey nowadays often undertakes the basic research for royal commissions or committees, and sometimes for bodies outside the government. For instance they undertook an inquiry into the pay of doctors and dentists for the royal commission considering the subject; a survey for the Road Research Laboratory of the Department of Scientific and Industrial Research, to find out the age and experience of motor cyclists; a report on the

[1] The surveys on Family Expenditure are in fact carried out for the Ministry of Labour, but the material is also used by the Central Statistical Office.

135

relations between the police and the public for the Royal Commission on the Police; a report on the Meals on Wheels Service for the National Corporation for the Care of Old People; and a study of the social consequences of a prison sentence for the Cambridge Institute of Criminology. They also did a great deal of work for the Robbins Committee on Higher Education, and have been asked to collect the basic data for the Allen Committee on the effect of rates on different groups of the population. The work of Social Survey is different, however, from most academic research. Most research organizations specialize in particular subjects whereas Social Survey specializes in the application of research techniques to any of the subjects which interest government. It is the customers who are the specialists. Ideas for surveys come from the government departments when policy decisions seem to require the study of a social or economic situation. Social Survey discusses with them the practical possibility of carrying them out. Every survey is therefore tailored to the needs of the department which asks for the work to be done. Every survey is individually requested by the sponsoring department to the Treasury, and the inquiry does not start unless the Treasury is satisfied that the work is necessary. So the sponsor of any inquiry has to take responsibility for the eventual use and application of the data emerging; and the inquiry must be shaped to serve some policy-making or policy-testing activity.

Social Survey has to be permanently available and adaptable enough to cover a wide field. Like any other part of the government, what Social Survey does must also be politically defensible—the subjects investigated and methods used must be able to be discussed and defended publicly. There are no statutory powers to collect the information and all those answering questions in a survey are volunteers. The inquiry must be so framed, and the interviewers sufficiently skilled, to attract the public's interest and to make sure that people understand its purpose. In fact the degree of co-operation obtained is high. In interviews, 80–90 per cent of those asked give the necessary information; and two-thirds of the people asked to keep records of their household expenditure for a fortnight, do so.

Social Survey relies almost exclusively on probability sampling applied to whatever register of names or addresses seems to be most relevant to the subject investigated. Its position as a central field research unit for the government ensures that there is a sufficient flow of work to specialize within the branch. There are five sections— the sampling section, responsible for working out the best samples of the population for survey techniques; the coding section, for the primary analysis of all material collected and checks on the field workers' accuracy; the tabulating and computing section responsible for the mechanical tabulation of survey material and the application of statistical techniques; and research officers who design the inquiries, supervise the other sections and write the final reports. Finally there is the section which selects and trains interviewers; Social Survey devotes a great part of its resources to this task—in fact other organizations use Social Survey's interviewer training manuals.

The Crombie report of 1949 said that one of the functions of information was 'to advise departments on the reaction of the public to a policy present or contemplated'. Social Survey is therefore sometimes used for research into people's opinions and reactions. In Britain survey techniques have become accepted for factual analysis; they are not yet wholly accepted for opinion reactions, although in the United States of America opinion surveys are used a good deal. Nevertheless, Social Survey has done a study of the relations between the police and the public[1] and on aircraft noise annoyance at London airport.[2] These were both surveys of opinions, not facts.

The value of Social Survey is to make sure that decision-taking is related to the facts of people's lives and not to some imaginary concept of them. But as Mr William Deedes, the former Minister co-ordinating the home information services, has said: 'Ardent sociology is the handmaiden of administration. It is certainly the prerequisite of sound government.'[3]

HER MAJESTY'S STATIONERY OFFICE[4]

Government departments naturally make large calls on the Stationery Office each year for all forms of printing and publishing services. The Central Office of Information's work accounts for about three-quarters of the Stationery Office's total expenditure on printing in the information field in the United Kingdom. The rest is the outcome of work undertaken direct for other government departments—usually for those leaflets and posters not linked with some special publicity campaign.

[1] Appendix IV to the Minutes of Evidence to the Royal Commission on the Police, 1962.
[2] Survey made for the Wilson Committee on the Problem of Noise, SS 337, April 1963.
[3] *Public Relations*, January 1963.
[4] See also above, Chapter I.

Information material received by the Stationery Office is normally in a finished state ready for the printer. The Central Office of Information or the originating department undertakes the editorial work, although the Stationery Office can also do the design and layout if necessary. The Central Office of Information and Stationery Office keep in close touch, however, over an information project from the early stages, and the Stationery Office offers its advice, especially on matters affecting the cost. It would be quite uneconomic for all government printing, involving the whole range of printing techniques, type faces and so on to be done directly by the Stationery Office on its own printing presses. The actual printing of information publications is therefore normally placed with commercial printers by the Stationery Office under term or *ad hoc* contracts awarded after competitive tendering.

The question of whether information material should be issued free or put on sale is determined at the time the project is discussed between the requesting department, the Central Office of Information, and the Stationery Office on whose Vote the cost falls. Only a very small proportion of the total information expenditure on printing is devoted to publications placed on sale, and the bulk of these come under the Home Information head. But some reference documents, primarily intended for free distribution overseas are also put on sale in this country. If the material is to be issued free, the number of copies to be printed is settled between the originating department and the Central Office of Information. If the material is to be put on sale, the number of copies to be printed is determined by the Stationery Office and they also decide the price in consultation with the originating department and the Central Office of Information.

The Stationery Office fixes the price of all its publications, including those produced for the information services, so that, as far as possible, it makes neither a loss nor a large profit. This requirement is not interpreted in a strict commercial sense, but it governs the basis on which publications are priced.[1] Information publications are priced individually on the basis of the estimated cost in each case, and where the Central Office of Information is involved, the cost on which the price is calculated includes an element for the Central

[1] An explanation of the pricing of publications is given in the First Report from the Select Committee on Estimates, Session 1956–7, p. 3, para. 22. Government publications are priced to cover the cost of printing, paper, binding, overhead expenses and selling discounts, but nothing is included for the cost of authorship. Some publications are priced below cost, e.g. *Hansard*, but the general aim is to ensure that the publishing business as a whole is self-supporting.

Office of Information's own costs, e.g. studio services. The cost of printing information publications is recorded against the department concerned, less the recoupment from sales.

Departments, in general, do not repay the Stationery Office for printing and other supplies, but a record of the value of the supplies is maintained and provided in the Stationery Office Estimate. A statement is prepared each year of the estimated cost of the information services, department by department, and this is forwarded to the Treasury for inclusion in the appropriate table of the Financial Secretary's memorandum. Detailed records of actual expenditure on information printing are maintained and notified to the Central Office of Information, or to the originating departments in the case of direct printing. Individual departmental totals are allowed to vary from the Estimates within reasonable limits, but the total sum authorized for information printing is not allowed to exceed the Estimate amount without Treasury authority.

EXPENDITURE ON THE INFORMATION SERVICES

As most government expenditure on the information services is provided on the Votes of the two common service departments it seems appropriate to discuss it briefly in this chapter.[1] Each department has its own Vote for information expenditure, but this only covers information staff salaries and operational expenses. All expenditure on the actual media of publicity appears on the Votes of the Central Office of Information or on that of the Stationery Office for printing costs.

The expenditure was divided in the estimates for the financial year 1963–4 as shown in Table 1.

Thus more than half the total expenditure on information was spent by the two common service departments—the Central Office of Information and the Stationery Office.

When the Central Office of Information Estimates are prepared, they are based on requests received from departments for spending on information campaigns. These proposed programmes are discussed with the departments and agreed with the Treasury before the final Vote Estimate is drawn up.

The Central Office of Information has general responsibility for economy on publicity matters—it advises user departments on the financial aspect of proposed schemes or campaigns as well as being

---

[1] See Appendix A for a detailed account of Expenditure and Budgeting.

responsible for scrutinizing its own costs and those of any commercial contracts placed.

Some of the services provided by the Central Office of Information, notably that of the regional organization, are not individually requested by departments and therefore are not divided financially between them. The news distribution and regional service, for example, are common services to all departments.

TABLE 1

Home Information Services 1963-4*

£(000's)

On Department's own Votes: Staff salaries and operational expenses on information in all government depts.	2,430
Central Office of Information†	2,347
Her Majesty's Stationery Office	379

Total 5,156

* See Table 6 in Appendix A for a detailed analysis of these figures, department by department.

† This is just under half the total Central Office of Information budget. The rest is mainly for the Overseas Information Services, see Appendix A, Table 3. For overseas expenditure, proposed programmes of expenditure are agreed between the Central Office of Information and the overseas departments and are submitted to an official committee on which the Treasury is represented. This committee is concerned with the detailed allocation of expenditure within a ceiling figure determined annually for overseas information as a whole.

Usually expenditure by the Central Office of Information is incurred as an allied service, that is, a service performed by one department for another without payment. The expenditure appears on the Central Office of Information Vote without any inter-departmental accounting.

There are some exceptions, however. Some departments pay the Central Office of Information for their publicity expenditure. The Post Office, for example, being an organization conducting services on a commercial basis, bears its publicity expenditure on its own Vote and, in so far as the Central Office of Information and the Stationery Office handle Post Office publicity work, they are employed on an agency basis, i.e. they are repaid by the Post Office. Other departments pay direct for some specific part of publicity connected with their activities, for example publicity for the National Health Service appears on the Ministry of Health Vote, and the Ministry of Transport makes a grant to the Royal Society for the Prevention of Accidents. The Stationery Office finances publicity for the National Savings Committee, but the Central Office of Information does not. The autonomy of the National Savings Committee is partly historical in origin, and partly because it is a voluntary committee and its function is to stimulate the voluntary savings movement. Publicity is a large part of its work.

Spending on the information services is of course only a small part of all government expenditure. How big is it? Of about £7,500 million spent a year, about £27 million is on information, and of that, about £5 million is on home information. Or to put it in another way —for every £1,000 spent by the central government, £4 is spent on information; and only 15s 0d of that is spent on the home information services.[1]

[1] Before the French Committee cuts in 1949–50, of every £1,000 spent by the government, £5 went on the information services, £1 on the home side. In 1955–6, after the cuts, of every £1,000 of government spending £3 went to information, 10s on the home side.

CHAPTER VII

Staffing the Information Services

SETTING UP THE INFORMATION OFFICER CLASS

We saw in Chapter II that between the wars first one government department and then another began to feel the need to provide an information or public relations service. In some departments members of the Executive Class were allocated to do this work; in others, outside specialists were appointed as temporary civil servants, but without being included in any particular civil service class.[1] The people holding these posts were variously known as Information Officer, Public Relations Officer, or Press Officer. Some of them had a small staff to help them.

Information and press work expanded enormously during the Second World War. By the end of it, the Ministry of Information alone was employing nearly 7,000 people—about half of them abroad.[2]

During the five years or so after the end of the war, there was a major reconstruction of the Civil Service, just as there had been after the First World War. The Professional and Technical Classes of the Civil Service, in particular, were the subject of a great reorganization which raised their status and substituted a series of general service classes (with linked Departmental classes) for the chaos of Departmental classes that had existed before. This whole post-war reconstruction sought to rationalize and unify the various groups of specialists who had come to be employed as the work of government departments developed; the review of the status of those engaged on information work formed part of this general reorganization.[3]

[1] See Table 2, pp 160-1 for a definition of civil service classes, etc.

[2] Select Committee on Estimates, Session 1950, 5th Report. *Government Information Services*. Memorandum by the Central Office of Information, Table IV, p. 256 and footnotes.

[3] A special committee of the Civil Service National Whitley Council—the Committee on the Structure of the Post-War Civil Service—began its work in July 1945. Its final report appeared in April 1949. *Whitley Bulletin*, June 1949, p. 8.

When the Central Office of Information came into existence in April 1946, it was considerably smaller than the wartime Ministry of Information. There was a total staff of just over 1,500 of whom half were in the clerical, typing, messengerial or other subordinate grades.[1] In addition, there were the 330 people (excluding the subordinate grades) employed in the Information Divisions of nearly thirty Ministerial departments.[2] This meant that, leaving aside the information work done abroad by the overseas departments, there were about a thousand civil servants above a subordinate grade engaged in information work. Some of them were in the general service Executive Class, and some were in special Departmental technical and professional grades (particularly at the Central Office of Information). All these came under consideration during the government's post-war reconstruction of the Civil Service.

In November 1946 the Treasury appointed a committee of officials to consider 'the recruitment, remuneration and conditions of service of Departmental Information Officers' and 'the organization and staffing of Information Divisions in Departments; and to make recommendations'. This committee is generally known, after its chairman, Mr J. I. C. Crombie, as the Crombie Committee.[3] In its report, which was produced in July 1947,[4] the Crombie Committee considered the functions of departmental Information Divisions and examined the existing structure and staffing of these divisions. It came to the conclusion that while all the Information Divisions, except those of the overseas departments[5] and the National Savings Committee, had a broadly common pattern, the existing organization failed to provide any coherent system of promotion. This led

[1] Figures provided by H.M. Treasury from the Departmental Quarterly Staff returns.

[2] H.C. Deb. (1946–7), 432, c. 296–8.

[3] The other members of the Committee were Mr Robert (now Sir Robert) Fraser, then Director-General of the Central Office of Information; Mr Ivone (later Sir Ivone) Kirkpatrick of the Foreign Office; Mr Francis Williams (now Lord Francis-Williams), then Public Relations Adviser to the Prime Minister; and three other officials.

[4] The Report of the Crombie Committee was not published. It was eventually issued within the Service as an appendix to a Treasury instruction (Establishments Circular 5/45 of August 20, 1949). See *Whitley Bulletin*, October 1949, pp. 176–82.

[5] The Committee found that the work of Information Officers in departments dealing with overseas publicity was sufficiently similar to that of other civil servants within the department that the staffs could be interchangeable. The Committee therefore did not propose that its recommendations should apply generally to the officers working on information in the overseas departments.

to difficulties in filling the higher posts because there was a shortage of officers with the 'necessary wide qualities', and the retention of specialists in the lower posts from which, in a particular department, there might be few opportunities for promotion. To remedy this state of affairs, the Committee proposed the creation of a new general service class for civil servants engaged on information work; and 'for the purposes only of recruitment, transfer and promotion, the Departmental Information Divisions should be regarded, with the Central Office of Information, as one Information Service'. The introduction of a special information service of this kind would, the Committee considered, increase the chances of securing good candidates from outside.

There was no discussion in the Report about the extent to which the work of the departmental Information Divisions could be regarded as similar to the work done at the Central Office of Information. The reader of the report is left to assume that the union of the Central Office of Information and the departmental Information Divisions for staffing purposes was known to be appropriate and practicable, from the fact that the Director-General of the Central Office of Information was a member of the Crombie Committee. There were, after all, about twice as many staff in the Central Office of Information as there were in information work in all the other departments, and their unification meant that there were enough people in the class to make it viable. The actual work done by the Central Office of Information and the departmental Information Divisions is, of course, all directed to common ends even if the nature of the work differs, and it is the tendency of the Civil Service to prefer standardization to departmentalism.[1]

Considering that it is the first basic document for the Information Officer Class of the Civil Service, the Crombie Report seems curiously incomplete in its attention to the problems of such a Class and of the organization of an Information Service. But this feeling may be the result of looking at it seventeen years later with the benefit of hindsight. The Report is clearest in its recommendations on the functions and recruitment of Chief Information Officers. A departmental Information Division, it said, should be in the charge of a Chief In-

---

[1] 'Standardization is tidier than departmentalism, and economizes time spent on negotiation; it may also be more equitable, and on the whole, the Civil Service Unions see advantages in the policy. There is, therefore, a continuous trend towards the creation of new Treasury classes of specialists.' W. J. M. Mackenzie and J. W. Grove, *Central Administration in Britain*, Longmans, 1957, p. 95.

formation Officer who should be responsible to a senior adminitrative officer—the Permanent Secretary, a Deputy-Secretary or an Under-Secretary—but having direct access to the Minister. He should be consulted at the earliest stage on matters relating either to the information of the public or to the response of the public. The qualities to be sought in a Chief Information Officer were defined as: 'experience in the art of communicating with the public; the mental capacity to understand the full range of the work and needs of the Department and to discuss them with the highest officials; the attributes which make a good Civil Servant.'

The recruitment of Chief Information Officers was not to be limited to any particular field but, unless an officer was being promoted from within an Information Division (or had served in one before), a suitable candidate was more likely to be found outside the Civil Service; he should, if possible, have had experience of more than one medium of publicity. The Committee recognized that it would be necessary to weigh the advantages to the Information Service of recruiting fresh blood against the damage inflicted to the promotion prospects of subordinates within the service. It was also conscious that some of the best people would not be attracted by the salaries that the Civil Service could offer. Suitable candidates for posts as departmental information officers might, from time to time, be found in the Central Office of Information—'but unless transfers are made both ways, Departments will benefit only at the expense of the efficiency of the Central Office'.

The Committee also had something to say about the recruitment of Press Officers: 'A Press Officer should normally have a first-hand knowledge of the ways of Fleet Street. It is rarely that he will be able to acquire the requisite touch, or to be fully acceptable to the Press world generally, without having worked at one stage of his career as one of them.'

Press Officers should therefore, they recommended, be recruited from among qualified journalists at a fairly early age. On the other hand, the Committee felt that it might eventually be possible for staff to be trained within Information Divisions as Press Officers.

Nothing further was said about the qualifications for the rest of the staff in the Information Divisions and the Central Office of Information, except that recruits to the basic grade of the new class should, in the main, be enlisted through the ordinary Executive Class Examination and should be paid according to the scale for Executive Officers.

Other points made in the Committee's recommendations were:

the need for a clear line of promotion from one grade to the next; the transferability of officers among departments and the Central Office of Information; and the maintenance of a proportion of the staff on a temporary basis so that there might be 'a turnover of ideas'. It also suggested that officers from other divisions in departments might with advantage have a period of service in the Information Divisions and vice-versa. 'This would promote familiarity in the rest of the Department with the work of the Information Division and would sometimes result in the filling of a post in the Information Division.'

In November 1947 the Treasury, wishing to consult the representatives of the Staff, made the Crombie Report available to the Staff Side of the Civil Service National Whitley Council.[1] At that time the civil servants engaged in information work were not organized through a staff assocation, but the Institution of Professional Civil Servants,[2] to which some members of the Central Office of Information belonged, was authorized to conduct negotiations with the Treasury on behalf of all information officers.

The Institution of Professional Civil Servants had already been involved for several years in the post-war reorganization of the professional, scientific and technical classes of the Civil Service. In these classes entry was by means of a recognized professional qualification, such as a university degree, or a five years' apprenticeship

[1] Whitley Councils are representative bodies for negotiation and joint consultation between management and staffs; the Councils are named after Mr J. H. Whitley, former Speaker of the House of Commons and chairman of a committee which investigated industrial unrest from 1916 to 1919. The Civil Service Whitley Council Staff Side consists of representatives of all the recognized staff associations in the Civil Service. For a short explanation of the machinery of joint consultation in the British Civil Services, see *Negotiation and Joint Consultation in the Civil Service: The Whitley Method*, being extracts published in *Whitley Bulletin*, July 1960, pp. 100–106, from two lectures given to the Royal Institute of Public Administration in 1953 by A. J. T. Day (now Sir Albert) then Chairman of the National Staff Side and A. J. D. Winnifrith (now Sir John) then a senior treasury official.

[2] The Institution of Professional Civil Servants which was formed in January 1919 is the staff association whose membership is open to any non-industrial civil servant, established or temporary, who is engaged on professional, scientific or technical work. Its membership, which started at 1,534 had by 1962 reached a total of about 57,000. It includes architects, accountants, legal and medical personnel, scientists, technicians, artists, cartographers, photographers, librarians, and a variety of surveyors and engineers. In July 1949 the Institution of Professional Civil Servants reached an agreement on joint membership with the National Union of Journalists to which many former journalists working in the Civil Service belong.

in engineering. It was not a simple matter thus to identify the specialists employed in the Information Divisions and in the Central Office of Information since there were no recognized professional qualifications in their professions. Nevertheless, the Institution of Professional Civil Servants maintained that the work done was clearly recognizable as being something quite different from the normal run of Civil Service Executive Class duties, and therefore requiring the employment of specialists. They wanted the Treasury to agree that the new information grades should be recognized as a specialist class and that only specialists should normally be appointed to it, although exceptionally, an Executive Class Officer with a particular flair for the work might be transferred to the Information Class. Negotiations between the IPCS and the Treasury went on from 1947 to 1949.

Meanwhile, an inter-departmental committee, the Wardley Committee, which had been set up within the Civil Service to advise on the implementation of the Crombie Report, had produced its recommendations in the form of a draft Establishment Officer's Circular. The Institution of Professional Civil Servants, with the support of the Advertising Association, the Incorporated Advertising Manager's Association, the Institute of Public Relations and the National Union of Journalists, secured certain changes in the draft circular but they felt that the circular did not go far enough in reserving the new Information Class for specialists, and would produce an Information Class with too many non-specialist civil servants in it. Despite the changes secured, the Institution of Professional Civil Servants continued to regard the Treasury circular as wrong in principle and it was finally issued without the agreement of the National Staff Side being attached to it, as is usually the case with the Establishment Circulars. The National Staff Side never has agreed to it.

The Treasury issued the circular in August 1949. It set up the new Information Officer Class[1] which was to comprise 'Officers of all grades above the clerical grades engaged on information work in all departments, including the Central Office of Information but, at first, excluding the Overseas Departments and the National Savings Committee'. The grades in the new class were named as follows, beginning from the bottom: Assistant Information Officer; Information Officer; Senior Information Officer; Principal Information Officer; and then two higher grades which were not given names in the circular but subsequently became known as Chief Information

[1] Establishments Circular 5/49 of August 20, 1949. *Whitley Bulletin*, October 1949, p. 176.

The Government Explains

Officer (B) and Chief Information Officer (A). The present salary
scales of these grades are shown in Table 2, from which it can be
seen that up to and including the rank of Chief Information Officer
(B) the grades are equivalent to those of the Executive Class; the
grade of Chief Information Officer (A), that of the Chief Information
Officer in most departments, is equivalent to that of Assistant Secretary in the Administrative Class. There are, in addition, six special
posts of higher rank than this: the Director-General of the Central
Office of Information and his two Controllers (Home and Overseas);
the head of the Treasury's Information Division; the Public Relations Officer of the Post Office; and the Prime Minister's Adviser on
Public Relations.

The Treasury instruction provided that recruitment to the new
Information Officer Class, after the first procedures for settling the
terms of employment of the existing staff had been completed, might
be from a variety of sources. For the basic grade of Assistant Information Officer, recruitment might be by promotion from the Clerical
Grades or through the normal competition for the Executive Class.
In fact, Assistant Information Officers were never recruited from the
normal Executive competition and this method of recruitment was a
dead letter. Vacancies, whether for Assistant Information Officer or
for higher posts, might also be filled by transfer from the Executive
or any other class, or, of course, by promotion from within the
Information Officer Class; also for those posts which required
specialized qualifications not to be found within the service, recruitment might be from outside the service by special open competitions
to be arranged by the Civil Service Commissioners. Further, departments might, if they chose, fill vacancies in any grade by a temporary
appointment of a candidate from outside; those given temporary
appointments[1] could not later be established except by being successful in an open competition.

These arrangements still left the way open for a proportion of the
posts to be filled by ordinary civil servants from the Executive or other
classes and did not go as far as the Institution of Professional Civil
Servants would have wished in reserving the new class for specialists
recruited from outside. In practice, however, as things have worked
out in recent years recruitment has gone much more in the direction
desired by the advocates of 'professionalism' in the information
service than could have been foreseen from reading of this first
Treasury instruction. At the present time although the 'civil service
element' exists, i.e. those who have been transferred into the In-

[1] For the meaning of 'temporary' appointments in the Civil Service, see Table 2.

148

formation Officer Class from the Executive Class or have been promoted from the Clerical Class, it is very much in the minority.
Nowadays, the vast majority of posts in the Information Class have
been filled by people with specialized qualifications, gained by some
years work on a newspaper, in a publishing house, with a documentary film company, in an advertising agency, with an exhibition
contractor, or in some other part of the press and publicity worlds.
Most departments have come to accept the arguments for 'professionalism' in the government's information services—that is the need to
employ people with special experience and specialized talent.

One of the main points made by the Crombie Report had been the
value of transferring members of the Information Officer Class between the various departments. Although the Treasury agreed this
in principle, in fact very few transfers took place until nearly ten
years later, when a pooling system was introduced in August 1958.[1]
This meant that all vacancies in 250 specified posts were to be
'trawled' in future; that is, details of the vacant posts were to be
circulated to the information staff of other departments by the
Treasury, and would therefore be filled by recruits from outside the
Civil Service only if no suitable candidates could be found within
it. The reasons given for introducing this procedure in 1958 were to
'ensure that such posts will be filled by the best available candidates
in the Service; that there will be a greater flow between Departments of people and ideas concerned with information work; and
that members of the Information Officer Class will gain wider experience of Government information work and will accordingly be
more fit for filling senior information posts'. This shows that official
policy regarding the Information Officer Class was still governed by
what had been the chief consideration of the Crombie Report, namely
that the main object of creating a single Information Service was to
encourage the interchange of staff between departments because this
would, by widening their experience, increase the chances of finding
within the service people of sufficient ability to fill the top posts: but
this 'trawling' system has only been in operation for six years, and
sufficient time has probably not yet elapsed for its full effect to have
been realized.

Staffing figures show that out of the 593 established members of
the whole Information Officer Class (in 1963) only 14 per cent
had served in more than one department. At the top of the class
fifteen out of the forty-three established Chief Information Officers
(i.e. 35 per cent) had served in more than one department; some of

[1] EC 25/58 of September 26, 1958. *Whitley Bulletin*, December 1958, p. 173.

these had made more than one move. However, of these fifteen, only eight had served in more than one department *before* attaining the rank of Chief Information Officer.[1] Likewise, among eighty established Principal Information Officers, sixteen (i.e. 20 per cent) had served in more than one department; but only nine had done so before reaching the grade of Principal Information Officer.

An analysis of the departments between which these moves had been made is not available, but it can be said that there were four or five Chief Information Officers in the Information Divisions today who were formerly at the Central Office of Information, and there were two Chief Information Officers out of fifteen at the Central Office of Information who had served in the Information Division of a home department; three others were formerly in the information service of an overseas department.

Even in the few years since the trawling system started, there would appear to have been a good deal of movement of information officers from department to department, including the top posts.

REDUCTIONS IN THE INFORMATION SERVICES IN 1951-5

Soon after the new Information Officer Class had been created in 1949 the information services, and particularly the Central Office of Information were subjected to very drastic cuts as a result of the French Committee recommendations.[2] In April 1951, after the posts that were to be designated as information posts had been sorted out, the total staff of the Central Office of Information was 1,473, of which 401 (27 per cent) were in the new Information Officer Class.[3] During 1951, however, the general contraction of the activities of the Central Office of Information, particularly in the field of films, exhibitions and the Social Survey, slashed the staff by almost a half, to 876 by August 1, 1952, a reduction of about 600 posts in eighteen months.[4] Staff continued to decrease more slowly until 1955 when the total staff at the Central Office of Information was 755, of whom 261 were in the Information Officer Class.[5] From 1955 (the year of the Conservative Government's second return to office, with Sir Anthony

[1] Figures supplied by H.M. Treasury. They relate only to established staff, but at the top of the Class the temporary element is too small for the absence of figures for temporaries to affect the picture.

[2] See above, Chapter III.

[3] Figures supplied by the Central Office of Information of actual staff in post.

[4] Select Committee on Estimates, Session 1959–60, 3rd Report. *The Central Office of Information*. Appendix 9, Memorandum by the Treasury, p. 280.

[5] Figures supplied by the Central Office of Information of actual staff in post.

Eden as Prime Minister in succession to Sir Winston Churchill), the staff of the Central Office of Information was steadily built up again. The total staff of the Central Office of Information is now almost back to what it was before the cuts were made, 1,409 by September 1, 1963. But there are more staff now in the Information Officer Class—40 per cent instead of 27 per cent.[1]

THE PRESENT STRUCTURE OF THE
INFORMATION OFFICER CLASS

At present, the whole Information Officer Class in the Central Office of Information and the departments amounts to over 900 staff of all grades; as general service classes of the Civil Service go, this is rather small. The class as a whole divides into three main groups: those employed at the Central Office of Information, amounting to nearly 60 per cent of the total; another 30 per cent employed in the Information Divisions of the home departments and the Service departments (about 20 per cent in the home departments and 10 per cent in the Service departments); the remaining 10 per cent is at the Commonwealth Relations Office and the Colonial Office (both in the Information Divisions at the London headquarters and at the information posts overseas).[2] There are also four Information Officer Class staff employed in the Foreign Office.

The Information Officer Class is made up of people engaged in an extraordinarily wide variety of occupations. In the Information Divisions there are some staff who specialize in relations with the press, the BBC and the commercial television networks; there are others who are concerned with advertising, films, booklets or exhibitions. At the Central Office of Information there are few direct dealings with the press;[3] but they employ 500 information staff en-

---

[1] Figures supplied by the Central Office of Information of actual staff in post.
[2] These percentages are based upon an examination of three sets of figures:
  (i) Figures supplied by the Treasury from the Civil Service Central Staff Records which relate only to established staff.
  (ii) Figures contained in the Memorandum by the Financial Secretary to the Treasury which is published each year with the Civil Estimates; these are estimates of the staff that departments expect to employ during the coming year.
  (iii) Figures compiled by the Institution of Professional Civil Servants from returns made by their representatives in each department.
[3] There is one Departmental Press Officer at the Central Office of Information's headquarters and about 100 journalists employed on press work for the overseas information services; at the Central Office of Information's Regional Offices there are a number of press officers dealing with the provincial press; these

151

gaged in a very large number of different activities that are all concerned with the production or distribution of some kind of paid-for
publicity material or service.

It is obviously an administrative convenience to have all these
different kinds of specialists serving in common grades with a single
salary structure. They are not, though, united by the possession of
any common professional basis in the way that the other Professional
Classes of the Civil Service are. Some of the specialists are much more
specialized than others[1] and their jobs cannot be open to other members of the class for transfers, nor do those recruited from outside
to do the more highly specialized jobs necessarily have the kind of
experience or background which would cause them to be considered
for the more senior posts. Although there are not a great many of
these highly specialized posts, it does mean that the field from which
candidates for the top posts can be selected is not quite as wide as
the total figure for the class might lead one to suppose.

Another unusual feature of the Information Officer Class is that a
high proportion of it is temporary—about 40 per cent in the Central
Office of Information, and between 15 per cent and 20 per cent in the
departmental Information Divisions. The Crombie report had suggested that temporary staff should be employed 'so that there might
be a turnover of ideas', and it was intended that there should be
temporaries in all grades right to the top. This has not happened.
There are many more temporaries in the lower grades than in the
higher ones—about 60 per cent of the Assistant Information Officer
Class, but only 10 per cent of those above the rank of Senior Information Officer are temporaries.[2] The pattern seems to be that the
majority of recruits are taken on as temporaries in the lower grades
but many are established later when they have been proved suitable.
This system has had advantages, especially in the last few years when
the information services have been expanding. Not only has a specialist to be found from within a fairly narrow field, but the new recruit
must be turned into a good civil servant with respect for the rules and
traditions of the service. By giving the new recruit a temporary appointment it is possible to discover whether he can adapt the skill
that he has acquired outside to the special needs of the government's
information services. Those who are suitable and who would like to

journalists are eligible to be considered for vacant press posts in departmental
Information Divisions.

[1] Some examples of specializations are artists, typographers, photographic re-
touchers, exhibition designers, etc.

[2] Same source as footnote 2 on page 151.

settle in the Civil Service are able to compete for establishment in the annual open competitions,[1] which involve an interview, with reports on previous employment, including that in government service, also taken into account. There always remains, in the lower grades a temporary fringe of those who have not yet tried to become established or who have been unsuccessful so far. At the Central Office of Information particularly it is useful to have a cushion of temporary staff so that the different publicity media can be given more or less staff as publicity needs change.

THE SENIOR POSTS[2]

While the structure of the Information Officer Class as a whole as analysed in the preceding section might be thought to have a certain lack of unity, the structure of the top third of the class, if analysed separately, appears much more balanced. There are nearly a hundred Chief Information Officer and Principal Information Officer posts, more or less equally divided between the Central Office of Information on the one hand, and the Information Divisions of the home departments and the Service departments on the other. In addition, there are just under thirty of these posts in the Commonwealth Relations Office and the Colonial Office.

As elsewhere in the Civil Service, and indeed in most large organizations, the tendency is to fill the top posts by promotion from within, thus providing career opportunities for the best people in the service. The view of the Treasury and of the departments is that by and large the experience and knowledge of the information service and the department's needs gained in the middle grades provide an invaluable foundation for the progression to the more senior posts, and give people already in the service an advantage over outsiders, however

---

[1] These annual open competitions are held by the Civil Service Commissioners although an independent outside expert in the appropriate specialized field also sits on the interview board. These competitions are advertised in the national press and do result in a few outsiders being recruited direct to established appointment as well as in the establishment of those already holding temporary appointments within the service. Since 1957, sixteen Principal Information Officers have been recruited by Open Competition all of whom were already serving as temporaries. Of ninety-two Senior Information Officer posts in the open competition, ten went to outsiders. In the last two years seven out of sixty-nine Information Officer posts went to outsiders and four out of sixty-one Assistant Information posts. (Figures supplied by H.M. Treasury.)

[2] Table 2 at the end of the chapter should be consulted for the Civil Service classes, grades and salaries.

gifted they may be.[1] Recruitment direct from outside to the grade of Principal Information Officer and Chief Information Officer does happen, although not very often.[2] It occurs more often at Senior Information Officer level.

The prospects of promotion in the Information Officer Class up to the level of Chief Information Officer (A) are quite good; that is for those who possess sufficient general ability to rise out of their particular specialization. The ratio between the Chief Information Officer (A) posts and the rest of the Class is 1:34. This compares well with most of the other specialized classes of the Civil Service.[3] It is certainly far better than the promotion prospects in the Executive Class of the general civil service, where the ratio between the posts equivalent in salary to Chief Information Officer (A) (Principal Executive Officer) and the rest of the Class is 1:470. But for Chief Information Officers (A), that is, in most cases the head of the Information Division, the prospects are not so good. In the Administrative Class of the Civil Service, the ratio between posts at this salary level, which is the level of Assistant Secretary, and the total of posts in all the top grades is just over 1:2. In the Works Group of Professional Classes it is just under 1:2; in the Scientific Officer Class, it is about 1:9; in the Executive Class it is 1:4. In the Information Services there are six higher posts to which the twenty-four Chief Information Officer (A)'s might be promoted; this gives a ratio of 1:4.

This is as good as the prospects in the Executive Class, but the Executive Class has an outlet into the Administrative Class—every year quite a number of the Executive Class secure promotion into the Administrative Class. What can and does happen in the ordinary classes of the Civil Service is that a man can join the service in one of the Clerical Grades, can work his way up into the Executive Class and from there can secure promotion into the Administrative Class where his way is open to the very top. Within these three Classes the Civil Service can provide parallels to the private soldier who rises to be a General or Field Marshal, or to the office boy who becomes Managing Director or Chairman. The specialized classes of the Civil Service offer parallel but distinct ladders of promotion. Some of them, for example the Scientific Officer Class, the Legal Class, the Medical

[1] Most of this paragraph is derived from a statement by the Treasury.

[2] Four Principal Information Officers were recruited direct from outside between 1961 and 1963.

[3] There are some specialized classes with better opportunities—the Scientific Officer Class, for example, has a ratio of 1:4 between the posts equivalent in salary to Chief Information Officer (A) and the rest of their Class.

Class, and the Works Group of Professional Classes, have, at the top, posts that are as well paid or nearly as well paid as the Permanent Secretary of a department. The Information Officer Class does not have such a top level structure. Of the six higher posts that exist at the head of the information services, three are outside the Central Office of Information and three are within. The salaries of five of the posts are more or less the same, and rank below that of Under-Secretary in the administrative class. The post of Director-General of the Central Office of Information is higher and carries the same salary as a Deputy Secretary but there is no post with a salary equivalent to a Permanent Head of a Department.

When one comes to look at their functions, however, there are considerable differences between the work of all the Chief Information Officers in the Ministerial departments and of the Public Relations Adviser to the Prime Minister on the one hand, and the two Controllers and the Director-General at the Central Office of Information at the other. The qualities and experience that make a good Chief Information Officer in a department are not necessarily those that make a good head of a department in the Central Office of Information and vice versa. Nor would a first-class Chief Information Officer who was interested in the political or the press side of his job necessarily be attracted to a job within the Central Office of Information. So that promotion for a Chief Information Officer who wishes to continue to work in his own field is limited to three posts, instead of six, and he would exclude himself from the highest of all—the Director-General of the Central Office of Information.

The head of an Information Division, then, has a much shorter ladder of promotion than the other specialized classes in the Civil Service. It is possible, in theory, to transfer from the Information Officer Class into the Administrative Class, but it does not happen.[1]

The average age of Chief Information Officers (both A and B together) at present is fifty-one; the average age of Chief Information Officer (A)'s alone would presumably be rather higher but the figures are not given separately. This means that if a man reaches the rank of Chief Information Officer (A) in his early fifties, and if he sees no chance of securing one of the six top posts, he faces the prospect of staying in the same job for ten or fifteen years. He can move along the line into another Chief Information Officer post for the sake of a change without promotion. It is also true that if the Chief Informa-

[1] The only case of an Information Officer moving into the Administrative Class was when an Information Officer was accepted in an open competition for Principals.

155

tion Officer decides to leave the Civil Service and seek promotion outside, he is qualified to practice in a field where employment is fluid and flexible and where he should have a good chance to earn more money if he is prepared to give up the security and other advantages of the Civil Service. He is not, however, so sought after as some of the scientific and technical members of the Civil Service.

To sum up the general position of the Information Officer Class, it has been seen in the earlier part of this Chapter how the Civil Service found itself after the war with a large number of people engaged in many different functions all directly concerned with some aspect of publicity, press relations or information. It was decided that the best way to fit these people into the Civil Service staff structure was to make a single Information Service and to create an Information Officer Class to contain the staff employed in this service. The arrangements laid down for recruitment to this new class were left very open and flexible. In the early years of the class there was not very much recruiting because, owing to a change in government policy in 1951–2, the staff of the information services were severely reduced. During the eight years or so in which the information services have been expanding again (1955–63) the pattern of recruitment has been developed so as to make the class a predominantly specialized one consisting of people recruited to the junior grades from outside for particular experience and talents. It has been the general policy to fill the senior posts by promotion from among these specialists after they have spent some years in the Civil Service. This pattern appears to have been accepted by the Treasury and by most government departments, partly because it is useful to have information experts with their own outside contacts in the press and television worlds. It must owe something, too, to pressure from the Institution of Professional Civil Servants who represent the interests of the specialist Information Officer Class and do all they can to see that borderline posts are classsed as Information posts wherever possible and are not filled by civil servants who have no specialist qualifications.[1]

Nevertheless, there are quite a number of promotions from the Clerical Class to the Information Officer Class and of transfers or promotions from the Executive Class. Nor are all the senior posts filled from below; some Principal Information Officer and Chief Information Officer (B) vacancies have recently been filled from outside in the Central Office of Information, the Treasury and one or two

[1] For example the IPCS have recently protested against the reservation for soldiers of the Public Relations Officer's post at the War Department.

other departments; the Ministry of Aviation has even recruited a Chief Information Officer (A) from outside in recent years.

Most senior posts are filled by promoting specialists who are already in the information services, but sometimes people are brought in from outside the Civil Service altogether. Sometimes junior posts are filled from the Clerical or Executive Class. Except for the 'trawlable' field, recruitment policy is to find the best person available at the time whether they are inside or outside the Civil Service.

THE EXCEPTIONAL DEPARTMENTS

There is, however, one home department which up to 1963 engaged in information work on a considerable scale without using the Information Officer Class.[1] This is the Ministry of Agriculture and Fisheries which has a large Information Division but does not, in the main, employ the Information Officer Class.[2] Three posts within the Division are designated as Information Officer Class posts, but two of these are at present occupied by officers of the Executive Class who 'happen to be qualified to meet the requirements of the job'.[3] The rest of the division is staffed by members of the Executive Class, with Administrative Class officers at its head. The most significant point here is not whether the information effort of the Ministry of Agriculture and Fisheries is better or worse than that of departments whose Information Divisions are staffed by the Information Officer Class, but the demonstration that if a department prefers not to, it need not use the specialized Information Officer Class at all. The fact that most other government departments do use the Information Officer Class shows, therefore, that they have preferred to do so.

The three Service departments and the Ministry of Defence, while they employ Information Officer Class staff in their Information Divisions have, in recent years, reserved the post of Head of the Division for a serving or retired officer. The Crombie Committee had allowed that there might be a case in the Service departments for

[1] In a number of other departments which have information work done by people who are not in the Information Officer Class, e.g. the Customs and Excise Department, the Export Credits Guarantee Department, the Board of Inland Revenue and the National Assistance Board, the information work done either does not amount to a full-time job or is of such a technical kind that it is more important to employ someone who is an expert on the subject; for example an expert on income tax rather than on publicity.

[2] One Press Officer from the Information Officer Class was appointed in 1964. Until then no members of the Information Officer Class at all were employed.

[3] Information supplied by the Treasury.

recruiting their Chief Information Officer from the service concerned. The argument here is that it needs a senior officer of the Armed Services to understand and have the confidence of the services and that a professional information officer would not be able to establish the necessary close relationship with the service. But this view has not always been held by all the Service departments and before the war both the Air Ministry and the War Office employed civilians as departmental Press Officers. The post-war arguments have been resisted by the Institution of Professional Civil Servants who from time to time pressed the Heads of the Service departments to appoint a professional man who would, apart from anything else, be able to stay longer than the two or three years tour of duty which a serving officer does.

The other notable exception to the use of the Information Officer Class for information work is the Foreign Office, which has never made use of the Information Officer Class in its extensive overseas information services.[1] This is not the place to discuss the problems of the overseas information services which are outside the scope of this book. Nevertheless, it should not pass unnoticed that the largest of the three overseas departments has for many years conducted its information services with ordinary civil servants in the departmental grades that correspond to the Administrative and Executive Classes of the Home Civil Service and has not thought it necessary to employ the Information Officer Class. The Head of the News Department in London is normally a member of Branch A of the Foreign Service. Although it may be agreed that the Foreign Office has special information problems, the fact that Foreign Office staffing policy for its information services is the exact opposite of that adopted by most departments calls for comment. The Foreign Office and the Ministry of Agriculture and Fisheries use their own administrative staff for information work and appear to be satisfied with these arrangements.

Other departments do not use administrative staff at the head of their Information Divisions; indeed it seems reasonable to suppose that the Ministers who rely on their Chief Information Officers for expert advice on press and public relations would not find a member of the permanent civil service so useful. It may be wondered whether those responsible for the two different policies in the Home Informa-

[1] The Commonwealth Relations Office and Colonial Office have used the Information Officer Class for their overseas services, but the Report of the Committee on Representational Services Overseas (Cmnd. 2276, Feb. 1964) recommended that they should adopt the staffing policy of the Foreign Office.

tion Services have come together to discuss their rival merits and to compare the results within recent years.

CONCLUSION

When it comes to looking towards the future, it must be remembered that during the last fifteen years or so the status within the Civil Service of the Chief Information Officer in particular and of the Information Service in general has steadily risen. It is possible that in the future we may see some Chief Information Officer posts upgraded from their present level of equivalent to Assistant Secretary, to the equivalent of an Under-Secretary or something approaching that. If this is a possibility, it gives even more force to the suggestion that the present policies for staffing the information services should be examined to see if they are really producing people of the qualities and calibre needed for the future and if, out of the various policies that exist, one seems to be producing better results than the others.

The present arrangements for filling Information Officer Class posts are pretty flexible; at this time when there is so much talk about bringing new blood into the Civil Service, it is as well to remember that this is one class where the import of specialists of various ages and backgrounds is quite common at all levels. It is not always easy to do this. One of the problems of bringing people in from outside at a senior level is that it damages the career prospects of those already in the service. It is also possible that departments may feel reluctant to bring in at that level of the service someone from outside when there is the risk that he may turn out to be unsuitable. And if, after a year or two's service on a temporary appointment, he does come to be regarded as suitable for establishment he then has to be submitted to the procedure of the Civil Service Commissioners' open competition. Departments may feel reluctant to do this at a senior level, or potential candidates may be reluctant to be exposed to it. Another possibility which should perhaps be considered is the possibility of filling some of the senior posts in the information services from among members of the Administrative Class (Assistant Secretaries or Principals) on a tour of duty. The damage to the promotion prospects of those within the class might, in this case, be offset by giving Information Officer Class staff a tour of duty in the Administrative Class. There are at least two points of view currently held in the Civil Service that have prevented the use of the Administrative Class for the Information Services (except in the Foreign Office and the Ministry of Agriculture and Fisheries). First there is the view of those

TABLE 2

GRADE AND SALARY SCALES OF CERTAIN CLASSES OF THE CIVIL SERVICE

The non-industrial Civil Service is made up of a number of classes, each class containing a series of grades. The main classes are the Administrative, Executive, Clerical and Typing Classes, and the Professional, Scientific and Technical Classes. The Information Officer Class is included in 'Other Classes'.

The figures of staff given below include both permanent and temporary civil servants. Permanent civil servants are established and pensionable and are recruited by the Civil Service Commission by means of various kinds of competitions consisting of written examinations or interviews, or both. Temporary civil servants, who do not qualify for pensions but are eligible for gratuities, are normally recruited by the department concerned. No qualifying examinations are required to become a temporary, but temporary civil servants can enter the competition of the Civil Service Commission for appointments to permanent service.

INFORMATION OFFICER CLASS			EXECUTIVE CLASS (General Service Only)			ADMINISTRATIVE CLASS		
Grade	Annual Salary Scale £	Numbers in Grade	Grade	Annual Salary Scale £	Numbers in Grade	Grade	Annual Salary Scale £	Numbers in Grade
Director General of the COI	4,950	1				Joint Permanent Secretaries to Treasury and Secretary to the Cabinet	7,450	3
						Permanent Secretaries	6,950	31
Controller, COI; Public Relations Adviser to Prime Minister;	3,863	2	Various Special Posts	up to 4,050	20	Deputy Secretary	4,950	65
Public Relations Officer, Post Office;	3,650 to 3,863	3				Under Secretary	4,050	239

Class	Salary (£)	No.	Grade	Salary (£)	No.	Grade	Salary (£)	No.
			tive Officer	3,150	83	Secretary	2,800–3,500	741
CIO (B)	2,542–2,800	28	Senior CEO	2,542–2,800	258	Principal	1,839–2,569	1,213
PIO	2,109–2,434	105	CEO	2,109–2,434	897			
SIO	1,568–2,001	233	SEO	1,568–2,001	2,845	Assistant Principal	768–1,271	232
IO	1,271–1,487	353	HEO	1,271–1,487	9,188			
AIO	476–1,200	233	EO	476–1,200	25,016			
Total in Class		983			38,307			2,524

Source: Civil Estimates 1963–4; *Memorandum by the Financial Secretary to the Treasury*, p. 37; Cmnd. 1965, March 1964.

Notes:
1. This table shows the number of staff that it is estimated will be employed on April 1, 1964, and the salary scales in force at that date.
2. All rates of pay shown are 'National' rates.
3. Staff employed in the Post Office are not included. Figures of Post Office staff are published separately in the Annual Report and Accounts of the Post Office.

who wish to reserve the information posts for 'professional' information officers, arguing that ordinary civil servants do not have the qualities or knowledge needed to carry out information functions and conversely, that information officers would not make good civil servants. Secondly, there is the view of those who control the Administrative Class that information work is not of sufficient importance for it to be possible to spare, from the other demands upon the class, a good man to take charge of the Information Division.[1] The exclusion of information work from the field of activities conducted by the Administrative Class may be considered to give tacit approval if not encouragement to the view of information work as a by-way among departmental functions and not as something that is genuinely important in itself. It may be that government departments still do not put a high enough value on public relations and information work.

If departments wished to do so, it would be possible to make use of all or any of these suggestions: the recruitment of more people from outside into the more senior grades; the use of members of the Administrative Class, on a tour of duty, in the top information posts; the posting of Information Officer Class staff to tours of duty in other parts of their departments; giving Information Officer Class staff the opportunity of securing transfer into the Administrative Class; and the up-grading of some of the top jobs in the Information Service to give a better promotion ladder.

---

[1] It used to be considered that all work done by the Administrative Class should be the kind of work that could be done by all members of that class. This is no longer as true as it used to be because the work now undertaken by members of the Administrative Class has grown increasingly varied, and some of it makes special demands for qualities or temperaments not present in every member of the Administrative Class, just as the demands of the post of Chief Information Officer would do.

CHAPTER VIII

The Training of Civil Servants for their Relations with the Public

Although in the last six chapters we have been looking almost exclusively at the information services, it was pointed out at the beginning of the book that the government's public relations are not confined to information officers. Of all the channels of communication that exist between the central government and the citizens, the basic channel in which everybody shares is the one that is made up of all the numberless contacts between individual citizens and individual officials, in person, on the telephone and by letter.

All civil servants are concerned in this sense with public relations, because their job is public business. In this chapter, therefore, we look at what is being done to train the ordinary civil servant—including information officers, in so far as they need such training—to conduct their relations with the public with efficiency, speed, courtesy, and a proper understanding of the needs of each private citizen.[1]

It is impossible within the compass of this book to make an analysis of all the types of training which are provided for all grades in all departments. It seems most valuable in this limited space to concentrate upon what is done to train civil servants in the departments where there is most contact and most direct contact, that is the Post Office, the Ministry of Labour and the Ministry of Pensions and National Insurance; but even within these limits, only some examples can be given, and on the whole we shall concentrate on the training given to the lower grades, who are the officials most people meet in their everyday transactions.

There is another problem which presents itself when a description is to be given of the training arrangements that exist in any large organization, because there are two main methods of training. First, there is training on the job whereby a person is not only told what work he has to do by an experienced colleague or by a supervisor, but is guided into the best ways of doing it; and second, there are the various kinds of formal organized training courses conducted by

[1] See also Appendix B for further details of training schemes.

fulltime instructors at a school or training centre. The second form of training, because it is conducted to a fixed programme, is much more easily described and, when described, sounds more impressive than the gradual and continuous tuition of training on the job. But these two forms of training are complementary and organized training courses can never realize their full value if they are not closely linked with training on the job, which ought to be kept up long after the course is over. Yet to try and make any valid survey of the extent to which properly managed training on the job is carried out even in one government department, let alone in many, would require more time and space than is available here. So, although it is realized that training on the job may be the most important part of any scheme of training, it will only be possible to refer to it in the process of describing the more formal types of group training courses that are provided.

CIVIL SERVICE TRAINING BEFORE 1945

It is only since the Second World War that planned schemes of training have been undertaken throughout the whole Home Civil Service. Before the war, there was no central study of the question of training in the Civil Service either by the Treasury or by any other central official body,[1] and during the 1930s training in the Home Civil Service was a very patchy affair. Some of the lower grades received no training at all and some of the departments which employed these grades were indifferent to the need to train them. Some departments practised training on the job with varying degrees of efficiency; some gave new entrants spells of duty in various branches of the department to give them a general understanding of the department's work. The Treasury appears to have taken no active interest in training except where a department developed a scheme which had financial repercussions; and their interest was then limited to the financial aspects of the scheme.

Certain departments, notably the Board of Inland Revenue, the Customs and Excise Department, the Ministry of Labour, the Prison Commission and the General Post Office, however, provided a considerable amount of formal organized training for some of their grades. The Post Office's training school for counter clerks (cor-

[1] Some unofficial studies were made, including a report by the Institute of Public Administration (now the Royal Institute of Public Administration) in 1933 and a monograph by Professor Walker of Ohio State University which was published in 1934. (Harvey Walker, *Training Public Employees in Great Britain.* McGraw-Hill, 1935. Commission of Inquiry on Public Service Personnel Monograph 6.)

rectly known as Postal and Telegraph Officers) in the London postal region was started in 1931; and at about the same time schools were established in London and in a few provincial centres for telephone operators.[1]

It was during the war that training first became an issue of importance in the Civil Service. This was partly because large numbers of new recruits had to be taught their jobs quickly in order to administer the vast wartime controls and regulations, so the need for training schemes became acute.[2] It was also because people from industry and commerce who joined the wartime civil service brought new ideas and a different experience of personnel management to the problems of the Civil Service. Training centres were started early in the war by the Ministry of Food, the Ministry of Labour and National Service and by the War Office and the Air Ministry.[3]

In 1943, the Chancellor of the Exchequer, as the result of certain suggestions made the previous year by the Select Committee on National Expenditure of the House of Commons,[4] appointed a Committee under the Chairmanship of the Financial Secretary to the Treasury, the Rt Hon Ralph Assheton, MP, to make an investigation into the training of civil servants.[5] The Assheton Report published in 1944,[6] was the original blue print for civil service training, and is still, nearly twenty years later, the basis of training throughout the Civil Service.

The Assheton Committee recognized that the increasing contacts between the community and the Civil Service needed 'planned and purposeful training' if civil servants were to improve in their own high standards of service.

Among the common criticisms of the Civil Service there is one of such importance as to call for particular mention in any statement of the objects of Civil Service training. . . . It is sometimes suggested that civil servants tend to form a class apart from the rest of the community and are apt to forget that John Citizen is a composite of innumerable individual John Smith's. Nothing could be more disastrous than that the Civil Service and the public should think of themselves as in two separate

[1] Harvey Walker, op. cit., Chapter IX.
[2] W. J. Mackenzie and J. W. Grove. *Central Administration in Britain*, Longmans, Green, 1957, p. 124.
[3] Cmd. 6525, para. 51.
[4] Select Committee on National Expenditure, Session 1941–2, 16th Report. *Organization and Control of the Civil Service*.
[5] House of Commons, January 28, 1943.
[6] *Report of the Committee on the Training of Civil Servants*, Cmd. 6525. HMSO, 1944.

camps. The inculcation of the right attitude towards the public and towards business should therefore be one of the principal aims of Civil
Service training. The civil servant must never forget that he is the servant, not the master, of the community, and that official competence
need not, and should not, involve the loss of the human touch. Many
civil servants who are brought most frequently into contact with the
public know and appreciate the value of the right attitude; others must
be raised to the same standard, since the Service is liable to be judged on
the basis of innumerable daily contacts between members of the public
and the government machine.[1]

The Committee made recommendations on the training organizations that should be set up at the Treasury and in the departments.
It also made a number of detailed suggestions about the types of
training that should be provided for the various classes of civil servants. Formal courses at training schools were considered suitable for
the training of the Clerical and the lower Executive grades. For the
training of similar grades who came into direct contact with the
public, the Committee drew special attention to the type of training
already being provided by the Post Office at the counter clerks training school where the emphasis was on active, realistic and practical
training with the use of role-playing sessions to demonstrate the
right and wrong ways of dealing with the public.[2]

The Assheton Committee did not overlook the fact that the
traditional method of training on 'live' work under the personal
supervision of an experienced officer was already in use in departments. They pointed out that this was a sound arrangement so long
as the experienced officer was a good teacher, and so long as full
allowance was made to him as well as to the trainee for the time
that would have to be spent on instruction. For the Administrative
Class, the Committee stated, this sort of training had, in the past,
been far too much a matter of 'hit or miss, sink or swim'.[3]

THE TRAINING ORGANIZATION AFTER THE WAR

As soon as the war was over, the recommendations of the Assheton
Report began to be implemented with the co-operation of the Staff
Side. In 1945 the Civil Service National Whitley Council appointed
a Joint Committee on the Training of Civil Servants[4] which has, since

[1] Cmd. 6525, para. 17.
[2] Ibid., para. 54.
[3] Ibid., para. 91.
[4] The First Report of the Joint Committee on the Training of Civil Servants is
contained in Treasury Circular 27/45 of November 9, 1945. *Whitley Bulletin*,
December 1945, p. 122.

then, been entrusted with the task of keeping the field of training under continuous review and of making recommendations to departments. In 1946, a Training and Education Division was set up at the Treasury under the direction of an Assistant Secretary. Other departments appointed their own departmental training officers. In 1948, at the suggestion of the Staff Side of the Joint Committee on the Training of Civil Servants, an official inter-departmental committee of training officers was appointed to examine afresh the whole question of the training of staff who had contact with the public. This committee, which reported in 1949,[1] in addition to making recommendations on the form and content of training courses, made two other important suggestions. First, they said, they were concerned about the need to create within every department the right atmosphere of courtesy and service without which the effects of formal training would eventually wear off; and they suggested that staff magazines, handbooks, posters, and leaflets could be used for this purpose. Secondly, the Committee reported that they found that the training of civil servants for face-to-face contact with the public was already getting a good deal of attention; they considered that this kind of training might well be extended to more of the staff and that more might be done for the training of doorkeepers, messengers, inquiry room staff and the Post Office telephone operators on departmental switchboards.

The training of Post Office staff was made the subject of an inquiry by a separate committee, the Post Office Training Committee, under the Chairmanship of Mr J. Scholes, CB, OBE, which met at about the same time as the Assheton Committee and made three reports between 1944 and 1946. Its main recommendations were about the need to co-ordinate existing training arrangements in the Post Office and to create a central Training Branch at Post Office headquarters. Like the Assheton Committee, the Post Office Training Committee recommended that the two Staff Sides that exist at the Post Office should be included on a permanent training committee. The Standing Joint Committee on Training and Education was therefore established and it subsequently set up separate panels to deal with the training of the various groups of staff employed by the Post Office.[2]

[1] *Training of Civil Servants who have Contact with the Public* (*Whitley Bulletin*, June 1949, p. 90) was the report of the Inter-departmental Training Officers' Committee under the chairmanship of Mr A. P. Sinker, then Director of Training and Education Division of the Treasury.

[2] J. V. Greenlaw, 'Training and Education in the Post Office', *Public Administration*, Summer 1957, p. 113.

Thus, within a few years of the end of the war, the machinery for civil service training had been set up and begun to operate in more departments than it had ever done before. However, the government decision in 1951–2 to cut public expenditure resulted in a setback to the development of training activities. The staff of the Treasury's Training and Education Division and the training staff of other departments were reduced.[1] Existing schemes for the training of new entrants continued, but other schemes had to be abandoned and it was the schemes for the training of the supervisory and senior grades that suffered.

But in 1954 the Crichel Down affair[2] threw a spotlight on some unsatisfactory aspects of some civil servants' attitude to the public. In the Report of a Committee appointed by the Prime Minister in connection with this case, it was stated:

> In present times the interests of the private citizen are affected to a great extent by the actions of Civil Servants. It is the more necessary that the Civil Servant should bear constantly in mind that the citizen has a right to expect, not only that his affairs will be dealt with effectively and expeditiously, but also that his personal feelings, no less than his rights as an individual, will be sympathetically and fairly considered.[3]

From 1955 onwards, training schemes, especially for middle and senior grades, began to expand again.

PRESENT CIVIL SERVICE TRAINING

Today training courses are mostly provided by the departments themselves, which employ altogether a staff of over 600 fulltime training instructors. The Training and Education Division of the Treasury, which co-ordinates the departmental training officers, also runs about fifty central courses to provide types of training which it is not possible for any one department to organize for itself.[4] About 2,400 civil servants ranging from Assistant Secretaries to typists attend these courses organized by the Treasury each year; most of them last a week or less but some—the new course for Assistant

[1] See EC 22/52 of March 14, 1952. 'Retrenchment in Civil Service Training', *Whitley Bulletin*, May 1952, p. 76.

[2] *Public Inquiry ordered by the Minister of Agriculture into the disposal of land at Crichel Down*. Cmd. 9176, June 1954. HMSO.

[3] *Report of a Committee appointed by the Prime Minister to consider whether certain Civil Servants should be transferred to other duties*. Cmd. 9220. July 1954.

[4] See Appendix B.

Principals, for example, is planned to last for three months or longer.[1]
Three or four courses a year are also run for departmental training
officers and their training instructors.

There is no planned training course in government information
work. People who are recruited to departmental Information Divisions from outside the service have the experience they have gained
in the exercise of their professions in the commercial or journalistic
world. When they arrive in the Civil Service they do not receive any
organized training in the special kind of information work performed by government departments, other than being taught their
work on the job by their superior officer. Information Divisions also
produce informal notes for the guidance of new entrants on such subjects as Parliamentary procedure, the Lobby and other specialized
groups of journalists and so on. The Central Office of Information
provides general background training for new entrants to the Central
Office of Information fairly early on in their careers. This training is
designed to tell them about the work of all parts of the Central Office
of Information and to give them a general picture of the information
services as a whole so they may understand where their own job fits in.
The Central Office of Information also provides training courses for
information officers who are going abroad.

A certain number of information class officials in the middle and
senior grades also attend various outside courses, including courses
run by the Treasury training division, but on the whole civil servants
working in Information Divisions receive very little training in their
special work.[2] Compared with other classes of civil servants, their
numbers, of course, are very small.

We can now turn to the training for public relations given to the
ordinary civil servants.

*Training in the Post Office, Ministry of Labour and Ministry of
Pensions and National Insurance*[3]
It is the large departments with nation-wide organizations that have
the most highly developed training organizations. The Post Office,

---

[1] See p. 178n.
[2] This is not true of the Regional organization of the Central Office of Information, where a good deal of the Regional Information Officers' time is spent on
training journalists, often recruited locally, to adapt their techniques to government information work.
[3] The National Assistance Board is not one of the government departments
which has been specially studied for this book. It must, however, be mentioned
that the National Assistance Board has had, since 1954, a highly developed system
of training for its staff, who every year are involved in well over 11 million

Ministry of Pensions and National Insurance, and the Ministry of Labour are three of the most active. The Plowden Committee on the Control of Public Expenditure[1] said that in these departments there was real appreciation of the scope for the application of 'management services', in which the Committee included training. The Committee did not think, however, that there was sufficient awareness throughout all the Civil Service of the contribution which management services could make to the efficiency of a department's work. It is probably both the size of their organizations and the extent of their direct contacts with large numbers of the community that have made these departments develop organized training. Fortunately, this means that the civil servants whom most people meet have been trained in how to conduct their relations with the public, since they belong to the large departments.

The officials of these three departments who are most involved with face-to-face contact with the public are the counter staff whom the public meets at the Crown Post Offices,[2] and at the local offices of the Ministry of Labour and the Ministry of Pensions and National Insurance; and the Visiting Officers, Inspectors and Welfare Officers of the Ministry of Pensions and National Insurance. All these officials belong to the Clerical and lower Executive grades of the Civil Service, or to Departmental grades that are roughly equivalent to them. The Post Office, for example, recruits about 2,000 a year—the Ministry of Labour about 800. Although the problems with which they have to deal in their relations with the public show considerable variations, their training arrangements have a good deal in common.

All three departments who employ these counter staff have headquarters training centres and a number of regional training centres throughout the country.

Most Post Office counter clerks have a five weeks' training course on entry which includes the detailed instruction they need in order to be able to handle all the many kinds of business transacted over

personal interviews. An account of staff training in the National Assistance Board by its former Departmental Training Officer may be found in the Winter 1961 issue of *Public Administration*—'Staff Training in the National Assistance Board: Problems and Policies' by H. R. Stowe. Other examples not mentioned in this chapter may be found in the Ministry of Agriculture, Fisheries and Food, the Customs and Excise Department and the Ministry of Transport.

[1] *Control of Public Expenditure*, Cmnd. 1423, HMSO, 1961.

[2] Crown Post Offices are the 1,800 Post Offices staffed by civil servants. There are also 23,000 sub-Post Offices, usually run as part of a shop, which are not staffed by civil servants. Training schemes apply only to staff at Crown Post Offices.

the Post Office counter. The Post Office has equipped its training schools with actual counters, complete with normal counter equipment and dummy money, forms and so on. This course is followed by supervised training on the job. The clerical officers of the Ministry of Labour and the Ministry of Pensions and National Insurance receive a background course of four or five days. After training at the desk, they also attend vocational courses (each lasting about a week) on the specialized knowledge needed for their jobs. Having acquired a good practical experience of the work, they normally go on a four-day course on relations with the public before being employed on counter or visiting duties.

In all these courses much attention is paid to the problems of communicating with the public and of dealing with them in an efficient, speedy, courteous and understanding way. The training techniques used for this purpose are common to all these departmental training centres; one department may favour one technique more than another and the techniques are adapted to suit the needs and tastes of individual training centres, but there do not seem to be any striking variations. Since the war, training courses have moved well away from the idea of straight lecturing to a passive audience. Instead, students are expected to remember the points by means of active and practical training, with the students taking a full part in the exercises.

Group discussion is the basic method used in all the training centres of these three departments; instead of the training officer telling the students what they ought to do, the students themselves are asked to suggest what should be done in some particular circumstance and then led to discuss each other's suggestions. The most widely used method of demonstrating the right and the wrong way of dealing with members of the public is the use of role-playing sessions. For example, in the training course at the Post Office counter clerk's school, there are three such sessions to demonstrate conduct at the counter: in the first session, two instructors play the parts of a counter clerk and a member of the public and show how things go wrong; in the next two sessions, the part of the counter clerk is played by one of the students. After each session the reasons for what happened and how things could have been done differently and better are discussed by the group of students. On some courses at the Ministry of Labour and the Ministry of Pensions and National Insurance, the part of a member of the public is taken by someone whom the trainees have not seen before. Another example, from the Ministry of Labour, is the case of the mechanical engineer calling at a local office to discuss the possibility of changing his job. The students are divided into two groups and put into separate rooms: for one visit the engineer arrives, straight from work, in his oily overalls; for the other visit he comes clean and tidy in an ordinary suit, having come from home on his day off; in both cases his behaviour is exactly the same. After the interviews are finished, the reactions of the two groups of students are compared and they may observe the danger of being misled by paying too much attention to a person's appearance.

At all these courses, the same kind of role-playing exercises are used to demonstrate how to manage telephone calls from members of the public. This is usually done by using an internal telephone line with the telephones in separate rooms. For both types of role-playing sessions, the whole action is often tape recorded so that it can be played back afterwards to help the subsequent discussion with the group. Films, sometimes made for departments through the Central Office of Information,[1] and film-strips (the latter often made by the instructors) are also used to demonstrate the problems of communicating with the public and the consequences of bad relations with the public. Both the Ministry of Labour and the Ministry of Pensions and National Insurance sometimes use recordings of dramatized incidents which are acted by members of the department's Dramatic Society.

All three departments, too, follow up the formal training courses given to these grades by supervised training on the job, attaching considerable importance to the training of the 'first line' supervisors, who do it. In the Ministry of Pensions and National Insurance, for example, detailed training guides have been prepared to instruct new or inexperienced staff in the law and procedure governing their work. The introduction of these training guides has done much to secure uniform standards of desk training throughout the department.[2]

Much of the advice and training given to the counter clerks of each of the three departments is similar. All counter staff are urged, both at the training centres and by means of leaflets and other printed matter to be clean, tidy and properly dressed. They are told to cultivate a pleasant and helpful manner; to avoid a non-committal or indifferent attitude; not to gossip, knit or read when on duty; to keep their temper in the face of provocation; to avoid the use of jargon and initials; and above all to know their job and supply accurate in-

[1] For example *Put Yourself in his Shoes* for the Ministry of Labour; *As others see Us* for the Treasury; and *Counterpoint* for the Post Office.

[2] The Ministry of Pensions and National Insurance has been a pioneer of this kind of analysis of work from the viewpoint of desk training, which was a major innovation in the Civil Service.

formation, since courtesy is no substitute for efficiency and accuracy. All these departments also stress that each counter officer, when he is speaking to a member of the public, is the representative of his department—to the caller, the counter officer is the Ministry—and furthermore, that he represents the whole Civil Service whose public relations so much depend on the behaviour of individual officials in their contacts with the public.

In addition to such general training, the counter staff of each of the three departments have special problems in their relations with the public.

Training in the Post Office. The Post Office has for a long time paid a great deal of attention to schemes that could contribute to good counter-relations with its customers. The new all-purpose counter service is a good example of a major change introduced with this object in view. Under all-purpose service, with very few exceptions, all clerks are trained and equipped to do all classes of business. Formerly the usual arrangement was to have two or three teams each doing different classes of business, and therefore unable to help each other out at times of pressure on one team. Not only was it annoying to wait in a queue in front of one clerk while another clerk was free but unable to help, but this team-working system often meant that the customer had to queue twice if he wanted to buy both a dog licence and a book of stamps. The decision to introduce the all-purpose system at most post offices was the result of one of the recommendations made by a committee known, after its Chairman, as the Taylor Committee appointed by the Postmaster General in April 1959 to inquire into the service at Post Office counters.[1] The Post Office had also commissioned a survey of public opinion on the postal service from the Social Survey Division of the Central Office of Information. From this survey, as well as from its own inquiries, the Taylor Committee concluded that while there were plenty of favourable comments on the service at Post Office counters, there still remained a hardcore of criticism levelled on the score of rudeness, off-handedness and inattention.

From the same sources the Committee also found that there were two main difficulties that stood in the way of establishing good

[1] Its full title was the Joint Committee on Service at Crown Post Office Counters; its members were representatives of the Postal Service, the Post Office Staff, the Department from whom the Post Office provides agency services, and the customer; its chairman was Mr L. J. Taylor, Regional Director, South-Western Region, GPO. Its report was published in 1960.

relations between the staff and the customers in the Post Office. The first was that many of the things which the public wanted to buy over the Post Office counter are not things that are wanted for their own sake—as are the things that one buys in a shop—but things that must be got and paid for because the government makes it compulsory; for example, motor, wireless and dog licences, national insurance stamps, and stamps for a variety of other taxes. These can only be bought at the Post Office; the customer is forced to trade there and when he gets there he may be kept waiting. The second main difficulty is that the counter clerks often cannot do what the customer wants because of some regulation of which the customer has never heard or cannot understand, and which the Post Office clerk cannot fully explain because it relates to one of the many agency services which the Post Office performs for other government departments. The counter clerk is not empowered to give advice on these subjects and he can only advise the customer to call upon or write to the department responsible for the regulation. An example of this, which is very troublesome to the counter clerk, is the customer who comes in to buy national insurance stamps, but does not know which of the many denominations of these stamps he ought to have. The counter clerk cannot possibly decide what a person's national insurance contributions ought to be, and he can only advise the customer to go to the local office of the Ministry of Pensions and National Insurance, which may be a long way away.

Although the criticisms, which were thought to arise mostly from the difficulties just described, came from a small percentage of the Post Office's customers, the Taylor Committee recommended that further measures should be taken to deal with the problem. It recommended that the theme of good relationships should dominate all the techniques used in the training schools for all subjects; and that some printed reminder of the need to try and understand the customer's point of view should be placed where the counter official would always be seeing it—perhaps on the cover of his portfolio of stamps. Finally, the Committee went further than this, and said that if, in spite of all the good service propaganda that had been directed at the counter staff for so long, the problem still persisted, then it was only reasonable, in a matter like this which was a question of human relationships, to ask whether the trouble did not sometimes begin on the other side—the public side of the counter. The Committee considered that if the customers were better informed about and understood the why and wherefore of the Post Office counter organization, regulations and procedures, they would be much more likely to be tolerant and to appreciate good service. It recommended, very positively, that the Post Office should undertake a publicity programme lasting for some years, if necessary, on the theme of 'Explaining ourselves to the customer'.[1] If such a publicity campaign would put an end to the misunderstandings which marred good relations, the Committee considered that the money spent on it would be money well spent.[2]

It is interesting to notice that, in this recommendation the Taylor Committee appears to be carrying to its logical conclusion the final remarks of the Assheton Committee:

> We rate high the need for civil servants to acquire the right attitude of consideration and sympathy towards members of the public, but would add that this attitude should be mutual. Public servants, like everyone else, respond to praise and blame, and enthusiasm and a spirit of service cannot be expected to flourish among them if they feel that their efforts are being disparaged, and their difficulties overlooked, by those whom they are endeavouring to serve. A more general appreciation by the public of the work of the Civil Service would go far to ensure that such appreciation was increasingly deserved.[3]

The Training of Counter Staff in the Ministry of Labour and the Ministry of Pensions and National Insurance. The special public relations problems of the counter duty staff employed by the Ministry of Labour and the Ministry of Pensions and National Insurance, are rather different from those of the Post Office. The duties of the counter officers (and of the various visiting officers and inspectors) bring them into contact of a far more detailed and intimate nature with the individual's private affairs than does any transaction carried out in a Post Office. The counter officers in local offices of the Ministry of Labour[4] have a variety of duties as well as finding jobs for all kinds of people. They include dealing with passport applications, applications to establish entitlement to unemployment benefit, and with special arrangements for youth employment and the employment of the dis-

[1] The Report of the Joint Committee on Service at Crown Post Office Counters, pp. 29–32.
[2] Post Office policy on this point, however, is still being considered, but some general publicity has been issued. Explanatory local press advertisements and posters in local offices based on the theme 'To save you time' were used as each Post Office was converted to all-purpose service; a leaflet was also issued to the staff. In addition, a number of explanatory leaflets about individual services, e.g. Premium Savings Bonds, Recorded Delivery, have been issued.
[3] Cmd. 6525, para. 120.
[4] Ministry of Labour Grade 6 Officers, who are equivalent to Clerical Officers.

abled. In the Ministry of Pensions and National Insurance, counter staff are called upon to deal with an extremely wide range of inquiries—from the sick and infirm, the war and industrially disabled, elderly and retired people, widows and mothers asking about National Insurance and Industrial Injury and maternity benefits and family allowances; and from employers and insured persons about the payment of contributions. Callers requiring a service on many of these types of business may have to be asked detailed questions about their private circumstances, and the counter officer will often be dealing with matters that are highly personal and of great importance to the person who has come to see him. The importance of personal callers at local offices and Ministry headquarters must not be minimized. Although the Ministry of Pensions and National Insurance, for example, deals with most people by post they still have twenty million callers a year.

The theory and practice of successful reception and interviewing of members of the public is set out in a clear and straightforward manner in a series of leaflets produced by the Staff Training Divisions of the Ministry of Labour and Ministry of Pensions and National Insurance. These leaflets are given to all students at the end of the course and are also distributed among officials already engaged in this work. The staff are advised that callers should never be kept waiting if it can possibly be avoided; to listen to the caller with patience and understanding; to try and see the matter from the caller's point of view; to explain clearly what has to be done and the reasons for doing it; and to be friendly and helpful. They are particularly warned to avoid interruptions and advised how to deal with them if they occur. It is assumed that the great majority of the interviews conducted in the Ministry's offices will have to be directed to setting the caller at ease.

But the quality of service depends not only upon the efficiency of the reception arrangements but also on the ability of the individual officers to explain complicated regulations in clear and simple language. Also it is equally necessary to provide a continuing internal information service so that staff are fully aware of the policies of their department and have this information in advance of public announcement. Only in this way are staff in a position to help and give clear explanation to their customers.

The Training of Visiting Officers, Inspectors and Welfare Officers in Ministry of Pensions and National Insurance. The Ministry of Pensions and National Insurance employs three types of visitor whose duties take them into people's homes and places of business. There are the Visiting Officers who are mostly engaged in visiting sick or injured people who are receiving sickness or injury benefit payments; the Inspectors who visit both homes and business premises on questions concerning National Insurance contributions payable by employers and insured persons, or on any other aspects of the schemes administered by the Ministry; and the Welfare Officers of the War Pensioner's Welfare Service. None of these officers may enter a person's home without an invitation to do so, although the Inspectors have a statutory right to enter business premises and to call for the production of wage records and contribution cards.

Visiting Officers and Inspectors have a duty to advise and help but, nevertheless, they may not always be welcome visitors. They may have to deal with complicated matters of obligations and entitlements which may involve considerable investigation, and if they are dealing with a disputed case or with evasion or fraud their call may lead to the matter being referred to an independent tribunal or to civil or even criminal proceedings. Each year these officers will make an enormous number of personal calls, and every day they will have to conduct quite a number of difficult interviews. The Welfare Officer, on the other hand, is a welcome visitor who is generally assured of a friendly reception from war pensioners and war widows; but he has to deal with them on a very personal basis and give practical help in a discreet and tactful way.

The Visiting Officers, Inspectors and Welfare Officers, particularly the latter two, have several weeks of technical training on their particular duties in addition to the general courses and public relations courses given to new entrants. The technical training courses, which occur at various stages of their career, usually proceed by means of discussion, the development of individual cases and role-playing sessions of the kind already described. They write detailed case studies as part of the exercise, which include descriptions of the characters, both of the Ministry staff and members of the public, involved in the incident.

Some examples of Training in Public Relations given to the Higher Grades[1]
The account given in this chapter of the various organized training courses has been mostly concerned with the training provided for the lower grades of the Civil Service who have to deal with the public.

[1] See Appendix B for a description of the general training given to Clerical and Executive Officers and Assistant Principals.

At the Post Office, the provision of formal training courses for these grades had begun before the war; at most of the other large departments, courses for the lower grades were started directly after the war. During the last ten years or so, the provision of training courses, both by the departments and by the Treasury's Training and Education Division, has increasingly been extended to the more senior grades—to the middle and top ranks of the Executive Class (Higher Executive Officer, Senior Executive Officer and Chief Executive Officer), and to the Administrative Class from Assistant Principal to Assistant Secretary, and to some people in the equivalent grades in the Professional and Scientific Classes.

In 1955 the Treasury initiated a series of one week courses, mainly for Higher Executive Officers and Senior Executive Officers, in 'The Conduct of Public Business'. These courses are now run by most large government departments for their own staff, the Treasury providing courses for the departmental instructors. The object of these courses is to awaken members of the middle ranks of the Executive Class to their responsibilities for relations with the public; for their relations with Ministers and Parliament; and for human relations with their own staff. The training methods used by departments on these courses usually include case studies, role-playing sessions and talks and discussions with outside speakers. At a recent one week residential course on 'The Conduct of Public Business' run by the Ministry of Pensions and National Insurance, for example, talks by outside speakers included a well-known Member of Parliament on 'Parliament and the Civil Service'; a Professor of Public Administration on 'Communication as a Problem of Government'; and the Editor of one of the largest popular Sunday newspapers on 'The Civil Service and the Press'.

The entry grade for the Administrative Class civil servant is an Assistant Principal, which is considered a training grade. Up to 1963 all Assistant Principals have had a three weeks' training course at the Treasury, usually after they had served one year attached to senior officers in their own department for training. The course contained sessions on 'Relations with the Press' and others on 'What Local Government or the Citizen expects from Whitehall'.[1]

[1] This course is to be extended in the future. The proposed new course marks a considerable departure in the general training of Assistant Principals in the Home Civil Service. In future, in addition to training on the job, all Assistant Principals in the Home Civil Service are to go to a Centre for Administrative Studies for a fourteen week course (twenty-one weeks for officers from departments with economic responsibilities) organized by the Treasury Training Division. The curriculum will include economics and the general principles of public

For the higher grades of the Administrative Class, the Treasury now provides a one week course in 'Management and Communications' for Principals, Chief Executive Officers and equivalent grades. There is also a two weeks' residential course, at a training centre in a country house, for Assistant Secretaries and equivalent grades on 'Organization and Management'. Both these courses take their texts from the Report of the Plowden Committee on *The Control of Public Expenditure* and are intended to improve the management efficiency of senior administrators. The course for Assistant Secretaries includes a session with a psychologist on 'Understanding People' and a session with a departmental Information Officer on Public Relations.

Training for Public Relations through Correspondence
A number of examples have now been given of the training provided for civil servants for the conduct of their relations with the public in person and on the telephone, two of the types of direct contact mentioned in the first paragraph of this chapter. The third type of contact, about which little has been said so far, is contact by letter.

Letter writing—the art of clear expression and the use of plain English—is taught to most of the grades mentioned in the preceding pages.

At all these courses, and generally within the Civil Service, the teaching of the use of English is based upon the works of Sir Ernest Gowers. Sir Ernest had been known for his interest in encouraging the use of good plain English in the Civil Service as long ago as 1929.[1] In 1948 the Stationery Office published his book *Plain Words* which had been specially commissioned by the Treasury as a guide to officials in the use of English. In the Epilogue to this book Sir Ernest says:

> The true justification for such a book is not so much that official English is specially bad as that it is specially important for it to be good. The efficiency of government, central and local, depends to an ever-increasing extent on the ability of a large number of officials to express themselves clearly. . . . I should be sorry to be thought to support the popular notion that officials write a language of their own of a uniquely deplorable kind. Undoubtedly they have their peculiar faults of style. So have journalists theirs. It is reasonable to attribute those of officialese in the main to the peculiar difficulties with which official writers have to

administration. (See H.C. Deb. [1962–3], c. 56.) This is a more ambitious scheme of training than any tried so far.

[1] Sir Ernest Gowers, 'Mainly about The King's English', *Public Administration*, Vol. VII, April 1929, pp. 182–91.

contend. As we have seen, much of what they write has to be devoted to the almost impossible task of translating the language of the law, which is obscure in order that it may be unambiguous, into terms that are simple and yet free from ambiguity. And our system of government imposes on them the need always of being cautious and often of avoiding a precision of statement that might be politically dangerous. . . .

It is generally recognized that, in their dealings with the public by post, government departments have made great improvements since a post-war House of Commons debate mentioning grubby acknowledgement slips and printed letters. The efforts made in the last ten years or so to escape from officialese have had some success. As well as training officials to improve their letter writing, much work has been done, sometimes by the Information Divisions with the help of the Central Office of Information, to make leaflets and forms simpler and clearer. Alterations in the rates of National Insurance contributions and the payment of increased benefits were smoothly administered largely as a result of efforts along these lines. The Post Office has recently reviewed all forms and letters addressed to the public to make them more friendly, easier to understand and better laid out.

However, once it is realized that civil servants do receive a good deal of training in letter writing and the use of clear English, it makes it even more annoying to find that, in spite of this training, it is still quite possible to receive a letter written in stilted officialese, or in a style so involuted that it is only understood with great difficulty by those who are reasonably educated.

There are various ways of accounting for the differences between the principles put over during training and the actual standard of some letters written to the public. First, it must to some extent be a reflection of the need for better, or more continuous, training on the job. Training on the job, as we emphasized at the beginning of the chapter, is probably the most important part of training. It is most likely that the effects of a training course, however good, will fade away if the principles taught on the course do not continue to be taught in the course of every day work for a long time after the course has finished. It may be too that many of those working in the supervisory grades have neither the time nor the ability to teach other people how to write better, simpler and clearer letters.

Secondly, departmental training officers complain of the declining emphasis the educational system puts upon grammatical construction and syntax, so that for example Clerical Officers entering the service with five GCE passes, need considerable training before they can do even simple drafting.

There is also the size of the problem. When the thousands of officials in the Clerical and Executive Grades and the millions of letters they write every year are considered, it cannot be surprising to find many letters that are not as well written as they ought to be. Sir Ernest Gowers makes the point strongly:

> . . . It is certainly wrong to imagine that official writing, as an instrument for conveying thought, is generally inferior to the lamentably low standard now prevalent except among professional writers. It is not only the official who yields to the lure of the pompous or meretricious word, and overworks it; it is not he alone who sometimes fails to think clearly what meaning he wants to convey by what he is about to write, or to revise and prune what he has written so as to make sure that he has conveyed it. From some common faults he is comparatively free. Most officials write grammatically correct English. Their style is untainted by the silly jargon of commercialese, the catchpenny tricks of the worst sort of journalism, the more nebulous nebulosities of politicians, or the recondite abstractions of Greek or Latin origin in which men of science, philosophers and economists too often wrap their thoughts. Sometimes it is very good, but then no one notices it. Occasionally it reaches a level of rare excellence.
>
> The fact is not that officials do uniquely badly but that they are uniquely vulnerable. Making fun of them has always been one of the diversions of the British public. . . . The field for its exercise and the temptation to indulge in it are constantly growing. . . . So many people have to read so many official instructions. These offer a bigger target for possible criticism than any other class of writing except journalism, and they are more likely to get it than any other class, because a reader's critical faculty is sharpened by being told—as we all so often have to be nowadays—that he cannot do something he wants to, or must do something he does not want to, or that he can only do something he wants to by going through a lot of tiresome formalities.[1]

CONCLUSION

Civil servants, as this chapter has indicated, are aware of the problems of relations with the public, and a good deal of effort goes into training officials, especially for the lower grades and especially for those involved in personal encounters with the public. Whether enough thought is given to training the top grades of the service, who do not come into contact in a very direct way with the ordinary citi-

[1] Sir Ernest Gowers, *Plain Words*, HMSO, 1948, p. 92.

zen but whose activities affect almost everything the ordinary citizen does, is more doubtful. There is some training for the higher grades, and the new course for Assistant Principals is perhaps a move towards teaching the techniques of good administration in a more formal and organized way. Nevertheless it may perhaps be a reflection of the Treasury's attitude to training that the offices occupied by the Treasury's own Training Division must be amongst the most dismal and most unwelcoming of all government premises visited during the course of this study.

CHAPTER IX

Comment and Conclusion

The information services are young compared with most parts of the administrative machine; they are a modern intervention in the process of communication between the government and the governed. The aim of this final chapter is to review the reasons for having government information services, and to show what difference their existence has made; and to suggest some ways in which their scope might be enlarged.

The account given in the earlier chapters of the work done by the information services should have convinced the reader that there is a good deal of officially inspired information around, perhaps more than he might have supposed. In the newspapers and in radio and television programmes there is factual information based on press releases from government departments, and there are political comments and general articles inspired by informal talks with Ministers or with press officers; advice on health education appears in women's magazines; there are 'Keep Britain Tidy' and Civil Defence posters in the streets; there are advertisements for police and prison officers, and for premium bonds. On the television screen we see 'shorts' on life in the Army, the need for foster parents, or blood donors; we get pamphlets explaining our duties and rights under the Welfare State, and our children get booklets about their careers; the local authorities get guidance about building standards for old people's housing; we can buy guides to Stonehenge, or to the annual Economic Survey. All these are the work of the information services.

THE NEED FOR A SPECIALIZED INFORMATION SERVICE

Without pressing the parallel too closely, some of the same reasons which nowadays put the public relations expert between the manufacturer and the consumer in the commercial world—namely the variety and complexity of goods offered, the increasing size of the general public and its increasing sophistication, and the growth of the mass means of publicity—apply also to the information officer in the Civil Service. It is not enough to chalk 'hands wanted' outside

183

the Employment Office to overcome a shortage of skilled technicians; if you want recruits for the army you don't put up a notice in the Athenaeum. Public relations has become more complex.

First, the information to be grasped nowadays is much more diverse and more complicated than that which our grandfathers had to digest. The modern informed citizen is expected to understand general economic problems, political events happening on the other side of the world, detailed instructions about his tax liability or his obligations and rights as a welfare state citizen. Secondly, the size of the interested public has also greatly expanded. On the one hand, there is universal literacy and a working class with more to spend; on the other, the modern state is much more concerned in economic activity and assumes responsibility for the health, education and general welfare of all its citizens. Explanations of these actions need to reach all citizens and reports of parliamentary debates do not meet the need. Thirdly, the means of communication have been enlarged. Besides the printed word, radio, television, and large scale advertising are all channels of communication, and they have voracious appetites. If they are to be fed, government departments have to be organized to provide a flow of accurate and reliable official news.

In fact, the information services grew up in response to a practical need. Some departments acted in response to pressure from the press itself; others acted in self-defence, as a means of defending busy administrators from the unwelcome attentions of journalists. In the Service Ministries and the Post Office there was something to 'sell' to the public which warranted a special section to do nothing else.

The information services proved themselves a convenience to the press too. Given the increasing complexity of public administration, it was frustrating and time-wasting for a journalist to have to find an informed source from the rabbit warrens of Whitehall every time he wanted to ask a question. Now, an inquirer can start off with the Press Officer and if he is knowledgeable about his subject he will not have much difficulty in learning what he wants to know, either direct from the Information Service or with their help from another branch of the Ministry. If the journalist is one of the groups—the Lobby, Diplomatic, Industrial or other special correspondents—he will expect and get a regular flow of news and comments from the appropriate Information Section.

Expanded data, an enlarged public and ampler means of communication combine to require specialization in the presentation and handling of news and publicity. Recruitment too is in direct competition with private industry and commerce. Private organizations compete with all the weapons in the public relations armoury, as well as offering better salaries and conditions of service than those which many of the social services can offer. The services of the expert publicist is needed for this, too. It is not that Ministers and civil servants could not master the techniques of handling news and publicity, but that the complexity and size of the task makes it compulsory to have fulltime practitioners.

In nearly every department, then, the work of information is the province of experts who have learned their skills on Fleet Street or in one or other aspect of the publicity world. Some administrators and executive officers may from time to time serve in an Information Division as part of their careers, but most government information work is in the hands of specialists.

The Position of the Chief Information Officer

But experts are not policy makers, and although the Chief Information Officer in most departments is the equivalent of Assistant Secretary in rank, and probably has, because of his special knowledge, more influence with the Minister and the officials at the head of his department than the ordinary Assistant Secretary, there is no transfer from the top of the Information Service into the administrative class. Nor probably would there be any such transfer, even if the rank of Chief Information Officer were raised to Under Secretary level.[1]

The Administrative Class is recruited from the best brains of the university, and a good Oxford or Cambridge degree is the usual preliminary to entrance.[2] Chief Information Officers are rarely graduates, and are even more unlikely to be graduates of the older universities. The status of the Chief Information Officer vis-à-vis the administrator, is, in the classic words of Kai Lung 'equal and below'.[3] He is a technician among the gentlemen amateurs. They will value and consult him as an expert, but he is not one of the administrative mandarins.

THEIR ADAPTATION TO POLITICAL CONDITIONS SINCE 1945

This general acceptance of the role of publicity or information in

[1] For civil service grades see Chapter VII, Table 2.
[2] It is true that many of the Administrative Class are nowadays promoted from the Executive Grade and may not have been to a university at all.
[3] It is significant that the highest honour awarded to an information officer was the baronetcy given to Sir Harold Evans, an honour which is usually reserved for non-civil servants.

departmental work has come about only gradually. As we have seen in Chapter III, in the early post-war days when the Information Divisions were first set up in their present form, there were doubts.

The need for *some* provision to be made for public information by government departments was not seriously denied. What was questioned, and very frequently during the Labour Governments of 1945–51, was whether the departmental information services were impartial or whether they were being used to put forward a specifically left-wing viewpoint, especially in economic matters, and especially by the Economic Information Unit of the Treasury. The existence of the Central Office of Information and the nature of the work it performed on behalf of other government departments on the home front was also criticized as unnecessary and extravagant. The Labour Government, using these services, said that the public had a right to be told how its money was being spent and a need to know the results of the national effort towards increased productivity and improved export figures.

It was only when the Conservative Party themselves took office that they accepted officially conducted publicity as a part of the apparatus of modern government, and continued to use the techniques of economic explanation and exhortation which they inherited. Information officers who had been implementing the Labour Government's economic information programmes continued in office; Conservative Ministers came to accept them as technical experts, not engaged nor interested in expounding a political point of view.

Having survived the change of government for well over a decade, the information services appear to be here to stay.

The information services have become established—in both senses of the word. The individual officers have become established in the technical sense as career civil servants, instead of temporaries who might go back to their original jobs if the Minister or the policy changed, and the information services have become established as part of the government machine. This has made a great deal of difference to the position and influence of information officers. They are accepted as servants of the department, like any other officer, who can be expected to serve his Minister without political bias, offering impartial advice as a professional in his own field.

New Ministers may need training in the delicate business of what is and is not party propaganda. With almost twenty years' experience behind them, information officers can speak with enough authority to be able to oppose a Minister if necessary, and Ministers have enough experience not to force the issue with borderline material, but to publicize it through the political party office.

There may possibly also be a more general reason why controversy over the activities of the information services died down between 1951 and 1964. Much of the sting went out of political controversy generally when the Conservatives came into power, and the information services shared in the relative peace. The more striking arguments of recent years—the Vassal tribunal and the Profumo case—were quarrels between Ministers and the press, and the information services were not involved.[1]

Nor does it seem likely that the old controversies will be raised again, even with the Labour Party in power and starting to pursue economic and social policies—like nationalization—very different from those of the Conservative administration. It would be impossible for a Conservative Opposition seriously to maintain that the information services which had worked under them for over twelve years had suddenly become politically biased the other way.

The information services, then, have been accepted by both the major political parties; and the press and the departments take for granted, for a variety of reasons, that government publicity is a good thing.

THEIR SIGNIFICANCE FOR THE MAJOR ORGANS OF GOVERNMENT

The term 'government' can be used to mean different things. Sometimes it means Parliament, sometimes the political party in power and sometimes the department. All three are the 'government'; and Ministers, as Members of Parliament, as members of their own party and as heads of their departments are concerned with all three. The information services are not. They are almost exclusively concerned with the last—namely communication between the department and the public. But they have some concern with the other two, and we will look at their relationships with all three.

Parliament

The constitutional theory is that Parliament is the main point of contact between government and people. The government's first duty is to the elected representatives of the people in the House of Commons. It is to Parliament—not the press—that the government makes its announcements and defends its policies. The Minister addresses to

[1] Except marginally, when information and press officers in the Service Ministries gave evidence to the Vassal tribunal.

his fellow Members of Parliament a statement of his government's proposals, and the public is informed of this through the press and radio and television reports. This is not only the theory; it is also the practice. But it is not the whole story. Government activity goes on all the year round, even when Parliament is not sitting, and therefore needs publicity all the year round. Again in the popular press, Parliament is often by-passed as a news focus unless the debate is a very important one. If an issue of great public interest is being aired, or if a debate may influence a government's standing, or even end its life, then it is true that people pay attention to it. But more often than not the monolithic party system means that most debates are unreal; the press and public are only mildly interested, if at all. The educative function of Parliament has shrunk.

The role of Parliament as Bagehot saw it—the nation's grand assize —is frequently lost amid the increasing volume and complexity of to-day's affairs. Moreover, even when government statements in Parliament have a bearing on the lives of ordinary citizens, they need interpretation. The Minister makes his pronouncements to 600 MPs, but they are intended to be understood by 40,000,000 other adults of very varied background and education. The press and broadcasting act as middlemen; but they in turn, with their problems of deadlines, need the information supplied to them at a time and in a form they can use, if they are to do more than print selections from or summaries of debates. This then, is one of the functions of the information services, as we have seen in Chapter I. When the Minister is to make an important speech, or issue a White Paper[1] or a Blue Book, it is the Information Division which sees that the press statement is drafted, the Lobby has had a background briefing and the White Paper or Committee Report has been circulated under embargo in advance. Indeed, it would be impossible for the press to report adequately on the contents of a long royal commission or committee report—sometimes several hundreds of pages long—without the interval an embargoed press notice and advance circulation afford.

These practices have grown up in response to the demands of press, radio and television and in recognition of public need. It might well be argued that they derogate from the prestige of Parliament in the sense that the 'informed comment' of the free media is based on confidential information and discussions to the detriment of straight reporting of Parliamentary debates. In practice, the choice

[1] White Papers themselves are increasingly becoming information documents addressed to the general public rather than exclusively to Parliament.

would normally be between reports assisted in this way by the information services, or none.

There is also another difficulty. The risk of using the mass media as the main means of communication is that the amount of space or time devoted to a subject depends in the end on what the editor decides. Information on serious matters is in competition with other forms of attention getting; it is often used only when it has entertainment value. The fact that *The Economist* or *The Times* publishes a series of balanced and well-informed articles about subjects of fundamental importance is obviously no evidence that the electorate in general is informed about it. The popular press and radio and television, aiming at a wide audience, find it natural to give ample publicity to proposals affecting the daily lives of large sections of the population. But public education in this sense should range wider than such matters as increased National Insurance and Health Service charges. It is important that there should be a well-informed public opinion on, for example, Commonwealth, Foreign and Defence matters. Indeed, whereas 'to educate our masters' might once have been regarded as a party political task, it is becoming increasingly agreed that it is nowadays a job that government information services should help to do. In this sense, the government information services and Parliament are on the same side of the fence; they are both trying to get the public's attention for more serious matters in competition with *Coronation Street* or the football results. Even ten years ago Parliament complained sometimes that too much information was being issued direct to the press, by-passing the convention that government announcements should be released only through the House. But Parliament itself is losing ground in competition with the increasingly effective attempts of other organizations of many kinds to achieve publicity. On the new medium, television for example, the proceedings of Parliament are sketchily reported and there is little visual impact to back them up. Parliament is in no situation to disdain its allies. In so far as the activities of the information services win press space and television time for the subjects which are discussed in Parliament, they are not a rival to it but a collaborator in getting the public's attention focused on what it thinks is important.

The Political Party in Power
The Dividing Line between Political and Administrative Action. One condition of their playing an effective part in educating public opinion, is that the information services remain free of political entanglement.

They inevitably have to deal with subjects which are controversial, but Chief Information Officers believe that the dividing line between the political and the administrative, the controversial and the non-controversial is in practice fairly easily drawn. No charge of political bias has ever been properly sustained against the information services. Furthermore, there are no known cases of individual members of the information services having engaged in political controversy.

The convention is that they do not anticipate the decision of Parliament nor do they normally discuss matters which are subject to Parliamentary privilege—when a Question has been tabled, for example. The information services should not be involved in justifying the government's proposals before Parliament has approved the policy. They should only be employed, in theory, in pursuance of agreed ends and for administrative efficiency.

This is the theory, but it leaves several factors out of account. Controversial matters under discussion in Parliament are the very subjects which are interesting to the press and broadcasters, and the information officers are likely to have to answer questions while they are still being debated. Both Ministers and Chief Information Officers themselves may have to talk to Lobby correspondents and give off-the-record background information to other interested groups of journalists, in advance of legislation.[1] There is also the practice of the deliberate 'leak'. Information officers thus do not avoid involvement in topics of considerable political controversy. What attitude should they take? There is the view that the information officer is the mouth-piece of the government; that he provides accurate information of what the government's views are and their reasons for holding them, and debate can start from the assumption that he is putting forward the government's case. The press is perfectly free to get the views of the other side, whether it is the Parliamentary Opposition or the National Farmers' Union, the trade unions or the Employers' Federation.

The other view is that in a democracy the public have a right to expect impartiality from the information services; otherwise, the argument goes, there is a real danger of the government machine being used to further political ends. 'It is the job of the Official Information

[1] The party political machine is very much concerned with these aspects of the Minister's relations with Parliament and the press, but information officers are undoubtedly also involved in the process. They are normally in attendance when the Minister meets the Lobby and themselves make comments to correspondents in the absence of the Minister; this is especially important in the case of the Prime Minister's Public Relations Adviser, who, after all, sees Lobby correspondents daily.

Services,' said Lord Swinton when he was Co-ordinating Minister, 'to give prompt and accurate information and to give it objectively day by day about Government action and Government policy. It is quite definitely not the job of the Government Information Services to try and boost the Government or to try and persuade the press to do so.'[1]

The whole question of impartiality is a very difficult one. A case is made by the very selection of facts, by their presentation, and by the omission of others. No educated person is unaware that apparently impartial statistics can tell lies. Even factual statements about the benefits of vaccination or water fluoridation offend small but vocal oppositions, who would not consider them impartial. How much notice should be taken of such opposition views? The views of Parliamentary minorities are usually taken into account; the views of every health crank are not. The information officer will often have to rely on his own judgement. It also depends on the occasion on which information is being given. There are different kinds of information 'statement' which an Information Division puts out, and different considerations apply to them. First, when the information officer is clearly acting as a spokesman for his Minister or his department's view, the press would not expect these statements to be impartial: the Civil Service, including the Information Division, is there to help Ministers. Oral comment is expected to be more free than the written word, and it is clear that on these occasions the information officer is putting forward his department's line or policy, usually on a non-attributable basis, and usually speaking fairly informally, for background information. But there are two other kinds of 'information statement'—press releases, and publicity in the paid media—books, posters, pamphlets, films and so on. How far should these make the government's case without giving any weight to opposing views?

Press releases should be, and usually are purely factual, although the press would not expect Ministerial press releases actually to make points for the Opposition.

Paid-for publicity material, on the other hand, should surely be impartial. The convention has grown up that the information services give the public, usually through the press and broadcasting, the background of facts against which proposed legislation—or other forms of action—can be set. Facts about matters under political discussion can be given to the press when they ask for it, but public money is not spent on producing paid publicity about a controversial subject still under consideration. There is a difference between spend-

[1] Conservative Party Conference, 1953.

191

ing only staff time on answering questions or supplying information for the press and broadcasting, and the deliberate spending of public monies to produce an advertisement or book or pamphlet to advocate or even explain government proposals. Comment in such publications should be conspicuous by its absence, and argument should be left to Parliament and the press.

By and large this convention has been adhered to since 1951, but there have been one or two exceptions. In 1953 the Ministry of Housing and Local Government issued a popular leaflet *Operation Rescue* to explain the Conservative Government's proposed Bill on Housing Repairs and Rents. This was issued before Parliament had had a chance to debate the Bill and not only was legislation in prospect, it was fairly imminent. The leaflet went somewhat beyond mere explanation of the proposed measures towards setting out the objectives of government policy on housing rents and repairs generally. The Opposition sharply criticized its issue. 'This is clearly a propaganda pamphlet published for the purpose of popularizing a Bill which has not yet been presented to the House of Commons', said the then Mr Herbert Morrison,[1] and went on to add that it was quite unlike the 'popular' Economic Survey, which was purely factual. Although they did not admit the pamphlet was wrong, the Conservative Government took the lesson to heart and has not been criticized since then for this kind of propaganda.

The second example of the problem of issuing impartial statements about the government's intention was the publication, in March 1962, by the Central Office of Information on behalf of the Treasury, of a booklet *Britain and the European Communities*.

The nearest parallel to the issue of such a piece of paid-for publicity on a subject very much under discussion in Parliament and the press at the time was perhaps the publication under the Labour Government of popular versions to explain the White Papers on the National Health Service and the National Insurance schemes.

Britain and the European Communities seems to have been different. Parliament had agreed that negotiations for Britain's entry into the Common Market should start, but no legislation was pending. The reason for publishing the booklet was, it is understood, that the press were asking the government to provide such a statement on the facts and figures behind the negotiations. If so, this would appear to have been a new kind of demand for information from the government about current issues, for popular consumption, and it came from sources which had previously taken the line that this was a job for

[1] Debate on the Address, November 1953.

newspapers and private effort only. The fact that the booklet sold well over 50,000 copies indicated that there was a real demand for such a factual background on a complicated subject.

The Treasury Information Division therefore issued the pamphlet, intending it to be an impartial assessment of the situation which could be used as a quarry for facts by anyone who wished to inform himself about the issues involved, whether he was for or against entry, and before the negotiations were finally settled. This again would appear to be a new departure; up to 1962 actual negotiations had only been explained by the information services after the event.

The reasons for issuing the booklet were then a departure from the usual course of events. No one would suggest it was a piece of deliberate propaganda trying to produce a climate of opinion favourable to entry into the Common Market, but its contents might also be criticized as being a somewhat selective array of facts.

No one would learn from this pamphlet that there were any economic arguments against going into the Common Market. The only economic point mentioned in the pamphlet on the other side was that food prices might go up. The prospects of an increase in imports was one of the matters omitted and the ultimate loss of Commonwealth preference for British goods another. Mr Gaitskell, in a speech three or four months after the booklet was published, rated the economic arguments for and against balanced at about fifty-fifty. A number of those who favoured British entry on political grounds would not have differed. It is not at all the conclusion to which the booklet pointed.

Some people believed, too, that there was a serious political risk of Britain losing its independence by joining Europe: this point, again, is not mentioned in the booklet. There is no need to labour in detail all the points which could be made showing that the information in the booklet was one-sided.[1]

It is true that the pamphlet was greeted with no public criticism, either by the press or by the Opposition in Parliament. The press only complained that the pamphlet ought to have been provided much earlier.[2] This was, no doubt, because when it was published opposition to entry into the Common Market had not crystallized along party

[1] For example by choosing 1954 as a base year, the figures used show the rapid economic growth of the Common Market countries, but do not reveal the fact that they grew faster in the three years before the Market started than the three years after.

[2] The Beaverbrook press gave the pamphlet a hostile notice, but a very brief one.

lines; if the booklet had been written after Mr Gaitskell's speech which expounded the case against entry into the Common Market, no doubt it would have been drafted differently. On the other hand, there is a real problem when a government department wants to give the public information about its future intentions. It may be that the interests of democracy are *not* always best safeguarded by the convention that matters are not publicized while they remain the subject of debate. It may also be argued that the public also has a right to be informed about legislative proposals before they become law, and about negotiations with other countries before they become a *fait accompli*. But surely the information services should not leave it to the Opposition to establish that there are two sides to a question.

The Existence of Government Information Helps the Party in Power. However impartial they are, and however much they try to avoid political entanglement, whether they issue plain statements of fact or explain policy, the existence of the information services undoubtedly helps the government of the day, and helps to get its policy accepted. It means that the party in office has a means of putting out information which is not available to the Opposition. The Opposition, it is true, has equally free access to the press, radio and television, but the activities of Ministers are nearly always more newsworthy than those of their opposite numbers out of office. Also, Ministers of the Crown are always much better briefed than their opposite numbers—either at press conferences or in debates. That is one of the advantages of being in office, and one of the advantages of being a Minister with the Civil Service working for you. The existence of the information services does help the government of the day, just as the existence of lawyers, statisticians and ordinary administrators in the Civil Service also helps them. It would be as unrealistic to treat this aspect of information work as a ground for the abolition of the information services, as it would be to argue that because an efficient Civil Service tends to increase the prestige of the government, the Civil Service should be either inefficient or abolished.

The Position of Ministers. All Ministers have a dual position as heads of their departments and also as members of their own political party; the line between the two is not always clear cut.

Information officers are not supposed to act as the personal public relations officers for their Ministers.[1] An information officer might sometimes be expected to defend his Minister in public on a matter of controversy, and letters sometimes appear from them in the correspondence columns of the press correcting mis-statements of fact. On the other hand, some newspapers—*The Times*, at one period—will not print such letters because they feel they should be written by the Minister himself, if at all.

Photographs of Ministers opening new schools, hospitals and colleges, plus glossy brochures about the armed forces and less glossy pamphlets about other careers, may contribute to the building up of a favourable ministerial 'image', but it also publicizes the new school and increases army recruitment. Moreover, the issuing of such copy by information officers does not ensure their publication.

When Ministers make speeches, the rule is clear—the government information services only operate on official occasions, and they publicize the speeches only by the issuing of a press statement. These statements are used extensively only when there is a strong non-political content in the speech; for example, when the Minister of Education appeals for married women to return to the teaching profession, or the Minister of Labour exhorts industrial firms to increase the opportunities for training and apprenticeships. If the Minister speaks on a party platform or on a party occasion, publicity must only be given through the Party Central Office; the Information Division does not give any press facilities for such a speech. Indeed there has been friction occasionally between Ministers and their Chief Information Officers on this point, but by now Ministers realize that political propaganda is the job of the press and public relations staff of the headquarters of the political parties themselves, not the Information Divisions. The Labour Party lost office in 1951 and the Conservatives won the next three general elections without anyone suggesting that activities of the information services had anything to do with either event.

So far as the content of a Minister's speech is concerned, practice varies from department to department. In some, the Information Division rarely writes or sees the Minister's speeches, in others—such as the Treasury with its specialized briefing section—material is provided for most Ministerial speeches and for some Ministers out-

---

[1] The Opposition is usually alert to point out any dangers in this direction, e.g. Mr Harold Wilson said in the *Journal of the Institute of Public Relations*, April 1962, 'I am not sure if some publicity conscious Ministers of the present government are not improperly using the public relations facilities of their departments.'

side the Treasury. The Treasury briefing section would also expect to provide basic economic material for a speech which the Minister could then use, if he wished, in a party political broadcast. But the difference would be that, for an official speech, they might prepare a draft of the whole thing—'including the jokes'. For party occasions, they would simply provide basic economic facts, which the Minister could use as he liked. Indeed, no doubt they would provide such basic economic facts for anyone who asked them, including Opposition spokesmen.

The Co-ordinating Minister. This dual position could be particularly difficult in the case of a Minister who held a job in the government as Co-ordinator of the Information Services and who also held a position of authority within his own political party. (The anxiety on this point which was voiced in some quarters during the early months that Dr Charles Hill was co-ordinating Minister proved to be unfounded.) The most important topic of any one week may well be discussed both at the meeting of the Chief Information Officers within the Civil Service, and by the party headquarters when back benchers are briefed at their weekly meeting, and the Co-ordinating Minister may be present on both occasions. But he does not brief the back benchers and the information officers' discussions would give the party no help in presenting their case or discussing their tactics. Co-ordinating Ministers have said that they felt no strain in filling both roles.

The Department
The Internal Effect on the Department. Experience has shown that when any organization starts a public relations department, the action ends by educating the organization itself even more than it affects the general public. 'The recoil effect is greater than the muzzle blast'.[1] The Civil Service has not proved an exception. The existence of an Information Division within departments has tended to set in order the department's own thinking about the public relations aspect of its work.

In a democracy, the citizens can reach informed and intelligent opinions only if they have the raw material on which to base them— and this is often not available from any except government sources. 'Departments now realize to a far greater degree than ever before the duty of making available to the public in an impartial and objective way, information and matters of general interest within their spheres;

[1] Rose Heilbroner, *Harper's Magazine*, 1957—an article on the effect of public relations on commercial organizations.

not with a view to supporting some particular feature of policy but rather to enable public discussion to take place against a background of improved knowledge.'[1]

Housing Information Divisions separately in each major government department and not in one central Ministry of Information has helped this 'recoil effect'. Administrators and information officers have had to live together and share the same problems. Public relations has become the concern of the whole department, just as the whole department is the concern of the Public Relations Division.

The Department's Effect on the Information Division. Conversely, with no Minister of Information, each Information Division is loyal to its own Minister and its own department. Information officers are nowadays established civil servants. They are not appointed or dismissed by a particular Minister, and they are independent of any particular party or policy. But they are independent only in the special sense that the Civil Service is independent of politics in this country. The information officer does not take a strong and independent line. He is the servant of his Minister and his department; he would not normally resign if called upon to support a policy of which he disapproved, any more than any other civil servant. The information services have proved that they can perform their functions for either political party without changing their apparatus or their personnel;[2] they have demonstrated that they are free of political bias.

It might be argued that a good information officer ought to be able also to stand aside from his own departmental 'view', if he is going to guide his Minister and his colleagues when they are influencing people through the organs of press and publicity, and if he is going to be able to tell his colleagues how their work looks from the outside. It is more difficult and more important for him than for ordinary civil servants not to be convinced of his department's 100 per cent rightness on all occasions, because the nature of his job forces him to seek publicity. This has nothing to do with political pressures—it may be about the expulsion of an alien, or a wage negotiation, or a piece of advice to a local authority. The criticism here is that at a time when people are becoming increasingly uneasy about the arrogance of the State when challenged by the individual, the information services, if they act entirely as advocates for their

[1] A statement made by Lord Bridges and quoted by Mr S. C. Leslie, 'Their Lordships Inform Us', *The Times*, June 16, 1959.

[2] With the possible exception of the post of the Prime Minister's Adviser on Public Relations.

departments, throw their weight on the side of bureaucracy. This danger is even more obvious in those areas of information where the government has a monopoly—in defence matters and in the field of government statistics generally. If a government department deliberately or inadvertently gives out wrong information in these fields, how can it be disproved? This is an indication of how far the Civil Service, at first suspicious of the new techniques, has nowadays adopted information work as part of its own thinking. Like the Chinese Empire, the Civil Service eventually absorbs most intruders and makes them its own. This is both a weakness and a strength for the information services. The strength is that Information Divisions have overcome the initial suspicion and gained the confidence and co-operation of their departments. The Chief Information Officers who have been interviewed have all emphasized the good relations they enjoy with their administrative colleagues and the feelings of mutual trust and friendliness they have. The disadvantage is that a Chief Information Officer perhaps could do more genuine information work if he could sometimes stand aside from the narrow departmental field of vision. The temptation to be 'one of the boys' with the officials of his own department can exercise a subtle pressure towards assuming that the department is always right.

THE CASE FOR EXPANDING SOME ASPECTS OF GOVERNMENT INFORMATION

There was at one time—and it is still sometimes heard—the view that a government department would be far better off without putting out any propaganda at all. The best refutation of this is the account which has been given of the information services' work in this book.

They issue routine publicity to make regulations intelligible to the outsider; publicity to persuade people to carry out tasks at the express direction of Parliament—what to do in an outbreak of foot and mouth disease for example; goodwill publicity to persuade people to use community services like pre-natal clinics or welfare foods; and informative publicity to make better known some work in progress. The practical value of, for example, DSIR research depends on what use is made of it by outside organizations or individuals.

The following suggestions for new types of action are not put forward as firm recommendations; this should be clearly understood. They are set down as possibilities, with supporting reasons.

Is There Too Much Reliance on the Free Media?

The kinds of publicity mentioned above cannot be left to the ephemeral pages of the daily press; recruitment for the armed forces and the social services must be continuous; laws and regulations must be constantly enforced and permanently available for reference. It would be unreasonable to expect the free media of press and television to carry out this kind of direct publicity for the government.

The information services are also concerned with encouraging the free media to give space and time to matters being discussed in Parliament, and to other serious topics which are the concern of their department. For most purposes, the free media normally serve the department well. Where public discussion is needed, the subject is usually newsworthy and, accordingly, a press statement or the abstract of a Ministerial speech will be fully utilized by the press, radio and television. The free media will also frequently follow up a government announcement or the publication of a royal commission report with feature articles and discussion programmes.

But the free media of communication are really free; they can publish what they wish, can seek out news whenever and wherever it occurs and can comment freely on it without government censorship. They can also, if they wish, entirely fail to give any space at all, or very little space, to something which they think would not interest their readers. Only the BBC is really free from the pressures of the market place, and they think about their audience reaction. If the free media fail to give enough attention to matters of moment, should the government information service remain content? Is it sufficient to leave the press and broadcasting to be the supreme arbiters of what is important for the public to know and what they shall be ignorant of? There is very little evidence to show that anyone but the top 4 per cent or 5 per cent of the public have much knowledge of the real issues of the day. If this is true, is it enough that the government information services should be regarded solely as disseminators of factual information and their role of public educators fall entirely by the wayside?

The state has an obligation to tell its citizens about their duties and rights as householders, as consumers and as beneficiaries of the Welfare Society. Should the information services go further than this to educate its citizens? If so—how? Is it right to produce paid-for publicity as a basis for discussion for proposed legislation or other government activity? Where should the line be drawn between information and propaganda? Should it be strictly factual only? Is it good enough to give the press background information and leave them to decide on the space and treatment to be given? What should Information Divisions do if there is a press silence on a topic which the government think is of vital importance—smoking and lung cancer, for example?

Moreover, if the government fails in its role of public educator, may there not be a risk that others—pressure groups, the political parties, or someone else—may assume this responsibility? And a government whose proposals offended a major and wealthy interest group might find itself faced with a barrage of adverse paid-for publicity with no means of redress, when the success of its proposals might rest on public confidence which had been eroded in advance. If one of the aims of the government information services is to supplement Parliament in its role of public educator, it seems invidious that the public should only be educated by them after the event of legislation.

Is Government Publicity Limited Too Much by Financial Considerations?
Government publicity is inevitably limited by finance. The nationwide distribution of literature and advertising when PAYE was introduced, for example, has nowadays been replaced by carefully selective distribution of information material. But it must get to the right place at the right time. When the National Insurance graduated pension scheme was being prepared it was not heralded by publicity on a national scale, but by the circulation to trade unions and employers of explanatory literature. Employers and employees had the job of discussing whether they would go in for the government scheme or whether they would opt out. The Ministry of Pensions and National Insurance relied on the employers and trade union leaders to disseminate the information supplied, and on the press to supplement this work.

It is doubtful whether this was really adequate. The scheme was a complicated one. It was covered by the press only when the necessary legislation was pending in 1961 and very little during the period when the groups concerned were having to decide, in 1960. The more serious press—*The Economist*, trade union journals and employers' journals—did, during this period, publish details of the scheme. But these journals have a very limited circulation. They do not reach the average rank and file members of the trade unions, or many small employers. Discussion at shop floor and union branch level tended to be ill-informed.

Concentration on selective publicity and information—on giving

information, other than through the free media, only to specified
groups or on request—has obvious advantages on the financial side.
But there are some subjects which involve the population to such an
extent that the 'right to know' should perhaps be regarded as of para-
mount importance.

The restriction of funds for paid-for publicity has further unfortunate effects. It may be a false economy to restrict advertising and
publicity for recruits to the home help services, for example, when the
alternative of taking more old people into care, may cost the community much more. In recruitment to these and other services the
government is in competition with private industry and commerce
and must act accordingly, even if it takes more money. Government
departments, too, offer many services to the general public which are
financed out of public funds. New employment exchanges have been
built and the Ministry of Labour provides disablement and youth
employment officers, factory inspectors and industrial relations
officers. The National Assistance Board exists to help those in difficulties. But the simple provisions of such services will not of itself
lead the public to use them, nor to give them a favourable image if
they are still considered as 'the Labour' or 'Public Relief'. It should
be the concern of Information Divisions if such a public image dis-
courages people from getting the help from government agencies to
which they are entitled. Also it should not be necessary for regional
officers of the Ministry of Labour to spend considerable amounts of
their own time, as well as their own money in some cases, to con-
struct exhibitions showing the services offered and work done by
Employment Exchanges. It should not be necessary, to give another
example from the Ministry of Labour, for a member of the public
actually to have to walk into an Employment Exchange before he
sees a poster informing him of the existence of the Professional and
Executive Register.

Is The Inward Function of Information Ignored?
Some people feel that the collection of information about the public
for the public's own benefit as well as the administrative convenience
of the department—what has been called the inward function of
public relations should be more emphasized—seems to have received
the least attention from government departments.

'Nor is sufficient time, trouble and skill yet devoted to finding out,
as opposed to judging, or just guessing, what people know and think,
how they live, what questions they are asking. "Study your public"
remains the first rule of public relations and the least observed' said

the Director-General of the Central Office of Information, referring to government information services in other countries as well as Britain.[1] Social Survey is one of the methods in this country which might be used more for the collection of such information.

Also, it is by no means general practice for the Information Division to be responsible for a department's dealings with the public. The press know the name of the departmental press officer and can go to him direct. The general public, on the other hand, are not always so served. Their letters go to the appropriate policy division, and telephone queries or personal visitors go to the inquiry point which may or may not be attached to the Information Division.

It is not suggested that public inquiries and complaints should be entirely the business of the Information Division—it is essential, in fact, that they should be dealt with by the policy divisions concerned. Much is lost, however, of the inward functions of public relations when the Information Division is isolated from the processes for dealing with the general public. The Information Division might seem to be the appropriate division at least to collate available records about the dealings of the department with the public.

Consideration might be given to attaching the inquiry point to the Information Division, where this is not already so, and to maintain a systematic record of inquiries and complaints. The only form of record which is at present in fairly general use in the Information Division seems to be the daily log book maintained in press offices which records the main queries from the press and the answers given during the day for the guidance of the evening duty officer. It might also be useful to read the number of standard letters sent out over a particular period, interpreted in the light of reports from regional officers and information about numbers of telephone queries and complaints. This could produce information of value to the department about its public relations. At present the evidence of a failure of communications between a department and its public is largely impressionistic—the numbers of letters the Minister gets from his constituents, or from Members of Parliament, or the number of Questions tabled.

SUMMARY

These are some of the directions in which information work could be extended. They may not all be practicable; it could be argued that

[1] Mr Fife Clark speaking at a European Conference on 'Public Relations and the Civil Service', in Brussels, November 1962.

Comment and Conclusion

they are not all desirable. There are risks both ways. The government has a duty to keep its citizens informed, but the information services must not go too far in pressing the government's case. Some criticisms of their performance have been made in this chapter, but it must be emphasized that these are exceptions which only stand out because of the high standards which are normally maintained. The dangers are inherent in the situation, and the information services are very well aware of them. In the final analysis, the standards of performance depend on a watchful Opposition and the clash of political parties. If freedom of debate is missing, the information services of any country can be open to abuse.

This book will have failed in its purpose if it has not indicated that the performance of our information service yields a large balance on the credit side. The impression obtained by the observer is of the good and valued service given to the press and broadcasting; of a wide and widely-used range of publicity issued to the public, and of the enthusiasm and integrity of the members of the service doing the job.

Expenditure on the Information Services

We will first describe the budgeting procedure of the Central Office of Information in more detail than was possible in Chapter VI; this will show how the money is allocated and control over information spending is exercised. We will then consider how information expenditure has varied—how total spending has fluctuated over the last few years, how it has varied between departments, and between the different publicity media.

BUDGETING PROCEDURE

We have seen in Chapter V that all expenditure on publicity is carried on the Vote of the Central Office of Information, and for printing on that of the Stationery Office. Departments' own Votes for the information services are for staff salaries and their own operating services.

As a first step in the financial programme, the Central Office of Information asks user departments, each September, to state their likely requirements in the next financial year. When it submits proposed programmes to the Treasury, the Central Office of Information indicates how its total expenditure, including staff, is expected to be allocated among the various requesting departments. The net provision on the Central Office Vote for Information Services to be provided on behalf of the various departments is set out in the Financial Secretary's annual Memorandum on Civil Estimates for Revenue Departments.[1]

Treasury scrutiny at the Estimates stage is primarily directed at the departments whose requests are the basis of the proposed expenditure. Special considerations apply to one large block of expenditure in the United Kingdom, namely the recruiting campaigns for the Armed Services. In this case, the total size of the programme in each year is considered by an official committee set up by the Ministry of Defence,

[1] See Table 6

and a figure is agreed by them with the Treasury, in the light of the individual Service department's requirements.

When the Estimate has been approved, the Central Office of Information requires specific Treasury authority for individual projects or services requested by other departments, unless the expenditure is within certain general limits of authority delegated to the Central Office of Information by the Treasury and can be carried within the Vote provision. Operational expenditure on projects for overseas and on publicity for Services recruitment may be incurred up to a maximum of £2,500 non-recurrent or £100 a month recurrent without notification to Treasury. Subject to prior presentation to the Treasury of a copy of a department's request letter for the particular service, the delegated authority is raised to £5,000 non-recurrent or £200 a month recurrent. In respect of expenditure on home information services, other than for Services recruitment, the limits are £1,000 non-recurrent or £50 a month recurrent without notification to Treasury, and £2,500 non-recurrent or £100 a month recurrent, after the submission of the request letter to Treasury. There are some exceptions to these limits. The Central Office has no delegated powers in respect of Social Surveys (except for surveys carried out on behalf of the Post Office); the delegated authority for the production of individual books and pamphlets for free distribution in the United Kingdom is limited to £500; the delegated authority for the production of films for overseas distribution and for Services recruitment is £6,000, and for other home films £3,000. All services for the Post Office and the British Council may be provided without prior reference to the Treasury.

In addition, the Central Office of Information has discretionary power to authorize proposed expenditure on services which, for practical reasons, cannot be classified as being on behalf of a particular department or other body, with the proviso that the services concerned are clearly within the recognized functions of the Central Office of Information and that the estimated operational expenditure on any one service does not exceed £2,500 non-recurrent or £100 recurrent a month. The delegated authorities relate to combined expenditure on the Vote of the Central Office and the Vote of Her Majesty's Stationery Office, where use of Stationery Office services is involved.

THE CHANGING PATTERN OF INFORMATION EXPENDITURE

In considering the pattern of expenditure in the post-war years there are several factors that must be taken into account. There is first the change in total expenditure. Secondly, there are changes in the proportion of expenditure on different media of publicity and information; thirdly, the change in balance between spending on home and overseas information; fourthly, there is the change between the individual departments and between them and the common service departments, that is the Central Office of Information and the Stationery Office. There have been significant changes in all these aspects of expenditure since 1946 as needs and policy have changed. If the basic Table 6 below is split up in different ways, and compared with earlier years, it shows how emphasis has changed over the last fifteen years.

Total Information Expenditure
Broadly, the changes in total spending have been the immediate expansion of the post-war years, the economic crisis and retrenchment of the early fifties, and then expansion again in the early sixties after the 1957 Defence White Paper proposed the abolition of national service by the end of 1962, with its consequent need for increased recruiting drives. It would, however, not be a true picture if the basis for comparison was set in 1946. This was the year in which the Central Office of Information was established and expenditure in the two or three years after the war may have been affected by the teething troubles of the new service as well as the continuation of a certain number of wartime activities. The best year on which to base the comparison is probably 1949–50—the Estimates for information spending which the French Committee considered too high. The latest available Estimates are for the year 1963–4, and if we also look at a year about half-way between, namely 1955–6, we shall see how total spending has changed:

TABLE 1

ESTIMATED EXPENDITURE ON THE HOME INFORMATION
SERVICES
(£000's)

1949–50	1955–6	1963–4
5,168	2,245	5,156

Thus it can be seen that spending was reduced by more than half after the French Committee cuts, but has since gone back almost to the previous figure, although in real terms, £5,168 million in 1949–50 would represent about £8½ million now.

Spending on Different kinds of Public Media
There have been changes in the pattern of spending in the various

media since the early days. Here we look at the main items in the breakdown of the Central Office of Information Vote, which is the main spending department in paid-for publicity. These figures include spending on both home and overseas information, but they give an indication of how the emphasis has changed:

TABLE 2

CENTRAL OFFICE OF INFORMATION ESTIMATES
COMPARISON FOR THREE YEARS
(£'000's)

	1948–9	1955–6	1963–4
Gross Vote	4,134	1,664	8,266
Vote Net of appropriations in aid	3,548	1,425	6,203
Of which:			
Salaries	896	585	1,714
Travel, telephone telegrams and freight costs	269	78	642
Advertising	1,605	539	2,797
Publications	214	5	26
Films	782	205	1,206
Exhibitions	207	40	772
Photographs	73	20	93
Overseas books, etc.	—	—	317
Other press and publicity services, mainly overseas	—	104	441
Social Survey	—	56	258
Other expenditure	88	32	—
Total	4,134	1,664	8,266

Summary of Above Table

	Per cent of Total Spending		
Salaries	22	36	21
Freight costs, travel etc.	7	5	8
Advertising	39	32	34
Films	19	12	15
Exhibitions	5	2	9
Social Survey	—	3	3
Other	8	10	10
Gross vote	100	100	100

After the 'French' cuts, spending on advertising was cut to one-third, on films to a quarter, on exhibitions to a fifth. This made salaries and freight costs, etc., a higher proportion of total spending. Today, spending on exhibitions is much higher than in 1948 both in absolute figures and as a percentage of the total, but although advertising expenditure has risen very sharply, and that on films a little, as a percentage of total spending they have both fallen compared with the earliest period.

Division Between Spending on Home and Overseas Information

If we look at the whole picture of expenditure on the information services, we can see more clearly what difference the French Committee cuts made. The cuts were made to the home information services only, while the overseas side remained at almost the same figure. In 1949–50, one-third of total spending was on the home side; by 1955–6 it was only a fifth, and this proportion has remained, although actual spending has more than doubled on both sides. If we look at the Central Office of Information Vote alone, that is the spending on paid-for publicity, the contrast is even stronger. In 1949–50, spending on home publicity was nearly three times bigger than that on overseas information. The economy cuts affected the home side much more—they were reduced to less than a half. In 1963–4, although the home side was nearly as big as it was before the economy cuts, overseas spending rose very much more. Spending by the Central Office of Information on home and overseas publicity is now about equal.

TABLE 3 (A)*
(£000's)

	1949–50	1955–6	1963–4
Total Spending in Home Information Services	5,209 (32%)	2,245 (18%)	5,156 (17%)
Total Spending in Overseas Information Services	11,038 (68%)	10,496 (82%)	25,780 (83%)
Grand Total	16,247	12,741	30,936

TABLE 3 (B)
Central Office of Information Vote only

	1949–50	1955–6	1963–4
Gross Home Expenditure	2,535 (73%)	1,034 (62%)	2,347 (42%)
Gross Overseas Expenditure	924 (27%)	630 (38%)	3,269 (58%)
	3,459	1,664	5,616

* Memoranda from the Financial Secretary to the Treasury. Estimates of Information Expenditure for the various years.

Pattern of Departmental Expenditure

The pattern of departmental expenditure reflects changes in the order of priorities. In so far as departmental functions are the same now as they were thirteen years ago and thus comparable, the only departments which have substantially increased their information expenditure are the three Service departments, the Department of Scientific and Industrial Research, and the Home Office. The recruitment campaigns explain the Service departments' increases. More than half of the total information expenditure in 1963–4 was allocated to them. Similarly the increase in Home Office expenditure is largely explained by recruitment drives—recruiting for civil defence, mainly, and on a smaller scale for the police, probation officers, foster parents and the prison service. The Post Office, whose spending is now on its own Vote and is therefore not shown in the Financial Secretary's Memorandum, is also now a big spender on publicity; this is because it is nowadays pursuing a very active policy in publicizing its services including the new Subscriber Trunk Dialling telephone system, and Telstar. As a big commercial department, its experiences are different from those of other departments.

As we have seen in Chapter III above, up to 1949 there had been a policy—exemplified by the setting up of the Economic Information Unit in the Treasury—of economic education for the general public by means of films, posters, and advertisements which involved the government in considerable expenditure in paid publicity. In 1949–50, the top six spending departments in descending order were the Treasury, Ministry of Transport, Ministry of Food, National Savings Committee, Ministry of Labour and War Office, all of them with Estimates of over £400,000 each, accounting for £3 million or 62 per cent of the total between them.

In 1963–4, War Office spending alone grew to £1½ million or about 30 per cent of total spending. The other five departments which used to be at the top between them only account for about 20 per cent of the total. In the latest Estimates, the biggest spending departments after the War Office are the National Savings Committee, Air Ministry and the Admiralty at about half-a-million each, and no other home department approaches the size of these allocations. Only the Home Office spends more than a quarter of a million. The increases in departmental totals, then, are very largely the result of the increasing emphasis placed on the need for gaining recruits to the Armed Services in particular, but also for recruiting for civil defence and policemen. Some of the increase, too, is due to greater advertising activity by a commercial department like the Post Office.

TABLE 4

HOME INFORMATION EXPENDITURE
TOTALS BY DEPARTMENTS*

	1949–50	1963–4
Agriculture	149 ⎫	126
Food	507 ⎭	
Aviation	58	61
Education	66	40
Forestry	2	11
†Health	171	128
Home	47	263
†Town & Country Planning/Housing and Local Government	32	155
Labour	459	71
National Savings Committee	501	571
Pensions and National Insurance	36	5
Power	162	12
DSIR	56	176
Scottish Departments	157	162
Trade	319	37
Transport	530	198
Treasury	553	99
Works	72	84
Other Departments	360	352
Total Civil Departments	4,237	2,551
Admiralty	145	523
War Office	460	1,501
Air Ministry	327	566
Ministry of Defence	—	15
Service Total	932	2,605
Total	5,168	5,156

(See Table 6 for further details of 1963–4 Estimates.)

* These figures include spending by the Central Office of Information and Her Majesty's Stationery Office on behalf of each department. Not all departments are listed here, e.g. in the earlier period, expenditure on home information by the FO, CRO, and Colonial Office was not split from their overseas expenditure.

† The figures for these years are not strictly comparable as many of the functions formerly performed by the Ministry of Health passed over to the Ministry of Housing ad Local Government.

The Proportion of Spending by Departments, as opposed to the Central Office of Information and the Stationery Office

The heavier emphasis, with a few exceptions, on the use of the free media of press, radio and television means that the money which is spent on keeping the public informed of the activities of central government is as much to be found, on the departmental Vote for the salaries and expenses of their information staff as on the Central Office of Information Vote.

TABLE 5

(£000's)

Estimates	1949–50	1963–4
Salaries and staff expenses	502	1,042
Operational expenses*	1,977	1,388
Total paid for by Departments†	2,479	2,430
Provision on COI Vote	2,535	2,347
Provision on Stationery Office Vote	155	379
Total on Home Information	5,168	5,156

* This includes such items as window displays in recruiting offices, hire of films from the Central Film Library, repayments to Central Office of Information, etc.

† Post Office spending is included in the 1949–50 Estimates but excluded from the 1963–4 figures since the Post Office now bears its information expenditure on its own vote.

The amount paid for salaries has nearly doubled since 1949, but much of this reflects salary increases rather than bigger staff numbers. The total paid for by departments shown in the Table is now very slightly bigger than that paid by the Central Office of Information, whereas it used to be slightly smaller.

TABLE 6

DETAILED ANALYSIS OF SPENDING ON HOME INFORMATION SERVICES*

(Estimate for Home Information Expenditure, 1963–4; Memorandum by the Financial Secretary to the Treasury for the year ending March 31, 1964, Cmnd. 1965)

(£000's)

Department	Provision on Department's own Vote		Net provision on HMSO Vote	Net provision on COI Vote	Totals
	Salaries & Staff	Operational expenses† (net)			
Agri., Fish & Food	67·6	39·7	6·2	12·8	126·3
Aviation	24·5	0·7	3·1	32·3	60·6
Colonial Office	16·7	7·2	14·2	5·4	43·5
CRO	37·5	26·5	15·7	5·4	85·1
Education	17·5	10·5	5·8	6·6	40·4
Foreign Office	30·0	3·5	2·9	2·8	39·2
Forestry	5·8	4·9	—	—	10·7

Department	Provision on Department's own Vote Salaries & Operational expenses to Staff	expenses† (net)	Net provision on HMSO Vote	Net provision on COI Vote	Totals
Health (and National Health Service, Eng. and Wales)	25·4	95·5	4·8	1·8	127·5
Home	16·7	38·7	35·4	172·3	263·1‡
Housing and Local Government	25·0	22·0	17·5	90·3	154·8
Labour	42·8	1·3	11·5	15·7	71·3
National Savings	26·0	500·0	45·0	—	571·0
Pensions and National Insurance	3·3	0·1	0·6	0·8	4·8
Power	11·8	—	—	—	11·8
DSIR	48·5	37·1	7·2	83·3	176·1
Scottish Ag. Ed. Home and Health Depts.	30·8	53·7	10·5	26·2	121·2‡
Scottish Savings	3·3	38·0	—	—	41·3
Tech. Co-operation	5·3	—	3·6	8·5	17·4
Trade	29·2	—	6·4	1·2	36·8
Transport	27·1	125·0	8·2	38·1	198·4‡
Treasury and Subord. Depts.	57·7	—	18·7	22·3	98·7
Works	32·7	2·8	9·8	39·0	84·3
Other Home	20·8	1·2	3·8	4·1	29·9
Resid. expenditure	—	—	4·8	129·0	133·8
Totals for Civil and Revenue Depts.	609·2	1008·4	235·7	697·9	2551·2
Admiralty	38·4	65·3	38·3	381·0	523·0
War Office	260·0	297·5	66·2	877·0	1500·7§
Air Ministry	119·4	16·7	38·8	390·7	565·6§
Ministry of Defence	14·7	0·5	—	0·3	15·5
	432·5	380·0	143·3	1649·0	2604·8
Total	1041·7	1388·4	379·0	2346·9	5156·0

* As the Post Office publicity expenditure is now on its own Vote, this figure does not now form part of the Financial Secretary's Statement. The figures also exclude commercial publicity for the Public Trustee and Her Majesty's Stationery Office (£24,000) and Export Credits Guarantee Department (£60,000).

† See note to Table 5 for details of what is included in this item.

‡ Including payments to the Royal Society for the Prevention of Accidents.

§ Includes expenditure by Territorial and Auxiliary Forces Associations and the cost of staff serving in overseas commands.

Further details of Training Schemes for Various Groups of Civil Servants in their Relations with the Public

The Treasury's Training and Education Division, which has a staff of twenty, co-ordinates the activities of some fifty departmental training officers and the 200 or so instructors for whom they are responsible. (Not all training officers are under the charge of the departmental training officers however. There are about another 400, mostly concerned with specialized and technical training, who are separately organized. The departments which have large training staffs that do not come under the departmental training officer are the Board of Inland Revenue, the Ministry of Aviation and the Admiralty.) The status of departmental training officers varies from Assistant Secretary at the Post Office, to Higher Executive Officer in some of the smaller departments; not all of them are engaged fulltime on training. About 80 per cent of the fulltime instructional staff coming under departmental training officers are employed in six departments. These are: the Ministry of Pensions and National Insurance (77 fulltime instructors); the Ministry of Labour (32 fulltime instructors); the Air Ministry (21 fulltime instructors); the National Assistance Board (17 fulltime instructors); the War Office (11 fulltime instructors); and the Customs and Excise Department (10 fulltime instructors).[1]

The instructors are ordinary permanent civil servants seconded from their normal duties for three to five years: they have mostly themselves been trained on instructors' courses run by the Treasury's Training and Education Division, although some training of instructors is done by departments themselves.

CLERICAL OFFICERS AND EXECUTIVE OFFICERS

In all government departments today, the Clerical and Executive grades receive some kind of general background training course,

[1] Information supplied by Training and Education Division of H.M. Treasury.

either on entry or at some time early in their career, and this will usually include some mention of relations with the public. However, the extent of this training and the way in which it is given varies enormously among departments. It is probably true to say that ıt is only in those departments which employ fulltime training instructors that the training of these grades is at all developed. Some of the larger departments offer places on their general background courses to Clerical and Executive Officers from the smaller departments, but this practice is not widespread and in any case its usefulness is limited by the differences between the work of one department and another.

For this study, examples have been collected only from four large departments: the Post Office, the Ministry of Labour, the Ministry of Pensions and National Insurance, and the Board of Trade.

Clerical Officers and Executive Officers at these departments all receive the general background course, which lasts for four or five days sometime during their first year of service. In the first three departments this is in addition to a certain amount of vocational training. The methods used to teach relations with the public by telephone and at a personal interview have been described in Chapter VIII.

Instruction is also given in the art of letter writing. The Board of Trade for example, since 1956 has provided a three-and-a-half day course on 'Clear Expression for Clerical Officers'. Here the case study method is used as an exercise in letter writing; letters to meet particular circumstances are also prepared and discussed in syndicate. In the Primary Background Course run by the Post Office for Executive Officers, Clerical Officers and Clerical Assistants there are two sessions on 'Methods of Work'. The first explains how to deal with correspondence and official papers in an orderly manner, and why it is necessary to keep written records. The second session deals with the use of plain words in correspondence; this is done by means of discussions, questions and actual exercises in letter writing. The Post Office provides a further Secondary Background Course for Executive Officers and Clerical Officers at a later stage in their careers, when the same subjects are treated at a more advanced level. The Ministry of Labour and the Ministry of Pensions and National Insurance provide similar training for these grades. During the instruction on letter writing that is given on these courses, the students are particularly urged to think from the point of view of the recipient of the letter and to adapt the language of their letters according to the sort of person to whom it is being sent. They are reminded that the recipient may be a business executive, a professional man, a housewife, an old person, a sick person, an uneducated person. Plenty of advice is given on good construction, punctuation, faults to be avoided, the general tone of the letter and on the need for each letter to be complete, concise and accurate.

ASSISTANT PRINCIPALS[1]

Up to 1963, the training for Assistant Principals was a three-week course, after which the Assistant Principal was moved round a series of jobs in his own department to give him as varied experience as possible until he was promoted out of the training grade to that of Principal.[2] The three-week training course included a session on Press Relations which consisted of a talk by a departmental Information Officer followed by a syndicate exercise in preparing plans for the press and publicity measures that would be needed to present a particular piece of new legislation to the public. There were also four sessions on Communications; during one of these sessions a number of recent letters, to other departments as well as to members of the public, were discussed and criticized in syndicate.

The entire second week of this course was taken up with a Project Study. In this exercise, teams of four Assistant Principals went for a week on a fact-finding and reporting mission to some large organization that had undertaken to co-operate with the Treasury. On a recent course, four teams of Assistant Principals went one each to a county borough, to the Independent Television Authority, to a large department store and to the Ministry of Aviation. Each of these organizations presented the team sent to them with a problem which was actually facing the organization and had not yet been settled. The teams were supplied beforehand with a certain amount of background information; they then had to ask for the rest of the facts that they considered necessary; to write a report on their recommendations for solving the problem; and finally to stand up to an oral cross-examination on their recommendations by members of the host organization. Quite apart from the experience of a week spent working with people who may have very different outlooks and experience from their own, the problems set for the Assistant Principals were normally ones that involved consideration of public

[1] See Chapter VIII, p. 178 footnote for a description of the new post-1963 training course for Assistant Principals.

[2] Some departments try to give the Assistant Principal a carefully planned series of experiences. See R. J. S. Baker 'The Training of Assistant Principals in the Post Office', *Public Administration*, Spring 1963, pp. 71-82

reactions and public needs. This use of practical and active training techniques by the Treasury for the training of Assistant Principals is a comparatively recent development.

POST OFFICE TRAFFIC STAFF

The Post Office gives special training to two of its special Departmental grades who are involved in a good deal of direct contact with the public. These two groups of staff, both employed in the Telephone Managers' Office are the Sales Staff and the Traffic Staff. The basic grade for the Sales Staff is that of Sales Representative. Before the war his main job was to sell as many telephones and associated equipment as possible in order to increase the size of the system. He had also the very important function of advising customers so that they got the best use and value from their telephone service. Since the war the nature of the job has varied with the inability of the Post Office to meet the demand for telecommunication services. At one extreme this means explaining why certain facilities cannot be offered. In contrast, much of the Sales Representatives' time is spent in selling those services which give a fair return on capital invested and which are readily available. The assessment of a customer's needs and relation of these to a variety of technical equipment remains an important advisory function which is now a recognized service given by the Post Office and handled by their sales staff. Before the war, the Sales Representative received no formal school training (although a correspondence course in salesmanship was provided). In 1948 in accordance with the recommendations of a Sales Study Group that had been appointed in 1944, a central sales training school was set up at headquarters. New Sales Representatives now spend a total of nine weeks at the central training school, sandwiched with periods of supervised training in the trainee's own area. The syllabuses of these courses contain a mass of detailed and special knowledge that the Sales Representatives must acquire in order to become both an expert on telecommunications facilities and to have a good background knowledge of the Post Office as a whole. He has also to be trained to become an expert interviewer, since he must be able both to find out what the customer needs and to explain what the Post Office can provide; these interviews may be conducted in people's houses or in their offices. The training must also equip him to write reports to the customer giving clear and accurate recommendations on the facilities to be provided.

It follows that an emphasis on the importance of good oral and

216

written communication runs through all the training. The kinds of discussion and role-playing techniques that have already been described in Chapter VIII are used in these courses. In addition, selling methods are examined in a variety of case studies, some of which are done individually, and some in syndicate.

The Post Office Telecommunications Traffic Staff are concerned with planning and operating the telephone and telegraph systems. They are responsible for the staffing and efficient operation of telephone exchange switchrooms in which over 50,000 telephonists and supervisors are employed. And, because they are broadly responsible for the quality of the service, they deal by letter, telephone and interview with customers, and can be said to act as local public relations officers. Experiments were made before the war in the school training of traffic staff, and in 1946 the Traffic Training School was set up at Post Office Headquarters. The school provides about a dozen different types of training course, including those devoted to the initial training of new entrants. These are recruited at two levels, Telecommunications Traffic Officer and Telecommunications Traffic Superintendent and they receive thirteen-week and twenty-three-week initial training courses, respectively. Although the initial courses also contain technical instruction, a great deal of attention is also paid to letter and report writing, human relations and the conduct of business with customers. The responsibility of the Traffic Staff for a good economic service is emphasized, and nearly every part of the course includes reference to and discussion of relations with the subscribers. There are also a number of sessions specifically devoted to direct contact with the public by interview, telephone, and public meeting.

POST OFFICE TELEPHONE OPERATORS

In a special class of their own, but very much in direct contact with members of the public, are the Post Office telephone operators. The training of these girls[1] has been the subject of a great deal of thought and investigation in recent years. Technical advances have made possible radical changes in the telephone system. The Post Office is trying to make sure, as the Postmaster General said when the Friendly Telephone Service was announced in 1959, that in a system

---

[1] In the daytime the telephone operators are all women, many of whom are under twenty years of age. During the evening and at night and on Sundays the bulk of the operators in the exchanges are men, about a quarter of whom, together with some women, are part-time staff employed only during the evening.

increasingly dependent on automatic techniques, the customer can get a friendly personal service when he needs one. This emphasis on friendly relationships with the customer followed the report of a Post Office team that had made a study of the telephone service in the United States of America. The report was issued in February 1959 under the title *Telephone Service and the Customer*.[1]

This report recommended that certain aspects of the British Post Office practice should be re-examined in the light of the practice of the American Bell system. Partly as a result of these recommendations, the training of day telephone operators, formerly given at centralized schools, is being progressively changed to individual instruction undertaken by first line supervisors at the exchange at which the girls are to be employed. All first line supervisors take part in this, and they continue to have a responsibility for the development of those individual telephonists whom they have trained. In the training of first line supervisors the trainees engage in discussion and practical demonstrations of the various things that can happen to make relations with the customer go wrong: for example, lack of knowledge or understanding; using jargon; keeping the inquirer waiting without explanation and speaking in an unco-operative tone of voice.

The training of the telephone operators incorporates the handling of 'live' telephone calls from the beginning. This makes for more realistic training in customer relations as part of the attainment of an operator's efficiency. Since the launching of the Friendly Telephone policy, in all training, in leaflets, posters, etc., and in group discussions and practices that the girls have with their supervisors, each operator is urged to think of the customer as a person. She is told to think what the customer wants, to listen patiently to what he has to say, to give him the service he wants cheerfully, and if his call is delayed, to tell him what is happening. She is told to try always to let her unseen customer hear the smile in her voice, to speak in a natural and friendly way and not to stick too rigidly to the standard phrases that she has been taught. Accuracy, speed and courtesy are the three qualities that are particularly stressed throughout telephone training.

The Post Office encourages the good public relations aspect of the telephone service amongst management generally. Its publication, *The Telephone in Business*, is directed to business firms but has also

---

[1] This report is known within the Post Office as the Ray Report, after Mr F. I. Ray then Director of the Inland Telecommunications Department who led the study team which visited the United States of America. The main part of the Report was published in the Summer 1959 issue of *The Post Office Telecommunications Journal*.

been issued to all government departments. It contains excellent advice on how to make the best use of the telephone service and deal efficiently and quickly—but politely—with callers; there is a special section of guidance for extension users.

Nevertheless, it must be confessed that the service given to an outside caller by the switchboard of most government departments leaves a great deal to be desired. The caller has to know the extension number of his contact as well as his name—and the extension numbers change every year or two—or go through a lengthy inquiry procedure. As no one below the rank of Assistant Secretary has a personal assistant, and the telephone operator is not allowed to take messages, the caller cannot ask to be rung back. If there is no reply there is frequently no one to tell the caller if the official has been transferred, is on sick leave, or has just stepped out of his room for a moment. There is often no one even to say there is no reply, and the caller is too often left hanging on to a dead telephone. There may be an excellent reason for the poor service given in any particular case; but a good telephone operator has been called the best public relations officer of an organization. It seems a pity that government departments are not more alive to the poor impression given by the system employed.

MESSENGERS

As the last example of civil servants engaged in frequent face-to-face contact with the public, we come to the Messengers who are employed, amongst other things, at most departmental headquarters in London for duties at the entrances and reception desks. These are the first people that a visitor to a Ministry meets (there are over 6,000 Messengers and Senior Messengers in the Civil Service) and they have to deal with all personal callers at the Ministry. The callers might be a newspaper-man, a member of the public just seeking information, or keeping an appointment with a civil service friend, or an indignant complainant who insists on seeing the Minister (occasionally with homicidal intent). The Messenger at the desk has to deal with these callers, be the doorkeeper and answer the telephone at the reception desk. Some Ministries have bright and attractive entrances and inquiry desks to receive visitors; some have little more than porter's cubby holes much pervaded by the aroma of sausage and onions and messengerial gossip.

In 1949 the Report of the interdepartmental Committee on the Training of Civil Servants who have Contact with the Public, had particularly suggested that more should be done about the training of messengers. In about fifteen departments today the Messengers get some new entrant and general background training to teach them the best ways of dealing with callers and of taking messages and to give them some general idea of the work of their department. This training is usually given by the Senior Messengers and by Office Keepers (the next grade above them). At the Ministry of Labour the Staff Training Branch has for the past five years been running special two-day courses for new Messengers on entry; the role-playing methods are used, with a recording to play back afterwards to help the group discussion. The Ministry of Labour has said they found that Messengers are a most rewarding group to train.

GEORGE ALLEN & UNWIN LTD

London: 40 Museum Street, W.C.1

Auckland: 24 Wyndham Street
Bombay: 15 Graham Road, Ballard Estate, Bombay 1
Bridgetown: P.O. Box 222
Buenos Aires: Escritorio 454–459, Florida 165
Calcutta: 17 Chittaranjan Avenue, Calcutta 13
Cape Town: 68 Shortmarket Street
Hong Kong: 44 Mody Road, Kowloon
Ibadan: P.O. Box 62
Karachi: Karachi Chambers, McLeod Road
Madras: Mohan Mansions, 38c Mount Road, Madras 6
Mexico: Villalongin 32–10, Piso, Mexico 5, D.F.
Nairobi: P.O. Box 4536
New Delhi: 13–14 Asaf Ali Road, New Delhi 1
Ontario: 81 Curlew Drive, Don Mills
Philippines: 7 Waling-Waling Street, Roxas District, Quezon City
São Paulo: Caixa Postal 8675
Singapore: 36c Prinsep Street, Singapore 7
Sydney, N.S.W.: Bradbury House, 55 York Street
Tokyo: 10 Kanda-Ogawamachi, 3-Chome, Chiyoda-Ku

ROYAL INSTITUTE OF PUBLIC ADMINISTRATION

PUBLIC SECTOR PENSIONS

GERALD RHODES

Demy 8vo.   *42s. net*

This book is of far wider interest than its title suggests, with its emphasis on the *public sector*, because the Public Services set the pattern for private enterprise in developing occupational pensions. This is the first book to offer a fundamental analysis of public sector schemes. It takes a new look at a whole range of problems affecting the retirement benefits of most of the population and ends with some very challenging, positive proposals.

After tracing the origin and growth of pensions in the Public Services, the book examines in detail the main features of twelve public sector schemes, describing both the benefits provided and the ways in which they are financed. It also makes comparisons with major schemes in private commerce and industry to see whether they can reveal ways in which the administration of public sector schemes could be improved.

POLITICAL AND ECONOMIC PLANNING

THRUSTERS AND SLEEPERS

A STUDY OF ATTITUDES IN INDUSTRIAL MANAGEMENT

Demy 8vo.   *35s. net*

This book is of compelling interest to all concerned with the good management of industry. It is a successor to the widely acclaimed PEP report *Growth in the British Economy*, which analysed the reasons for Britain's slow rate of economic growth. In the conviction that ultimately the prosperity of a national economy depends on the performance of the individual firm, PEP has turned its attention in this report to the attitudes of managers towards the problems that confront them.

As a result of these investigations PEP has formulated some suggestions as to how the gap between thrusters and sleepers might be narrowed to the benefit of the whole economy.

GEORGE ALLEN AND UNWIN LTD